D0936026

ELECTIONS WITHOUT CHOICE

The contributors

JOEL D. BARKAN, University of Iowa

JEAN-FRANÇOIS BAYART, Centre d'Études et de Recherches Internationales, Paris

GUY HERMET, Director, Centre d'Études et de Recherches Internationales, Paris

JUAN J. LINZ, Pelatiah Perit Professor of Political and Social Science, Yale University

DENIS MARTIN, Centre d'Études et de Recherches Internationales, Paris

JOHN J. OKUMU, University of Khartoum, Sudan

ELIZABETH PICARD, Centre d'Études et de Recherches Internationales, Paris

ALEX PRAVDA, University of Reading

RICHARD ROSE, University of Strathclyde

ALAIN ROUQUIÉ, Centre d'Études et de Recherches Internationales, Paris

PHILIPPE C. SCHMITTER, University of Chicago

ELECTIONS WITHOUT CHOICE

Edited by

Guy Hermet, Richard Rose and Alain Rouquié

Committee on Political Sociology IPSA/ISA

Contents

1. 'Approaches to the Study of Political Participation', a special issue of *Acta Sociologica*, vi, nos 1–2 (1962)
2. *Cleavages, Ideologies and Party Systems*, ed. E. Allardt and Y. Littunen (Helsinki: Westermarck Society, 1964)
3. *Party Systems and Voter Alignments*, ed. S. M. Lipset and Stein Rokkan (New York: The Free Press, 1967)
4. *Party Systems, Party Organizations and the Politics of New Masses*, ed. Otto Stammer (Berlin: Free University, 1968)
5. 'Social Structure, Party Systems and Voting Behaviour', ed. Richard Rose and Derek Urwin, a special issue of *Comparative Political Studies*, ii, no. 1 (1969)
6. *Citizens, Elections, Parties*, Stein Rokkan et al. (Oslo: Universitets forlaget; New York: D. McKay, 1970)
7. *Mass Politics*, ed. Erik Allardt and Stein Rokkan (New York: The Free Press, 1970)
8. *Opinion-Making Elites in Yugoslavia*, ed. Allan Barton, Bogdan Denitch and Charles Kadushin (New York: Praeger, 1973)
9. *Electoral Behavior: A Comparative Handbook*, ed. Richard Rose (New York: The Free Press, 1974)
10. *International Almanac of Electoral History*, Thomas T. Mackie and Richard Rose (New York: The Free Press, 1974; London: Macmillan, 1974)
11. *The Management of Urban Change in Britain and Germany*, ed. Richard Rose (Beverly Hills and London: Sage Publications, 1974)
12. *Contemporary Political Sociology*, 24 Sage Professional Papers Series 06 (Beverly Hills and London) 1974–77
13. *The American Intellectual Elite*, Charles Kadushin (Boston, Mass: Little, Brown, 1974)
14. *The Dynamics of Public Policy*, ed. Richard Rose (Beverly Hills and London, Sage Publications, 1976)
15. *Elections Without Choice* ed. Guy Hermet, Richard Rose, and Alain Rouquié, (London: Macmillan, 1978; New York: Halsted Press, 1978)
16. *Comparing Public Policies*, ed. Jerzy Wiatr and Richard Rose (Warsaw: Polish Academy of Sciences, 1977)

Preface

Elections are held in nearly every country in the world. Only eight of 136 member-states of the United Nations have not held a national election in the past decade. But most of these contests are elections without choice; only about one-third of United Nations members can claim to hold competitive free elections conforming to the classical liberal model of democracy.[1] The comparative study of elections without choice thus directs attention to the ballots most frequently held in the world today.

Conventional accounts of the development of elections emphasise the dynamic of democratic legitimacy, which has given citizens in Western countries the power to act as periodic arbiters of their governors. A very different course of events is observed in countries without competitive elections. Rulers have developed a technology of manipulation to give their regimes the appearance of legitimacy and consent by 'manufacturing' up to 100 per cent endorsement at the polls.

If one commences the study of elections by analysing elections without choice, then attention is immediately directed to the functions of elections for rulers of a state, rather than their significance for the individual voter.[2] The fact that elections do not have the same meaning when they are without choice is not evidence that they lack any meaning. Instead, it is an indication that their meaning is different. Rulers who do not rely upon election for their continuance in office can nonetheless use elections to mobilise public opinion and gain the appearance of legitimacy, in a world where election by the masses has replaced election by a Calvinist God as a token of authority.[2]

Any careful student of the evolution of electoral institutions in countries that now boast free competitive elections will soon come across much evidence of the extent to which these countries in the past did not meet standards that they now prescribe for other lands.[3] For example, Britain did not adopt the rule of 'one man, one vote' until a 1949 Act of Parliament abolished the extra vote for university graduates and some businessmen. The United States did not effectively enforce the right of blacks (and poor whites) to vote in the American South until after civil-rights demonstrations there in the 1960s. In France, overseas colonies have elected representatives to the Assembly in Paris continuously since 1871, but they have usually not conformed to the franchise laws or electoral standards of metropolitan France. In most European countries, universal suffrage is a twentieth-century innovation.[4] Moreover, in some areas, cultural, social or ideological restrictions continued long after suffrage was broadened, as did the influence of patrons upon local clienteles or the influence of landlords upon tenants. Moreover, when parliaments were divided into multiple and loose party groups, a general election could not present a verdict upon a government, but only choose individuals to negotiate the terms of a weak coalition government through parliamentary cabals.

The political preconditions for competitive elections are multiple and restrictive. Enumerating the attributes – freedom of speech and association, the rule of law, an executive responsible to an elected body, a neutral civil and military service, and so on – emphasises the extent to which these preconditions are confined to countries within the European political tradition. Outside Europe, competitive elections can most readily be found in those countries deriving their population as well as their institutions from European settlements. The failure of succession states of the British and French empires to establish or sustain competitive elections emphasises the difficulties of transplanting classic liberal political institutions to remote lands.

Competitive elections today are strongest where they have had longest to take root. But most independent states are of relatively recent origin. In their days as colonies or as subordinate regions within larger states, their rulers had no wish to promote lessons in the use of the franchise. Leaders of independence movements also had little interest in encouraging competitive elections. Instead, like European nationalist leaders, they wished to promote unity by coalescing support behind a single independence party. It would be unrealistic to expect every new state without previous experience of free elections or their political prerequisites to achieve in a decade or two a level of free choice that evolved gradually in Western nations. For example, in the period 1885 to 1914, one-quarter to one-third of parliamentary seats were often uncontested at British general elections.[5]

Just as countries without competitive eletions today may evolve toward free choice tomorrow, it is possible for a country that now has competitive elections to suspend them in the future, as part of a major transformation of its political regime. This is more often the case in Latin America than in North America. It has happened occasionally in Europe, most notably in post-war Greece and Czechoslovakia and in Spain and Germany in the 1930s. Such events are a reminder that competitive elections are not the final resting point in the continuing evolution of political institutions.

An awareness of the ætiology and pathology of elections in Western nations can inoculate a reader against applying unrealistic European norms when analysing non-competitive elections in other parts of the world. The differences between the two groupings are not so much differences between electoral institutions viewed in isolation, as they are differences between political systems and levels of social and economic development. Given that non-competitive elections are the statistical norm in the world today, it might even be argued that the practices of Eastern European Communist states provide a better ideal-type model for countries trying to develop and *control* elections.

This volume is meant to compensate for the political scientists' neglect of non-competitive elections, and complement the hundreds of studies that have paid homage to the practices of competitive elections. To investigate the vast field of elections without choice we first of all need intellectual signposts to identify the characteristics that competitive and non-competitive elections have in common (for example, nominations, campaigning, marking ballots), as well as how elections differ. Chapter 1, by Guy Hermet, provides a systematic outline of the differences between competitive and non-competitive elections, and, equally important, of the different types of non-competitive elections. It also identifies functions of elections additional to the choice of governors between competing parties. Chapter 2, by Alain Rouquié, examines the importance of clientelistic control of masses of voters, a system of influence that allows for an element of competition or electoral influence, but without meeting the liberal criteria of free choice. Juan Linz's analysis of the negative and positive functions of elections in inter-war Europe – concentrating upon Germany, Italy and Spain (Chapter 3) – emphasises an often-neglected point, the difficulties of free choice in a society where the polarisation of party politics offers voters 'too big' a choice between extreme alternatives, leading to the breakdown of the regime.

Case studies of individual electoral systems are necessary for two reasons. The first is that only by studying elections in a single country can we fully understand the connection between electoral and other political processes. The second is that there is more variety to be found among electoral systems lumped together as 'non-competitive' than there is among competitive elections. Each case study is intended to elucidate points of general significance, by considering in context why a country whose governors need not have an election to confirm their hold on power should hold elections at all. The fact that the outcome of the election is inevitable in an authoritarian regime gives such elections a banal character. Yet the recurrence of elections in societies where political decisions are not gratuitously made further emphasises the need to explore their latent significance.

The studies of Cameroun by Bayart, of Kenya by Barkan and Okumu, and of Tanzania by Martin (Chapters 4, 5, 6) each examine the interaction of modern political party and electoral institutions in more traditional, even tribal societies. In each case, modern institutions are concerned with making a nation, as well as with manufacturing an election result. The account of a Syrian general election by Picard (Chapter 7) calls attention to the problem of governors consulting the public after a military coup.

Even generals relying upon bayonets also wish to invoke forms of popular endorsement. The practice is common in Latin America as well as in the Middle East. Philippe Schmitter's study of elections in authoritarian Portugal (Chapter 8) analyses how electoral institutions worked in an authoritarian European state, as well as providing valuable insights into electoral traditions in a country that since 1974 has sought to make a rapid transition to elections with choice.

The review of elections in Communist party states by Alex Pravda (Chapter 9) emphasises the philosophical gulf between Communist and liberal ideologies, for the former assumes that under socialism there are not the competing political interests taken for granted in liberal states. Pravda's article shows that, notwithstanding this, a limited element of choice is increasingly found in Eastern European elections. The concluding chapter (10), by Richard Rose, examines the limits of choice in two parts of the Anglo-American world – the American Deep South and Northern Ireland – where majority rule by free elections institutionalised the power of one social group – Southern whites or Northern Ireland Protestants – over a black or Irish Catholic minority. It shows that majority rule is not the only touchstone by which political systems can be judged.

As the title page and table of contents make evident, this book is the product of international collaboration on a grand scale. It is one of a series of election studies undertaken by the Committee on Political Sociology, a research group of the International Political Science Association and the International Sociological Association, of which one contributor, Juan Linz, is chairman, and another, Richard Rose, the secretary. The volume is in the first place an outgrowth of a colloquium organised by Guy Hermet, Juan Linz and Alain Rouquié at the Centre d'Études et de Recherches Internationales of the Fondation National des Sciences Politiques, Paris, on 17–18 May 1976, with the assistance of a grant from the March Foundation. Sixteen papers were presented at the colloquium, but, unfortunately, not all of them could be reported here. Papers about elections in Iraŋ, Indonesia and the United States, and a French-language version of the chapter by Philippe Schmitter have, however, appeared in the *Revue française de science politique*, XXVI, no. 5 (1976), and XXVII, no. 1 (1977).

In preparing the papers for publication, we are particularly grateful to Dr Anthony Mughan, now of the University of Wales, Cardiff, for making initial translations from the French of papers by Rouquié, Bayart, Martin and Picard, and to Mrs Rosemary Rose for the initial translation of the paper by Hermet. Mrs R. West and Mrs K. M. E. Liston of the University of Strathclyde, and Mrs Sylvie Haas of the Centre d'Études et de Recherches Internationales provided the invaluable staff assistance without which this book could not have been brought out so promptly by editors and authors scattered across countries and continents.

GUY HERMET
    Director, Centre d'Études et de Recherches Internationales, Paris

RICHARD ROSE
    Professor of Politics, University of Strathclyde, Glasgow

ALAIN ROUQUIÉ
    Research Scholar, Centre d'Études et de Recherches Internationales, Paris

1 State-Controlled Elections: A Framework

GUY HERMET

With sporadic exceptions, political scientists concentrate upon supposedly free and competitive elections while they loftily ignore those in which one candidate gains 99 per cent of the votes. The approach which justifies this bias in research is well known. On the one hand, holding free and competitive elections is accepted as a sign of pluralist democracy;[1] on the other hand, political science conceives itself as being primarily concerned with multi-party systems and with competitive elections. Postulating that one-party elections or other types of state-manipulated ballots are necessarily rigged leads to their being denied any significance. This removes the political scientist's obligation to examine how rigged these elections really are, or to consider the implications of electoral politics so dissimilar from the liberal democratic model.

Studies of competitive elections are often restricted, failing to take into account the full meaning of electoral processes. They focus heavily on voters' attitudes or electoral legitimation as privileged means of 'gentlemanly' control and change of government. Moreover, this concept implies an objective contempt for the numerous functions performed by elections departing from the classical competitive model.

Once it has been decided to explore the more or less unknown territory of non-competitive elections, the manner of doing so must be considered. This chapter outlines a methodological proposal concerning the limits of non-competitive elections and the analysis of one type of elections without choice: those controlled or 'made' by authoritarian regimes and their leaders. These proposals bear upon elections in Mediterranean lands, Latin America, South-East Asia and Africa south of the Sahara. Clientelistic electoral systems in Latin America and Eastern European elections are considered elsewhere in this book, by Professor Alain Rouquié and Dr Alex Pravda, respectively.

OUTLINING THE FIELD OF ANALYSIS

At worst, it may be argued that elections are inevitably undemocratic; a procedure allowing the cleverest and most powerful people to make the 'sovereign' people yield power to them in an acceptable way. From this perspective, the distinction between classical elections, thought of as free and competitive, and their unfree and non-competitive variants is of little importance, as both are said to rely on manipulation of the people's will. In that type of analysis, such manipulation can be avoided only through direct democracy or by a lottery selecting power-holders.[2] In his *La Guerre civile en France*, Marx, contradicting views advanced by him at other times,[3] denies the democratic validity of universal suffrage as practised in parliamentary regimes. He refers to the Paris Commune as the only democratic model in which those elected must be 'servants', always 'liable to be dismissed by their electors'.[4] Extending the Marxist criticism of representative liberal democracy, Antonio Gramsci emphasises the system of ideological domination which facilitates what he calls 'electoral putsches' of the bourgeoisie. Gramsci writes, 'All that is necessary is to have ideological supremacy (or, better, supremacy of passions) on the chosen day, in order to win a majority which will govern for four or five years in spite of the fact that the mass of the electorate would dissociate itself from its legal expression once passions have died down.'[5]

Elitist and liberal thinkers also express some scepticism about the free and competitive nature of elections. For Gaetano Mosca, 'The representative is not elected by the voters but, as a rule, has himself elected by them.'[6] According to Joseph Schumpeter, 'The choice of the electorate does not flow from its initiative but is being shaped, and the shaping of it is an essential part of the democratic process.'[7] For Anthony Downs, who agrees with Talcott Parsons' theory on parties and elections, competition does not exist between candidates in competitive elections. These involve competition only between interested parties who take only marginally into account the deeper freedom and dignity of the voters. 'Parties in democratic politics', writes Downs, 'are analogous to entrepreneurs in a profit-seeking economy. So as to attain their private ends, they formulate whatever policies they believe will gain the most votes just as entrepreneurs produce whatever products they believe will gain the most profit for the same reason.'[8]

These criticisms hold that totally democratic procedures are distant ideals, unattainable in view of the weight of economic, ideological, social and human factors. At best, elections are relatively free and competitive, as regards competition between parties accepting the rules of liberal democracy along with their economic and cultural assumptions. Even in the most democratic countries of Western Europe and North America, these conditions bring about a situation in which there are regularly uncontested elections, and elections with more or less predictable results where certain candidates have for years had no chance whatsoever of being elected. As Richard Rose's chapter illustrates, nomination can be tantamount to election, even in ballots in the United States and the United Kingdom.[9]

Although it is not easy to define an electoral system as democratic simply by looking at the formal requirements of freedom and plurality of parties, the fact remains that there is a wide range of electoral practices, running from ballots recognised by common agreement as free and competitive, to those in which coercion is notoriously linked with absence of competition between the candidates, or where candidacy is ordained by the power-holders. Two points *freedom of voters,* and *competition between candidates* – still constitute the most generally accepted criteria for distinguishing between 'classical' and 'non-classical' elections (the latter not allowing a free choice by votes and/or competition between the candidates). Nevertheless, a third concept should be introduced to complete the distinction: *the effects that the elections have on government policies*. Classical elections normally have direct effects on government, while non-classical elections do not.

In practical terms, the difference between free and controlled elections is indicated by the opportunity a voter has (1) to have his franchise recognised through registration; (2) to use his right to vote without being segregated into categories dividing the electorate and revoking the idea of popular sovereignty; (3) to cast his ballot free from external hindrance; (4) to decide how to vote, even to spoil his ballot, without external pressure; and (5) to expect his ballot to be counted and reported accurately, even if it goes against the wishes of those in power. Restricted elections are those which do not fulfil one or more of these conditions. In effect, the freedom of election is judged here by the voters' degree of freedom.

This definition omits the indirect social pressures exerted upon voters, especially by a dominant culture or ideology. In fact, we propose to consider whether cultural domination distorts the freedom a voter has, as no one living in a human society can hope to be totally independent of societal pressures common to any social system. To deny this is to deny the possibility of really free elections, and fail to recognise that total freedom is never more than an ideal.

The criterion of competition is obvious. It is reflected through the presence of several candidates for office or, in the case of referenda, through the existence of various options offered to the voters. From this perspective, it is a commonly held view that, whereas an election where only a single candidate – or a single list of candidates – is presented to the electorate is not competitive, an election which offers a choice among several candidates or lists of candidates – or between several options in a referendum – is a competitive election.

We recognise the oversimplification introduced by this twofold division.

In practice, perfect electoral competition represents as unrealistic a goal as absolute freedom of the voter. Even in multi-party democracies, two limits to competition generally remain. One is the economic limitation favouring parties with supporters controlling large amounts of money, thus handicapping groups which are short of such support. The other may be legal and ideological, expressed in many cases, such as in France, by the outlawing of extreme right- or left-wing groups, or autonomist or separatist organisations judged to be dangerous to national unity. But this is not the essential point for differentiating the intermediate and very composite category of elections which are falsely – or, to use a milder term, semi – competitive.

This intermediate category – no doubt the most normal if one equates normality with frequency – covers an enormous variety of limitations upon electoral competition. Whatever these limitations may be, they mean that the electoral system they affect fits neither the category of openly noncompetitive models in which restriction is manifested as an abject refusal to allow more than one candidate to stand nor the classical competitive model where direct coercion constitutes to some extent the exception which proves the multi-party rule. Electoral competition can be feigned – that is to say, suppressed by clientelist phenomena analysed in the next chapter. Moreover, faking electoral competition is also based in many cases on state or single-party intervention. For example, a government can impose a drastic limitation on the number of parties having legal status, thus preventing them from taking part in elections (as in post-war Turkey, Brazil after 1964, Iran before 1975, Egypt since 1976, Indonesia, Senegal, and so on); can add procedural barriers to check the growth of a few small legal parties or electoral groupings, tolerated only to reinforce the democratic legitimacy of a large government party (as in Mexico, in Portugal before 1974, or in some Eastern European countries); or may allow voters to choose from two or three candidates of a single party (as in Franco's Spain, many African countries, or Eastern European countries).

The effects of the ballots is the third criterion by which classical and nonclassical elections can be distinguished. In classical elections, control of office is normally determined by the outcome of the election. Replacing office-holders by leaders of the opposition is possible, and modifying government policies in a direction more in tune with the wishes of the electorate. The principle of alternating parties in government – though not of regimes – is the fundamental rule of elective representative democracy. In non-classical elections, results do not modify the control of power; power-holders claim to stand above parties and electors, and elections provide only, at best, a political barometer, the readings of which do not create any obligations for the government.

Classical elections combine, in a fairly coherent manner, these three variables: voters' freedom, multi-party competition, and results which affect what happens in government. Non-classical elections combine these three elements in so many ways that they induce a sort of taxonomic confusion – ranging from elections where the result changes nothing, through semi-competitive or non-competitive free elections with some political consequences, to elections which are not free and have no consequences for the voters, but where candidates compete to manipulate the electorate.[10]

One can illuminate this confusion by taking real examples and, in particular, by giving one variable, electoral competition, a prime position in relation to the other two. As the most readily measurable variable, electoral competition enables us to discern more precisely the two chief axes of this study of non-competitive elections: the electoral control exerted by the state, and the clientelist phenomena. While many attributes can help discriminate between types of elections, competition is of *first* importance. Thus it becomes possible to outline a qualitative scale of non-classical elections, considered fundamentally from the perspective of their manipulation by the state.[11]

This scale, or model, can be presented as shown in Table I.1, which adduces a large, but by no means exhaustive, series of examples from recent elections in non-Communist countries. Including classical electoral systems as a reminder, this empirical rather than logical schema relates particularly to two of the many forms of non-classical elections manipulated by the central sources of power. The first one is presented as 'exclusionary elections', those which Samuel P. Huntington and Kenneth F. Johnson call *liberal-machiavellian elections*,[12] while the second refers to a unanimity model and to a revolutionary or pseudo-revolutionary practice. In the case of 'exclusionary elections', the government aim is to prevent the authentic manifestation of popular wishes and pressures, while retaining a liberal façade which favours only those who support the existing order. In these situations, those in power dare not rely solely on the influence of an inadequately assimilated political culture, or technical strategies such as gerrymandering or adopting a favourable electoral system to obtain the right results. But neither do they dare simply to use dictatorial electoral practices, or limit voting through restrictive qualifications such as were applied in bourgeois societies in the nineteenth century. These coercive and restrictive strategies of two-party or multi-party systems are now favoured by an increasing number of strong governments, such as Brazil, Mexico, Turkey or Indonesia. Egypt is now travelling along the same road by introducing three 'political tribunes' into its one-party system, and the Franco regime was attempting such a reform in its last stages.[13] With the exception of Iran, which is just coming back from an exclusionary multi-party system to a one-party regime, pluralist coercive elections these days seem to represent the most frequent and modern electoral system for authoritarian conservative regimes.

TABLE 1.1
Types of Electoral Situations

	Control of competition by the state or a one-party bureaucracy	Examples	Extent and liberty of vote	Effective consequences on government issues
Classical elections	Prohibition of candidatures exceptional; influence of a dominant culture	Western Europe, North America, Japan	Universal suffrage effective, no coercion, and correct computing of results	Alternation of government and shift in policies possible
Non-classical, semi-competitive elections	Multi-party, excluding the right	Portuguese 1975 constituent elections	Universal suffrage with actual hindrances to the registration of electors residing outside Portugal	Immediate consequences limited by agreement between parties and Armed Forces Movement
	Multi-party with racial exclusions	South Africa	Universal suffrage limited to whites	Political consequences for white power structure
	Exclusionary and coercive multi-party elections	Turkey 1950–60	Universal suffrage, little coercion	Effective alternation of government
		Mexico, Brazil 1966–74	Controlled universal suffrage (with exclusion of illiterates in Brazil); results unverifiable outside large cities	Without direct consequences; no alternation of government
		Nicaragua, Guatemala	Full-scale coercion, official results unverifiable	Without consequences
	Coexistence of a state-controlled political movement and a residual multi-party system	Indonesia 1971	Controlled universal suffrage, strong coercion, official results unverifiable	Without consequences
	One-party system, but opposition lists tolerated	Portuguese legislative elections until 1974	Officially restricted suffrage, with alteration of electoral lists, strong coercion and forgery in results	Without consequences, as opposition cannot win any seat

Table I. 1, cont.

Control of competition by the state or a one-party bureaucracy	Examples	Extent and liberty of vote	Effective consequences on government issues
Declining one-party sytem, with competition among candidates representing several 'political streams'	Egyptian 1976 legislative elections	Universal suffrage with little coercion	Used as a political barometer by government
One-party system with competition among several candidates	Tanzania 1965, 1970, 1975	Universal suffrage with popular mobilisation rather than coercion	Used by government as a means of arbitration between political factions
	Spanish 1967–71 legislative elections	Para-universal suffrage with sporadic coercion; results unverifiable	Without consequences
Number of candidates does not exceed number of seats	Many countries of francophone Africa; presidential elections in Kenya, Burundi, Algeria	Universal suffrage with mobilisation of the electorate; results unverifiable	Confirmation of elections without other consequences

(The leftmost bracketed label reads: *Non-classical, one-party or no-party elections*)

On the other hand, though they are not alone in such practices, revolutionary or pseudo-revolutionary regimes of the Third World have a predilection for unanimity, with only one-party elections. Multi-party elections, even falsified ones, are rare, particularly in Africa. But it is also true that single-candidate or single-list elections are becoming less frequent, except in the case of presidential elections. The most commonplace example of one-party elections is now the advanced practice of competitive ballots among candidates selected either by those in power or by the single-party leader (see Chapters 5 and 6, on Kenya and Tanzania). Moreover, these non-pluralist but formally competitive elections frequently give some influence to the voters, especially in some states of East Africa where they resemble Jerzy J. Wiatr's consent elections, which 'do not decide who rules the country, but . . . influence the way in which the country will be ruled'.[14] This, no doubt, is the best means of influence offered to the voter by non-classical elections.

Our empirical schema relates only to national legislative or presidential elections, and neglects local or professional consultations, which may be of quite significant interest in some authoritarian or revolutionary situations. This model obviously ignores many electoral modalities which would complicate its premises to some extent, such as in distinguishing between the quantitative and qualitative aspects of the choice offered to the voters. It also ignores the individual voter's perception of elections inside the global political system. A more comprehensive model would undoubtedly make special reference to historical and socio-economic dimensions. For example, it is obvious that state-controlled elections do not have the same meaning in Spain as in Cameroun.

THE SIGNIFICANCE OF NON-COMPETITIVE ELECTIONS

Are elections, considered as one of the most significant fields of analysis in Western multi-party states, so deprived of meaning in other regimes that they are not worth studying?

Such a negative conclusion is unacceptable. The analysis of classical competitive elections fails to give just weight to certain dimensions of the electoral process particularly prominent in non-classical elections. In a sense, non-competitive and semi-competitive elections give an exaggerated insight into techniques of manipulation and centralised control, which are, to some degree, extreme manifestations of phenomena inherent in any electoral situation.

In the liberal democratic context, which is the usual area of study for classical behavioural electoral analysis in the United States, in Britain and in France, many aspects of the complex electoral reality are overlooked, such as the cultural or ideological processes underlying voting. It is not enough to wonder what determines the voter's choice, as if the value attributed to the ballot and to representative democracy were a matter of course for every individual and every social class. It would do no harm to undertake a parallel investigation of the different levels that may exist – social, historical, regional, international – in understanding and assimilating electoral practices. What do elections mean to citizens who are periodically called to the polls? What affective or rational price are they ready to pay? What feelings of deprivation (or benefit) would result if elections were held less (or more) frequently?

If the analysis of liberal pluralist elections presents some deficiencies, it is obviously insufficient in other areas. Because of generally questionable statistics, the British (Nuffield) qualitative style of electoral analysis is more appropriate than the French and American behavioural and quantitative approaches measuring the distance separating a particular non-Western election from the Western model.[15] However, the general unsuitability of such research tools for electoral systems found in a majority of countries around the world remains a matter of fact.[16] The study of non-competitive elections is not a scientific luxury for scholars in search of gratuitous originality: it permits a global insight into negative aspects of electoral processes in general, and constitutes one of the very few grounds for observing political management in more or less authoritarian regimes.

The analysis of non-competitive or pseudo-competitive elections increases our understanding of the development and nuances of electoral phenomena. When applied to industrialised or semi-industrialised countries whose electoral history has gone through various phases, often involving more or less successful liberal pluralist periods alternating with authoritarian periods, this analysis can illustrate the numerous twists and manipulations practised by those in power, and how the population perceives these manoeuvres. Do authoritarian or socially restrictive regimes really manage to block the political awareness of the masses or do they just redirect this political vitality, or even accelerate it? When applied to non-industrialised countries, particularly those of the Third World, the analysis of elections can also lead to a more extensive appreciation of the worldwide electoral process, especially by bringing to light the processes by which socially undifferentiated and tradition-bound peoples are or are not transformed into relatively conscious electorates. In the nineteenth century, this maturity was usually reached in the electoral purgatory of those who were excluded from voting under the poll-tax system. Because it was long sought after, the right to vote may have had a deeper meaning during this period than it has today, when the franchise is generally granted before any serious claim is made for it. Non-competitive elections, which often take place in countries with a socio-economic structure similar enough to that of mid nineteenth century continental Europe, represent another method to encourage, and at the same time control, the course of the political apprenticeship of the people. The analyst can discover in the slightly exaggerated example of non-competitive elections today the complex functions of socialisation, persuasion and social control displayed by voting systems, whether classical or not.

In another respect, the study of non-competitive elections represents one of the rare chances to analyse factually the public manifestations of the governments which control them. In the new states of the Third World, as well as in authoritarian regimes – whether populist or reactionary – established in countries that have reached the stage of industrial take-off, political conflicts are generally resolved in the secrecy of personal fights and confrontation coteries. Political life is generally concealed behind the opaque screen of a very small ruling circle which the Spaniards ironically called the Bunker, referring to Hitler's Bunker in Berlin. Non-competitive, state-controlled elections provide the analyst with an exceptional manifestation of a political reality which otherwise is almost always hidden.

Non-classical elections vary, reflecting very diverse social and historical contexts, distortions of European prototypes, new forms (invented by those in power) of popular involvement in politics, and distortions caused by clientelist phenomena. Unfortunately, the body of literature devoted to the various forms of non-classical elections is very small. In particular, informative and methodological research dealing with state-controlled elections, with which we are concerned, is unavailable in so far as the studies devoted both to coercive elections in conservative authoritarian regimes and to revolutionary or pseudo-revolutionary elections in former colonial states remain mainly descriptive and generally deprived of methodological innovations. In fact, some studies about Latin American, African and – less commonly – South-East Asian elections, have been done. For example, Brazilian elections are the subject of a body of literature similar in scale to that devoted to any European country. However, the authors of these studies still refer in general to the classical methods of Western electoral sociology, or, at best, to a clientelist interpretation of the election results, and do not on the whole try to find new ways of investigating the more original features of these elections, in particular the techniques of voter and candidate manipulation by those in power.

Finally, studies which really seek to create tools of analysis specifically adapted to the field of state-controlled elections are very rare and concern almost exclusively Africa south of the Sahara. Examples are the pioneering works by John S. Saul, Goran Hyden and Colin Leys, Joel D. Barkan, and Denis Martin.[17] The task of designing no more than a modest framework of analysis for non-competitive elections is still both huge and difficult. The excitement of discovery and the relative absence of scientific precedent may stimulate the political scientist, but it also exposes him to clumsinesses and traps, which inevitably confront those who venture into little-known sectors.

A FRAMEWORK OF ANALYSIS

The framework of analysis outlined here is no more than a departure point for a more systematic study of state-controlled elections. The first of these levels of analysis refers to the mere description of these elections, including the consideration of their cultural and institutional environment. To this end, the legal framework of elections will be examined as regards the extension of suffrage, the object, frequency and form of elections, the organisation of campaigns, the shaping of constituencies, the computing of votes cast and the making of results, as well as the importance that those in power publicly attribute to the voters. Moreover, this legalistic description must be complemented by the observation of actual campaign behaviour: the machinery, whether hidden or openly fraudulent and coercive, affecting the number of electors really allowed to vote; the content of propaganda; the ties between candidates and either those in power or some political coterie; the effective freedom of the vote; and the fairness of the count and the consequences of the elections. Finally, the relative honesty of some non-competitive or semi-competitive elections justifies consideration of their formal and public aspects, reflected particularly in the official election figures, while the extreme coercion of many others forbids any serious consideration of these aspects, especially in connection with electoral statistics.

The description of the formal and actual aspects of elections does not exhaust this complex field, since electoral practice is always embedded in a political tradition and a specific socio-economic and cultural context. The political awareness of the people depends very largely on the overall structure of the society. Non-competitive elections do not have the same meaning in a complex industrialised society as they do in a predominantly peasant country, the population of which is fairly homogeneous and largely illiterate. They also have a different meaning according to the electoral history of each country. In the Third World, some peoples, as in ex-Portuguese Africa or what was formerly the Belgian Congo, have had no experience of elections during the colonial period, while others had ballots organised by the British or the French. Moreover, some of these countries briefly experienced – before, and in various cases after, independence – comparatively free and competitive elections, while others never had such an opportunity. In the same way, relatively industrialised countries like Spain, Greece or Brazil had fairly free and competitive elections before shaking off authoritarian regimes and state-controlled elections,[18] while Portugal, for instance, never had really competitive elections with universal suffrage before the dictatorship of President Salazar and the enforcement of the manipulated electoral system described in Chapter 8 by Philippe Schmitter. The significance of non-competitive elections is obviously not the same in societies that have never experienced other types of elections as in those which formerly had competitive electoral regimes, especially when the political cutlure of the electorate is really influenced by the Western electoral model.

Descriptive analysis of those technical, socio-economic, cultural and historical variables that characterise non-competitive electoral systems constitutes only a prelude to the research as such. At this level of interpretation, what we might call a first-degree analysis can refer to the obvious – or relatively obvious – results and processes of elections.

The analysis of the voters' attitudes as they appear in electoral statistics is possible in only a few cases. At local, and sometimes national, level, there are non-competitive elections the results of which are not falsified, either because the government considers it unnecessary, or through its express wishes. In these situations, the proportion of votes attributed to each candidate generally does not matter very much, except in detailed studies of results by constituency, where it may be interesting to contrast the characteristics of the successful and unsuccessful candidates. More

promising is the analysis of abstentions. When the government gives no
opportunity to express an opposing view, withholding one's vote may be a
challenge to those in power. This is especially true when abstentions are on
a very large scale and clearly concentrated in certain regions or sectors of
society. In these circumstances, when abstentions can be interpreted as
politically significant, a cartographic representation even becomes possible, permitting an interpretation in terms of regional conformity towards
the government. In Spain, for example, juxtaposing the results of the
municipal and Cortes elections of 1970-1 and the Republican elections of
1936 shows a close geographical correlation between massive abstention in
1970-1 and the leftist vote in 1936.[19] In Brazil, maps of the 1968 and 1970
elections would also show a massive, and probably significant, abstention
in certain states.[20] Similarly, the primary elections of December 1969 in
Kenya were marked by a very noticeable escape from assent by the
electorate in the Western province and Nyanza province.[21]

   Although it may certainly be studied in nations other than Spain, Brazil
and Kenya, the analysis of significant abstention remains an exceptional
opportunity for research. In general, analysing the candidate-selection
machinery offers a much wider and more useful base for understanding
rivalries, compromises and manoeuvres for seduction or intimidation,
which frequently constitute the real purpose of non-competitive elections.
The composition of the list of candidates offered to the voter reflects an
infinite number of ideological nuances, even within nominally single-party
regimes (single-member constituencies; party list in each constituency;
several lists or sub-lists, representing varied political streams or groups; and
so on). In the same way, the observation and interpretation of the content
of electoral campaigns and electoral literature may be very helpful to the
analyst.

   In all these stages, non-competitive elections provide one of the few
occasions when those in power cannot avoid the public formalisation of
their programme and ideological positions, whether real or assumed, and
the revelation of their ability to mobilise mass-support. Although there are
many parts of the world where elections are not regularly held, few
political leaders can do without them for long periods, as was discovered by
President Fidel Castro of Cuba, who once declared, 'Revolution has no
time for elections.' More usually, for authoritarian governments, non-
competitive elections represent a necessary operation of pressure relief or
mass-mobilisation compelling them to unveil some of their political
conceptions. They may do so in a rather naïve way, as did the Indonesian
Minister of Information, N. Budiardjo, for whom elections and democracy
are 'a way to ensure order in the political, social and cultural life of the
nation'.[22] They may also rediscover the old theory about one-party
democracy, as did Tanzanian President J. K. Nyerere, who declared in
1963, 'Politics in a country ruled by a two-party system is not, and cannot
be, national politics; it is the politics of groups whose rivalries have

generally little interest for the great majority of the people. . . . When there is one party, and when that party is identified with the Nation as a whole, the foundations of democracy are more solid than they will ever be if you have two or more parties, each representing only a fraction of the community.'[23] In any case, non-competitive elections always reveal the ruler's ideology, as well as indicating the type of relations, coercive or participative, which the governing circles try to have with the population.

These remarks on the electoral dimension of the relationship between political power and society may lead us to what may be called the second-degree interpretation of non-competitive elections: an analysis of their latent significance rather than a description of their overt features. Here we focus on only two of the many possible ways of analysing this latent significance: the functions of non-competitive elections, and the role of these elections in class-relationships.

Competitive elections are expected to provide a peaceful succession of office-holders, to help legitimise leaders and government, and to effect control of their policies. In the opinion of Marxist or anarchist critics of liberal democracy, they also help to hide a class domination, in the name of equality of votes. The functions of non-competitive elections are not so clear. However, if they evidently do not affect the replacement and succession of office-holders, they do fulfil functions that are not so different from those, fulfilled by competitive elections, of legitimation and of eclipsing political domination. Finally, one of the great differences between competitive and non-competitive elections lies in the fact that, in the latter case, a government calling an election that it is not obliged to hold must expect such an event to have very specific functions or consequences. By contrast, the compulsory and multipurpose character of competitive elections does not require as precise a political calculation. Whatever the case, the fact of organising elections in a certain form and at a certain time never constitutes a gratuitous act. It is even more voluntary and meaningful in the case of 'non-obligatory elections', where the rulers must have serious motives for holding elections from which they, rightly or wrongly, anticipate certain benefits. The functional analysis of state-controlled elections seeks to ascertain these anticipated benefits.

In the state-controlled non-competitive context, the functions of elections may be identified through four categories. The first three refer to the relation between the government and the governed: first, communication role; second, education, whether stimulating or anaesthetising mass political participation; and, third, legitimation. Fourth, elections affect the internal equilibrium of the governing circles, and refer particularly to the compromise, hidden competition and intimidation that state-controlled elections assume among ruling 'coteries'.

(1) The communication function of these elections is the most factual and incontrovertible. Electoral processes normally provide an immediate

and solemn occasion for the transmission of orders, explanations and cues from the government to the population. They give also the opportunity to recruit intermediaries – or scapegoats – acting on behalf of those in power. In authoritarian regimes where public controversy is anathema, election time sometimes looks like a period of exceptional politicisation, albeit directed solely to the advantage of those who govern. Authoritarian leaders cannot escape the obligation of 'indulging in' politics from time to time, but they evidently do it in as directive, massive and unilateral a manner as possible. Moreover, the government of new states where illiteracy, linguistic fragmentation and lack of regular channels of information are hindrances to easy communication with the people can use electoral campaigns as an efficient though occasional means to reach the masses, who cannot be contacted by more permanent means. This is, above all, the case when the ruling party or administration is unable to ensure continuing nationwide political activity by its own elites. In cases of authoritarian regimes in either relatively industrialised countries or new states, communication can also take place from the periphery to the centre, offering voters the more or less fictitious opportunity of choosing – or, more precisely, endorsing – the nomination of prominent local people or members of traditional or new elites who act as their spokesmen in negotiation with the central government. But experience shows that those spokesmen are much more likely to be messengers of the state authorities.

(2) More controvertibly, the educational functions of state-controlled non-competitive elections reflect the paradox that, whereas the very exercise of the vote instils in citizens an awareness that they ought to have the ability to influence their rulers, it at the same time hides real inequalities of power through nominal equality at the ballot box. Summing up this function, the result of which is both educational and anaesthetic, coincides with the specific effect of elections in the process of socialising individuals and groups. Acting as the practical manifestation of a dominant or domination-oriented ideological set-up, it strengthens the long-term legitimation of an existing order, while creating the psycho-sociological conditions for smooth working.

It is of no use to repeat the denunciation that traditionalist as well as revolutionary critics have made of this function for more than a century. And it is even less useful to point out that this criticism of the alienating role of elections becomes really convincing only when the elections are manipulated by authoritarian governments to such an extent that they may be considered as no more than simple devices for propaganda and for opposition intimidation. Such was the case in pre-1974 Portugal, where on the whole the elections served to disqualify the opposition (which was allowed to campaign only one month before the ballot), and to feed the files of the political police with new information about anti-system politicians. Although typical of reactionary dictatorships, where every election takes on the appearance of a plebiscite[24] the results of which are known beforehand, such concealment of inequalities in power and wealth also occurs in new states with more or less radical façades. This is, for instance, the argument developed by John S. Saul about Tanzanian elections, which rank among the most democratic of African elections. 'The electoral system may also have had the effect of stabilising that Tanzanian class system', writes Saul, who later adds that he foresees 'the possibility that in an unreconstructed Tanzania one possible function of such an electoral system was an anaesthetising one'.[25]

In the short term, non-competitive state-controlled elections also display a socialising role, concentrating on more precise and analysable objects. In situations where governments seem to consider that general conformity strengthens their stability, elections tend to invalidate the opposition and, by contrast, to reinforce the institutionalisation of a single party. Alternatively, in those cases (fairly common) where the regime is strong and its rulers believe in the advantages of a certain amount of pluralism without freedom as a factor of social and political stability, state-controlled elections give the opportunity of trying various bipartisan or multipartisan exclusionary combinations. This allows them to force a more-or-less successful acceptance of the 'civic culture' by subjects whom they wish to transform into respectful and disciplined citizens. It is hoped that the population will get used to having no choice other than that imposed by the political planning of the government, or even that it will forget its former, less restricted choice and will thus learn moderate electoral behaviour, making control eventually unnecessary. Moreover, electoral socialisation tends to give individuals the feeling that they share the responsibility for decisions that bind them – even if it is only through casting a vote implying a general agreement with these decisions – and that they ought therefore to collaborate willingly in carrying them out.

(3) Even more controversial than their educational functions, the legitimation function of state-controlled elections can take two forms: national and international. In non-competitive state-controlled systems, international legitimation counts for at least as much as national legitimation. Elections are signs of good conduct to the outside world. This is true in new states, particularly in Africa, which pay homage to the former colonial powers in this way, as in conservative dictatorships, where elections may be frequent, if not decisive.[26]

Electoral legitimation varies considerably according to historical circumstances. In relatively industrialised countries under strong regimes, as in Franco's Spain or post-1964 Brazil, non-competitive state-controlled elections are meant to demonstrate political support, but are really only a form of confirmation or a safety valve. In these contexts, those in power do not fully trust their capability to mobilise the population; they only offer their own supporters largely artificial electoral opportunities in the guise of a discriminatory process which excludes dangerous elements. In these states, other aspects of electoral functions are much more important than the doubtful internal legitimation.

On the other hand internal electoral legitimation is commonly a political resource of the greatest importance in new states whose national unity is still fragile if not fictitious. In these countries, elections generally constitute the most efficient method for promoting a popular nationwide mobilisation transcending local and socio-economic cleavages. By simultaneous application of traditional political processes (e.g. palaver norms favouring unanimity, feudal patronage, and so on) and modern techniques (ideological references, single or dominant party with or without deferent and tolerated opposition, and the practice of votes) elections appear semi-festive and even cathartic; they become a sort of national festival the meaning of which has not yet been lost in the mist of time. As a result, they lend themselves to various interpretations suiting the rural populations as well as the uprooted town-dwellers, and the prosperous Westernised elites as well as the radical have-nots. By establishing for the first time a direct and apparently consensual tie between governors and governed, state-controlled elections in the new states finally legitimise the political and economic pre-eminence of the new national bourgeoisie and/or military bureaucratic coterie. Sometimes state-controlled elections can also help rejuvenate the legitimacy of a regime that predates the colonial period, as with the 1962 constitutional referendum in Morocco, which endorsed a government by secular monarchy when it was challenged by the champions of independence represented by political parties such as Istiqlal.

(4) Finally, state-controlled elections reflect and influence the distribution of power among the groups that control the government. In regimes where there is no fixed term for elections, holding them is often motivated by the need to give public sanction to the rivalries of the different factions of the elite, by the wish to capture new elements whose support is sought by the rulers, or, in some circumstances, by the will of those who govern to weaken the influence of traditional forces such as the religious forces (for example, in Iranian and Indonesian elections). The main though disguised purpose of state-controlled elections is sometimes 'consulting' the people in order to ratify an already-negotiated compromise. Thus in Pakistan, during the period 1962–9, the military – bureaucratic oligarchy allowed the political leaders and the bourgeoisie to have elections in reward for their support.[27] On other occasions, elections may serve to delineate the conditions of a future compromise by letting each protagonist assess his support, without making manifest the personal, economic or ideological implications of such a velvet-glove confrontation; such was the case with the Cameroun elections analysed by Dr Jean-François Bayart in Chapter 4. State-controlled elections may also help to reimpose a firm hand on anarchistic or unenthusiastic sectors of society by compelling their members to adopt greater political conformity, at least on the surface, or

else by attracting non-radical opponents by holding out the promise of reform of the system from within, as in the 1969 Portuguese elections. In the more peaceful instances when the more extreme electoral manoeuvres (leading to the overthrow of democracy) are not adopted, state-controlled elections generally help rejuvenate political elites, and/or weaken groups or individuals by conveniently isolating them.

It goes almost without saying that all elections are multi-functional to some extent, and that the four functions abstracted here can never completely characterise any of them. Nevertheless, one or two functions are generally more important, especially in the case of elections held in authoritarian regimes. Consequently, one very specific way of comparing state-controlled elections is to characterise them by the functions to which regime leaders give priority, and then assess the extent to which these functions are realised. This in turn may contribute to a better understanding of the issues at stake in the complex and often contradictory strategies of many authoritarian states.

The objectives of authoritarian leaders may introduce the problem of class relations, another aspect of a second level of analysis of state-controlled elections. Placing the electoral phenomena in their historical and structural contexts, on the national level as well as relative to colonial dependence, it relates the analysis of dominant relationships common to all social systems to objective and observable events. One can try to describe a social system in an all-embracing way, taking into account, for instance, its productive structure and its congruence of political and cultural super-structure; but it does not seem unreasonable to prefer another method of analysis: focusing on the investigation of immediate electoral facts which may vividly illustrate the mechanics of domination and social change.

A careful study of state-controlled elections would have a good chance of throwing a more accurate light on the strategy of regimes that are strongly divided between their desire to modernise through industrialisation and their conservative bias towards counter-revolutionary stabilisation. These regimes are usually found among nations, such as Franco's Spain, Brazil, Iran and Mexico, that have reached the threshold of industrialisation, but they also have partial counterparts in much less industrialised countries, such as the Ivory Coast or the Philippines.[28] All of them have a system of controlled elections, with varying success. But they also demonstrate a preoccupation with repressing popular pressure and subversive aspirations. Careful not to over-react to the desire of developing oligarchies or expanding middle classes for participation, and wishing to appear politically pluralistic in the Western world, where they aspire to win an honourable place, an increasing number of strong regimes resort to multi-party systems which nonetheless exclude any real opposition, as in Brazil, Mexico, Egypt and Senegal. In the same way, the waning Franco regime was getting ready to switch from a single-party electoral system to one of timid pluralism. Iran has taken the opposite direction: from coercive multi-party elections to a one-party unanimity system. A great many Third World countries remain faithful to this same formula, or to hybrid systems, tending to be 'unanimitarian', as in the Indonesia of Golkar.

In all these cases, the attributes of elections clearly illustrate the social limits of more or less authoritarian states. In exclusionary as well as in mobilisation systems, electoral analysis emphasises the nature of conflicts between the traditional elites (feudal, landed proprietors, local political bosses, cultural or religious dignitaries, and so on), the new elites (businessmen, entrepreneurs, newspaper-owners, engineers, university people, leaders of formal or informal parties, and the like) and the bureaucratic – military core which constitutes the real government. Such an analysis should provide actual examples concerning the basic question of the autonomy of the central power faced with oligarchies whose counter-claims it is supposed both to evaluate and to represent.

2 Clientelist Control and Authoritarian Contexts

ALAIN ROUQUIÉ

'Chief, I have done everything as you asked me to. Now, I would very much like to know who I voted for.'

'My son, never ask me that kind of question and above all do not forget that the vote is secret.'

Dialogue between 'Colonel' Chico Heraclio and a Limoeiro voter, state of Pernambuco, Brazil.

The political scientist's interest in electoral dynamics should not be limited to the liberal pluralist framework. The analysis of public opinion is not worthwhile when universal suffrage has been adopted in social contexts differing greatly from modern industrial societies. A global electoral sociology requires methods and techniques unencumbered by 'occidental-centric' prejudices.

At first sight, the analysis of so-called non-competitive elections seems to present more pitfalls than interest. To define the characteristics of an institutional mechanism by negation implies that the competitive elections peculiar to Western pluralist democracies are an ideal standard for comparison. Moreover, it implies that non-competitive elections equal the modern authoritarian systems of non-Western nations, a residual grouping of countries on the road to the political perfection of the industrial democracies.

If this were the case, the analysis of elections would hardly be justified. The study of the working of electoral mechanisms alone is not the best way to understand distinctive political systems in which elections are artificial, ornamental or without real political meaning. But to look upon elections as a heuristic instrument does not make it necessary to value them by norms alien to the nations analysed. One can doubt the sociological merits of a division between competitive and non-competitive elections, and this dichotomy cannot refer to the usual distinction between 'pluralist democracies' and 'authoritarian regimes'. The purpose of this paper is to examine the *real* use of electoral processes in certain social contexts.

The competitive character of classical elections raises problems. Can electoral competition be unambiguously defined by simple and indisputable criteria or is it simply an ideal aspiration after the fashion of economic competition in the market economy? Is definition a question of a formal, even ideological, distinction open to analysis, with an operational value beyond theoretical premises idealising liberal, representative regimes?

External criteria are of little help, and global analysis of the actual functioning of universal suffrage weakens its significance. The technical regularities of the vote (access to the ballot box, counting of the votes, and so on) evidently do not guarantee its competitive character. Nor does a plurality of candidates or alternatives and the absence of impediments to candidates and the casting of one's vote. Pluralist regimes are known in which coercion plays hardly any role in the conduct of electoral consultations but which none the less have elections that are to all appearances non-competitive. This is the case, for example, in those political systems that can be called 'semi-competitive'.[1] Moreover, formally free elections are not *ipso facto* competitive, unless electoral and political freedom is likened to the Manchester concept of the 'free fox in the free hen-house'. But if freedom is dissociated from the means of exercising it, no election is fully free. In fact, the disparity in resources between candidates and parties that permits those supported by the state or economically powerful groups to invoke through a vast propaganda campaign promises, threats or effective pre-election measures is not compatible with perfect competition.

The radical criticism that some Marxist writers have voiced concerning the neutrality of electoral processes particularly underlines the elements of domination behind the processes of apparently free competition. For Gramsci, free elections measure only the influence of different groups on an electorate, and not the state of the latter's opinion, still less the sum of individual opinions.[2] The group that dominates the means of influence can manipulate political opinion and 'bestow on itself an emotional majority of the electorate'[3] on polling day. Viewed as a communication phenomenon, the expression of popular sovereignty is limited by the dominant culture and ideological conformism, which work to the advantage of the ruling class. There is no need at all to violate peoples' consciences. The inculcation of dominant values through multiple ideological mechanisms makes for the permanent consent of the mass of the electorate.

If one takes this same critical perspective, advanced industrial democracies or post-industrial societies today exemplify common types of limitation to electoral competition. These integrated and consensual societies, where anti-system forces, legal or not, are of negligible importance, and which have been characterised by a unidimensional profile, have elections in which a plurality of candidates is matched by very moderate differences between electoral programmes. Are elections that do not offer a choice between different social models or governing elites, but only the simple alteration of interchangeable teams representing the same social stratum, fully competitive? But to say that without fundamental choices between alternatives there is no meaningful choice boils down to approving only those political situations in which the election stakes are dramatically increased – for example, in Chile from 1964 to 1973, or today in the Mediterranean countries of Europe. Thus, paradoxically, the only really competitive elections would take place in the nations where political-development experts and writers wedded to the polyarchic ideal see only unstable or endangered democracies. This would refute all who consider low stakes in electoral competition to be the *sine qua non* of political systems founded upon bargaining and compromise.

The competitive/non-competitive distinction, then, is perhaps not as artificial as it appeared. But the notion of non-competitive elections can be operationalised generally only on condition that it does not depend on multiple and equivocal criteria. Schumpeter, discussing the classical theory of democracy, reproaches it for attributing 'to the electorates an altogether unrealistic degree of initiative . . . which practically amounted to ignoring leadership'.[4] Instead, he proposes a broad and simple definition of democratic practices that is able to inform our argument. According to him, 'democracy means only that the people have the opportunity of accepting or refusing the men who are to rule them'.[5] A non-competitive election can then be defined as one in which the majority of the voters is unable to reject the leaders proposed by the governing power, whatever the freedom of the vote and despite the existence of alternative and competing candidates. In other words, a non-competitive election is a consultation the outcome of which is known in advance, not because of the majority of voters' constant and informed preferences, but as a result of manipulation on the part of the governing power or of insurmountable social constraints.

AUTHORITARIAN CONTEXTS

Non-competitive elections thus understood are not peculiar to authoritarian states alone. If one is not restricted to a national focus or a purely constitutional approach, elections in representative democracies are sometimes not the result of an autonomous choice on the part of the voters. In the United States, within the bipartisan national party system, non-competitive elections are not rare. In numerous counties and towns, there is only one party organisation. This absence of political choice is not limited, as is generally imagined, to the once electorally solid Southern states.[6] Examples of single candidatures or pseudo-pluralism in Western democracies could be multiplied.[7]

Very often, political systems that offer all the appearances of liberal democracy and where a plurality of groups coexist and, in theory, oppose each other on equal terms, experience competitive elections only through nationwide aggregation of results from one-party locales or regional systems of domination. Huge numbers of unanimous votes at the level of villages or even vast territorial constituencies exclude individual choice. Thus, in the Colombian countryside, electoral competition between Liberals and Conservatives is often of the most limited kind. Liberal villages oppose Conservative villages;[8] the unanimity of the vote in each does not reflect a choice between clear political options but an inherited, traditional attitude. In a Nigeria proud of its multi-partyism before Biafran secession, each party tended to confine itself to a particular regional and ethnic area in which it enjoyed quasi-monopolistic control. Opposition parties were rejected as foreigners – that is, representatives of another region.[9]

Such manifestations of non-competitive elections within a formally pluralistic framework are prevalent in societies where the modes of relationship favour *primary* groups, while secondary groups are weakly developed, even non-existent. The preponderance of primordial links (family, ethnic group, language, religion, province) over voluntary groupings favours the ascendancy of traditional local authorities and hierarchical structures of command. More generally, in the absence of horizontal solidarities based on common socio-economic interests or conceptions, vertical authority patterns of dependence and domination crystallise.

We shall describe as *authoritarian contexts* those local or regional societies marked by the preponderance of relationships founded upon vertical solidarity, whether based upon economic, social or ethnic sources. When this type of situation is predominant in a nation, it may give rise to a unique political system differing from both the democratic pluralist model, in which consent plays a decisive role, and from authoritarian regimes, where coercion tends to be the decisive factor. But such a system, *at least locally*, has the same features as single-party regimes have with regard to political competition. It is structurally authoritarian, but does not have recourse to institutional authoritarianism. At the extreme, the governing power may find it necessary to resort to private or local violence, but not to forced mobilisation or the centralised coercive demobilisation procedures of authoritarian systems.

The *vertical* nature of social relations permits the authoritarian use of democratic pluralist institutions in the sphere of the vote. These common types of social control exclude opinion-based voting. In authoritarian contexts, votes are more collective than individual. Therefore, floating votes do not exist, since voters are always firmly directed by those above them.

CLIENTELIST CONTROL OF THE VOTE

Where it is impossible to dismiss a political leader – or to choose another one – through an election, this is likely to be because the governing power has laid down conditions that limit candidates' and voters' freedoms and falsify the results of the election. One is then dealing with what is conventionally called an authoritarian regime. But it can also arise from social control of voters in authoritarian contexts. For convenience, we propose to designate as 'clientelist control' all the different types of social domination that allow the imperative control of electoral choices.

The patron – client relations or clientele systems principally studied by anthropologists cover a wide range of vertically organised forms of co-operation. They constitute 'relations of mutual advantage between unequal partners'[10] or 'a dyadic contract of reciprocal obligation between individuals of unequal socio-economic status'.[11] Clientelism always consists of three elements: a relationship between two parties of unequal status, 'an exchange of non-homogeneous goods and services'[12] and an interpersonal relationship based upon particularistic criteria regulating this exchange.

Basing their conclusions on a limited range of communities, some anthropologists have at times overestimated the affective character and voluntaristic aspect of clientele relations. The *do ut des* relationship ('I give to you so that you give to me') rarely arises in the 'lopsided friendship' model used by Pitt-Rivers in his study of patronage ties in Spain.[13] If the clientele relationship represents a kind of instrumental orientation, occasionally even being founded on some rational calculation,[14] it is no less fundamentally asymmetric. This asymmetry conditions the whole relationship. The exchange is more unequal than reciprocal; thus, the powerful figure can offer his protection to the weak in exchange for a multitude of actions of social and political support. It is the patron who 'directs the relationship and determines what must be exchanged and when'.[15] Notwithstanding face-to-face contact and the proximity of the 'contracting' parties, the patron's need for a clientele is marginal, especially in prestige and power. For the deprived and vulnerable client, however, the need for patronage can be critical, even a matter of life or death. The hierarchical relationship founded on subordination and command through personal dependence[16] is so stable that only a social upheaval or the disappearance of one of the partners can challenge it. This dependence is not always tied to exploitation, but it is often characterised by coercion, which becomes all the stronger as clientelist legitimacy weakens.[17]

The clientelist vote is not reducible to the phenomenon of non-competitive elections. A continuum stretching from a captive to a freely expressed vote covers various types of dependent votes, occurring sometimes in open pluralist contexts and sometimes in strictly non-competitive ones. Thus, even European democracies can have patronage networks to varying degrees. According to region, electoral results are more or less characterised by the importance of clientelist votes. If the circumstances are favourable, local political authorities can create genuine patronage relationships through the multiplication of personal favours or individual interventions with the public authorities. The vote, in the direction specified by the powerful benevolent notable, exhibits both gratitude and the willingness to preserve a situation that has been judged favourable. Equally, direct or indirect economic pressures and individual pre-election presents sometimes come to take over from these legitimate means of influence. However, the complex characteristics of modern, liberal societies (urbanisation, relatively full employment, social security, and so on) reduce the possibilities for personal domination.

By contrast, in countries where the social context is dominated by vertical authority patterns, some more secularised areas, such as the urban districts, generate 'clientelised' partisan competition that allows the voter a very profitable freedom of choice. This was true in the Philippines, where, before the Marcos era began, elections were hotly contested and political attitudes were largely independent of socio-economic variables. The free voter, living in urbanised areas, 'sold' his vote to the highest bidding party.[18] This is equally the case in several South-East Asian and Middle Eastern countries with political pluralism. The distribution of the vote does not reflect a choice based on opinion, but, within certain limits set by confessional or ethnic allegiances, blends into laws of the market, and mirrors the parties' differing economic resources. Such situations are hardly long-lasting, either because horizontal groupings come to alter the rules of the clientelist game, or because the winner-take-all ethos becomes politically dominant by the introduction of a ballot that does not allow partisan competition.

When the clientelist vote is responsible for non-competitive elections, it divides broadly into two extreme ideal types. At the one extreme is the *sold vote* and at the other the *gregarious vote*. These are differentiated by the voter's degree of autonomy *vis-à-vis* his patron. The distinction is not absolute. In reality, the vote that we have labelled gregarious almost always comprises some degree of gratification, while the sold vote is rarely without a minimum of coercion: it is an obligation to sell, especially when an anti-system alternative appears.

In the case of the sold vote, the vote is a commodity of exchange with no political meaning for the person who has it in his possession. It is precisely a question of an 'economic valuable given for a political right'.[19] The vote is not always exchanged for money but rather for scarce goods. This can be alcohol, as on the Colombian Caribbean coast;[20] food and clothing, as in Naples under the monarchist mayor in the 1950s;[21] or even sewing machines, as in 1962 elections in the Brazilian state of Ceara.[22] The goods received are more often a job, a place to live, credit or irrigation for crops, or proper payment for the sale of agricultural produce. Control over the voters is effected through multiple actors electing agents, functionaries of specialised or commercial bodies, of local politicians or large landowners, transport entrepreneurs or majordomos.

One thing is certain: the sold vote is not a free vote. The monopoly purchaser exercises dominance over the citizen who sells. Delivery of the vote does not pay off the debt contracted by the latter. Except in the case of an anonymous and proportionate exchange – for example, a vote for a food package – a durable dependence tie is established. A clientelist network is founded upon a continuing grant of personal favours, but favours that can always be revoked by the patron.

In contrast to the sold vote, which is individualistic in character, the gregarious vote is collective and passive. Groups of voters are organised to ballot. They are transported, lodged, fed, entertained and may even receive small presents. The election is a festival that breaks the monotony of their days. Feasting and drinking reward organised civic zeal. The citizens are herded to the ballot boxes. Brazilian electoral vocabulary, rich in terms to designate this type of election, has baptised the gregarious vote the *voto de cabestro*, the 'vote of the herds'. The important thing, particularly in north-east Brazil, is to pen the election contingents carefully in *quarteis* or *currais* while awaiting polling time.[23]

The election result, which is known in advance, depends for the magnitude of its success on the discipline or indiscipline of the assembled voters. This type of operation, which is not peculiar to pre-1964 Brazil, sometimes is carried off with a good deal of violence. Election agents, the patron's right-hand men, are occasionally heavy-handed. Beware the voter refusing the delights of patronal generosity and preferring to vote in another direction. The *capanga* in the Brazilian north-east or the Mafia in Sicily not long ago would have punished such a dangerous anti-social citizen.

Thanks to a vigorous organisation, the painful surprises of universal suffrage are avoided. The patron, often the biggest landowner in the area, in effect owns a large bloc of votes that the parties and governing power buy from him. They have no need to conduct a campaign for the benefit of atomised floating votes. It suffices to address the 'vote banks', i.e. the herdsmen who direct flocks of gregarious voters.

In such contexts political participation reflects not the state of individual opinion, but that of society, and the election result registers not the political attitudes and choices of voters, but the reality of social relationships. In authoritarian systems the teller is often the voter. In authoritarian contexts, it is the patron who plays the role of voter-in-chief, rich in his clientele.

THE SOCIAL AND INSTITUTIONAL CONDITIONS OF THE CLIENTELIST VOTE

The granting of universal suffrage is as much a condition for the clientelist vote as it is for competitive elections. Limited franchise system or authoritarian regimes do not need complex techniques to achieve a result that is identical in appearance. But the establishment of a clientele network is not possible in every social environment. Personal dependence is not a cultural and psychological phenomenon; it is a response to specific social structures.

Before analysing concrete situations, one can try to specify the conditions underpinning the electoral manifestation of clientelism, as contrasted with the competitve vote. In the sense that we have defined them, competitive elections assume not only formal political equality but also that the social distance between the haves and the have-nots, even if it is considerable, does not appear natural and legitimate. An egalitarian ideology, realised most notably through the possibilities (even if limited) for social mobility or the impartiality of the state, seems indispensable. By contrast, one of the characteristics of an authoritarian context is to be found in the predominance of ascribed and hereditary conditions over achieved status. Perfect competition, however, would assume the homogeneity and nearly absolute secularisation of society, as well as the unhindered mobility of its members. It seems risky to define by per capita income the chances for a stable pluralist democracy. If an economic variable must be introduced, this can only be the stage of development of the economy that largely determines the nature of social relationships. Thus, clientelism very often appears tied to the 'incomplete capitalist rationalisation of the economy'.[24] This is a broad definition which does not cover all forms of patronage.

The social context in which clientele relationships predominate presents three closely related characteristics, which we shall separate for the purposes of this analysis: insecurity, isolation and the privatisation and concentration of power.

(1) *Insecurity.* Anthropologists emphasising the voluntary dimension of clientelism have shown how patronage relationships create security. The client relation provides a kind of insurance for peasants in poorly developed regions, 'an antidote for the precariousness of existence and the feeling of insecurity that accompanies it'.[25] It is behaviour intended, through the quest for a protector, to reduce anxiety, distress in the face of calamities, and threats.[26] Clientelism develops in areas where the problem of survival is faced daily. Traditional rural areas are not the only places affected. Periods of social disorganisation in urban milieux are also favourable to clientelist structures. Immigration, the exodus from the countryside, and a high level of chronic and structural unemployment all multiply the number of 'civic incompetents'[27] whose short-term expec-

tations lead them to appeal for assistance – which it is easy to politicise. The shanty-town and the slum as well as the *latifundio* are the breeding grounds for patronage-based elections.

Scarcity of the necessities of life and vulnerability of economic status are the two mainsprings of insecurity consolidating vertical solidarities. Just as there is a politics of abundance, there is a politics of scarcity.[28] A monopoly of scarce and precious resources gives a patron the capacity for total domination. This is the case, for example, with water in irrigated lands under cultivation. The person who controls the water supply in hydraulic despotisms has the power of life, if not death, over his vassals.

The most decisive and widespread means of control and domination is employment. A permanent and structural high level of unemployment is often responsible for clientelism, whatever the nature of a country's institutions. When 'work is an ancestral aspiration' appearing most often as 'a sort of favour that . . . falls from the sky through a benefactor's act of grace',[29] clientele relationships are inevitably to be found at the centre of social and political life. This is the case whether it is in Naples, Calcutta or Recife. In an environment marked by a structural labour surplus, the person responsible for employment or giving out jobs certainly has some political power, even if he does not monopolise it. This is true not only of the large landlord and his agricultural workers, but also of any public-service employer. The latter can work in the state alcohol industry, as in Colombia,[30] or other state industries[31] or even in the municipal school service, a source of patronage in southern Italy. The electoral exploitation of the anguish of the unemployed is a permanent feature of the politics of scarcity. In every case, unemployment is a decisive component of the authoritarian context.

The influence of the landed property system and of types of tenure has been found in almost all corners of the globe, even in countries where public opinion is a reality independent of patronage relationships. Thus, André Siegfried in his *Tableau politique de la France de l'ouest* pointed to the non-possessing classes' dependence in the large landowning areas as being a function of the mode of cultivation, share-croppers being more sensitive than farmers to the 'owner's' solicitations.[32] It is the same in southern Italy, in the relations between *mezzadria* and clientelism. In other respects, the more unstable the peasant's status, the greater is the patron's power; precarious tenures granted in exchange for non-remunerated work, a relatively frequent form of exploitation in Latin America, create a personal dependence that is even stronger than share-cropping. The recruiters of day-labourers, the Andean *gamonal* or Sicilian *caporale*, who grant or refuse work in the absence of the owner or without his knowledge, are particularly effective election agents.

The difficulty of establishing horizontal solidarity organisations such as trade unions or agricultural co-operatives is evident. The fatal reality of underemployment encourages clients to wish to be looked upon favourably by their patron rather than to organise on the basis of common categorical interests. It is the politics of each man for himself, of favour and recommendation, a politics that corresponds to the perception of society as a cake of fixed size that has to be shared among a growing number of starving table companions.[33] Therefore, it is not paradoxical that in countries and regimes where the distribution of income is flagrantly unequal, where social injustice reigns as master, class conflicts and oppositions are weak in intensity.[34]

Structures based upon the quest for protection and personal dependence express the penury of those with work and without land. At some point economic modernisation provokes the emergence of new patrons or at the very least directs client attitudes towards new social authorities, such as civil servants or engineers, sometimes even against the authority's will.[35] Since debts to the patron are paid by votes, the changing allegiance resulting from the intrusion of new patrons (public works, credit organisation, industries, state agricultural institutes) can have decisive political consequences. Nevertheless, a clientelist model remains dominant.

(2) *Isolation.* André Siegfried has observed that scattered living patterns favour the ascendancy of local authorities. In the same way, communication difficulties increase the need of the weak for protection and mediation. The benevolent patron 'bridges the gap between village and town, between villagers and governmental elites'.[36] He serves as mediator between the centre and the periphery. But very often this intermediary acts 'to remedy social and geographic discontinuity [only] so as to preserve it indefinitely'.[37] The closed society engenders social domination. In Mexico, local chiefs (*caciques*) have been known to oppose the building of roads and railways: the mobility of their subjects threatens their power.[38] This is the practice principally in rural areas, when the basis of domination is commercial, as the patron is the principal purchaser of the local produce. Thus, we have the local chief, a coffee-buyer in an isolated Colombian village, who threatens to lower the price of coffee paid to peasants who do not vote in the right direction.[39] The large isolated landholding, communicating with the town or village only through the patron's telephone, is the ideal picture of the clientelist microcosm. In some Latin American countries, it is not unusual for the patron to open a general store, and even distribute alcohol more or less freely on Saturday evenings so as to avoid all outside contact and maintain a monopolistic control over his human resources.[40]

The free market and the horizontal mobility of economic agents are conditions of competitive elections. But isolation can be social, even psychological: transplantation to a culturally foreign urban environment and the use of a minority language often have the same effects as geographical isolation and are susceptible to political use in the same way. Clientelism is thus tied to the difficulties of national integration.

(3) *The state and the privatisation of power.* Clientele relations develop especially, but not exclusively, in social contexts where durable and impartial status and guarantees of security do not exist. Neither the means for a rudimentary existence nor those for effective social protection are provided by impersonal institutions. The minimal and distant state does not attend to the welfare of its citizens. It intervenes as little as possible in socio-economic relations. It delegates its power to private territorial authorities in return for their keeping order and providing electoral support. This was the case with the Brazilian *coronelismo*, where rural chiefs controlled both land and men and determined the latter's vote.[41] In such a case, the weak and the poor can expect nothing from the central government.'The Commander is stronger than the government', declared a Brazilian peasant of the Nordeste to a journalist, with regard to a police officer who had improperly acquired great areas of land in the state of Pernambuco.[42]

In fact, the government, when it makes its presence felt, by no means guarantees everybody's protection under the law, either because of a pact with local notables or because of underadministration. The ruling power is sometimes even a threat operating through the gendarmes' and tax-collectors' exactions, against which it is advisable to find the protection of a powerful private guardian.[43] There is also a third case: the state substitutes for the multiple patrons, and sets up a mass clientele system that, without abandoning the particularistic criteria of protection and dependence, gives a more impersonal dimension to the mechanisms of non-competitive electoral mobilisation. That is, the public body and the 'state-controlled' union replace the big landowner or influential professional. This intervention of the state is usually accompanied by a transformation of the economy and of social relationships. The traditional society gives way to a mass society, but the insecurity of existence is no less. The ruling groups strive to identify the regime with the welfare state that they claim to be establishing. This is a new manifestation of the privatisation of power. The type of state, clientelism and non-competitive elections are therefore three closely interdependent aspects of the same phenomenon.

TYPES OF CLIENTELIST CONTROL

Following Alex Weingrod, one can distinguish between 'patron – client ties' in a narrow sense and 'party-directed patronage'.[44] The latter takes several forms.

(1) Traditional patronage rests on a system of domination exercised by local notables over protected and obligated clients. This type of primary vertical solidarity develops especially in an agrarian environment with a hierarchical status system, where wage-earning is not widespread. The

gregarious vote of organised election contingents occurs in this situation. Unrestricted universal suffrage is not even necessary. On the contrary, when any restrictive clause whatever is introduced (a literacy criterion, for example), the system functions all the better, because the patron chooses the voters. The vote then becomes a distinction, proof of confidence and a reward for fidelity.

This type of clientele relationship is not primordial. The directed vote is only an adaptation of a command structure with diffuse economic, social, political and sometimes military functions. The patron – client relationship is multiform and diffuse. The vote is only a supplementary factor in a system where power depends less on wealth (that is to say, production) than on the number of clients or vassals who are producers and soldiers, as well as voters. This kind of 'paternalist group relations'[45] is rarely to be confused with party structures. In the same way that the patron chooses his voters, he also chooses the candidates or party to which he will deliver the bloc vote at his disposal. Usually, following some hard bargaining, the patron delivers his fiefdom's votes to the party that offers the most. Competition thus takes on a very peculiar meaning: parties compete for a patron who gambles with his electoral capital.

Sometimes very loose alliances of enfeoffed notables can make up a political group that has it own electorate. Some parties in Nigeria and Brazil at the time of multi-partyism there illustrate this type of adaptation. But traditional patronage can also occur in modern forms of partisan representation. Thus, even theoretically class-based doctrinaire parties sometimes contain clientelist configurations within their structures.[46] According to W. F. Wertheim, this is the case in Indonesia, and especially in Javanese society, because of its vertical divisions into broad ideological segments (*aliran*). In Sukarno's time, the Indonesian Communist Party (PKI) was a 'mass party run by village leaders using their traditional prestige'. Like other Javanese parties, the PKI's followers were poor peasants and its leaders often rich ones. In elections, the villages frequently voted unanimously for the PKI or for such and such a *santri* or *non-santri* religious party. The discrepancy between theory and practice cause by grafting a modern partisan content onto traditional forms of relationship is also found in other societies.

More frequently, modern multi-class parties rely on a clientelist structure without integrating it into their organisation. The Union Progressiste Senegalaise (UPS) fits this description: Leopold Senghor's party benefits from the support of the Maraboutique notables while remaining separate from the Moslem fraternities.[47] This is a borderline case, since it is not easy to distinguish personal patronage relations from properly so called party-directed patronage.

(2) The patronage role of parties is found in all political systems. Its importance varies from system to system. While marginal or residual in an opinion-based regime with competitive elections, it can be the keystone of a

semi-competitive system in which competition is only accidental. In fact, party clientelism is found in full play in some pluralist democratic states because of the *de facto* suppression of electoral competition in them.

Theoretically, at least two models of partisan patronage can be distinguished: on the one hand, machine patronage; and, on the other, the clientelism practised by parties of social integration. Broadly speaking, they correspond to two types of state. The machine, a product of a form of party that is in eclipse, usually develops within the framework of a liberal state. Parties of social integration, having multiple collateral organisations, are better suited to welfare and social interventionist states.

Machine politics assumed its classical form in institutional contexts of competitive pluralism, notably in the United States before and after the First World War. Founded on the power of the 'boss' exercising power without responsibility, the election machine functioned thanks to the boss's services to a population that was often outcast and vulnerable.[48] The boss brought often-indispensable assistance to immigrants and foreign minorities in crowded city areas; they used their vote as a piece of merchandise. The precinct captain, himself an entrepreneur and client of the boss, delivered the votes on polling day. When a machine was thoroughly entrenched in a ward, the opposition party did not even bother to organise there. Thus, there was not only a non-competitive election, but also a single party. The authoritarian context, deriving from a concentration of needy and docile voters, could even lead to the establishment of a kind of local dictatorship. Frank L. Hague, the Democratic boss of New Jersey, or the picturesque Huey P. Long of Louisiana are the most well known of authorities based upon well-run electoral machines. Corruption and authoritarian manipulations supplemented them, thus passing from clientelist control to the ruling power's direct intervention in the elections.

The historical North American example helps identify the mechanisms and conditions under which political machines emerge. Their emergence is a question of an organism responding to particular demands in exchange for votes. Their preferred terrain is the big city in periods of accelerated urbanisation owing to an exodus from the land or external immigration. It was in a period of massive immigration that the great American machines such as Tammany Hall became entrenched. The isolation and anonymity of urban life resulting from atomisation and immigrant uprootings are equally responsible for the success of the Radical Party machine in Buenos Aires at the beginning of the century, although the right to vote was granted to foreigners very rarely. The district chiefs (*caudillos de barrio*) provided help, charity and credit. Party committees even sold low-priced food, known as 'Radical bread' and 'Radical milk'.[49]

The protection furnished by the political machine mitigates the absence of governmental protection. Sometimes the electoral machine even blends into the official government party, since the latter prefers a broad social base of support, channelling its 'distributive capacity' through the party. A favour or a service creates bonds of personal dependence tying the citizen to his benefactor. Rights guaranteed by laws impersonal in essence offer fewer political dividends.[50] In the case of single or dominant parties that have only a weak mobilisation capacity and do not play a permanent social control role, this type of political machine is one of the most rudimentary forms of state clientelism.

The permanent parties of social integration differ in their clientele relationship from political machines by virtue of the means employed. The end is the same: to make people vote, and direct them in a manner that is quasi-irreversible. This type of party in power – for the resources of power are necessary to their operations – grips the state and society in a clientele network of extreme density. This is accomplished through collateral organisations (trade unions, peasant associations, cultural associations, and so on), on the one hand, and through public bodies, on the other. The two are often closely interrelated, distributing goods or services according to particularistic criteria implying a political *quid pro quo*. Clientelism is superimposed upon *parentela*, the inbred ties linking the party, the state bureaucracy and pressure groups.[51]

This tentacle-type party can dominate a system that is fundamentally pluralist and open. In this case, the secularisation of social relations, resulting particularly from economic development and cultural modernisation, blocks the clientelist machinery, even increasing the polls' competitive character in some reputedly authoritarian contexts and delivering a fatal blow to the preponderance of party government. Contemporary Italy largely conforms to this situation. In other societies, the dominant party is synonymous with the regime. All forms of political competition are restricted to the system's periphery and the system itself can evolve only by changing its nature. Non-competitive elections are not regional or residual exceptions affecting only areas where the simultaneous confusion between traditional structure and legal – rational ones has perpetuated an archaic political culture.[52] These elections constitute the essence of a semi-competitive type of political system that has as its principle that the issue of who holds governing power should not be brought into question, and state clientelism as its prime means of realising this principle. Contemporary Mexico and its Partido Revolucionario Institucional would be a good example of this model.

Because it has been best studied, the Italian case can provide us with some insights into the functioning of modern clientelist parties. According to Luigi Graziano, the dominant party is a mass-patronage party. But the electors' relations with the partisan bureaucracy, which is in particular the distributer of state jobs, are dependent on a quasi-contractual arrangement. In that respect, the relationship is more balanced and less effective than in traditional clientele systems.[53] In a democratic system (i.e. operating on the basis of universal suffrage) characterised by clientelism and 'paternalism', every institution is more or less clientelised. Savings banks, agricultural friendly societies and all credit establishments in general, as well as the state industries and the social security and superannuation funds, constitute a 'Pharaoh-like' empire of colossal clientelist interests, which form the regime's foundation.[54] State resources are not only employed so as to exercise a collective influence over the electorate, as in reputedly competitive opinion-based regimes, but also used to make each elector individually dependent upon the partisan bureaucracy. Therefore, it is the nature of the entire state that is ultimately affected by the modalities of electoral control. This is true in complex industrial societies as well as in less differentiated ones.

THE FUNCTIONS OF CLIENTELIST CONTROL AND POLITICAL DEVELOPMENT

Non-competitive clientelist elections can have the same political functions as results obtained through the intervention of the governing power. Of the four functions stressed by Hermet, two appear to be better filled by clientelist control of electors. Pluralist elections, without excessive restriction on opposition rights or the fraudulent manipulation of results, assure the regime a legitimacy much superior to that afforded by a plebiscite or a single-list consultation. Clientelist control presents more risks for power-holders, because of the discretion it offers. Observers can be mistaken: the hold on the elector is less apparent than when manipulating the ballot boxes. The 'anaesthetising' role of this type of election is particularly marked, but it is often devoid of educational content, for the ideological dimension is secondary or non-existent. Anaesthesia derives from the satisfaction of short-term demands in return for political support and votes, a process that acts to the detriment of long-term change. These individualist demobilising favours keep fundamental problems in society hidden, and channel a gratitude towards the master and power-holders that is very useful for the maintenance of the *status quo*.

It is in fact in social relations that clientelist control of the vote has its most significant effects. In the political use of social domination, the clientelist vote articulates the fundamental configuration of society through the institution of universal suffrage. As a mechanism of control, patronage and clientele relationships ensure a certain social peace. The partial satisfaction of immediate individual needs serves as a safety valve in situations where the distribution of income is profoundly unbalanced. The favours dispensed by the patron reinforce his hold over his clients. The fidelity reward exchange perpetuates a funnel structure in which the person situated at the top of the pyramid goes unchallenged. The system legitimates the concentration of wealth in its private form as well as corruption in the public realm.

The context of insecurity in which dependence networks develop makes horizontal bonds of social solidarity almost impossible. The association between classes of people appears as a high risk with uncertain benefits. The client prefers to minimise his losses at the expense of his independence rather than seek class autonomy.[55] Thus, the vertical organisation of 'clientele systems is one of the most important obstacles to the outbreak of social revolutions'.[56] All the evidence points to its being the same with traditional solidarities.[57] Party clientelism, although more apt to evolve, fills the same role.

However, these mechanisms can be perpetuated, especially in their modern form, only if they are periodically brought up to date. Thus, the election is an important time in the clientelist system. It is the means of affirming the loyalties that make the elimination of electoral competition possible. The electoral exchange reinvigorates the vertical solidarities that otherwise lose their edge. If the notable, the machine or the party and its parallel hierarchies guarantees a minimum of social protection, the election enables the client, by paying his debt, to deserve a patronal largesse once again. In addition, the patronal potlatch and the reminder of obligations erode the temptation of common interest groups and horizontal ties.[58] The electoral drama again spreads the net of the primary group, the framework of unquestioned domination. The non-competitive poll can also reflect a vote of identification. Clan, ethnic, village or province consciousness sweeps the nascent class consciousness aside. Domination is reaffirmed by it.

TABLE II. 1

From Clientelism to Intervention by Governing Power

	Traditional rural society or society complex with authoritarian contexts	Transition to mass, secularised society	Conservative breakdowns and authoritarian modernisation
Social relationships	Primary, vertical	Categorical, horizontal	Secondary, vertical (neo- or pseudo-corporative)
Social control	Clientelist	Impersonal, objective influence,-consent	Coercive
Elections	De facto non-competitive	Competitive	De jure non-competitive;-intervention by the governing power

The importance can be illustrated by certain accidents of political developments that affect modernising traditional societies. The disaggregation of primordial clientelist solidarities, and sometimes the failure of state or party clientelism, entails the establishment of 'emergency bureaucratic regimes' *after* the temporary introduction of competitive elections in the wake of mass secularisation (Table II.1). The crisis of the authoritarian context ends up in the creation of an authoritarian system. Brazil in 1964 and Indonesia in 1965 followed this evolutionary pattern. From the electoral point of view, the loosening of clientelist control and the first results of electoral competition stimulated the governing power's intervention. Authoritarian modernisation was invoked to guarantee the social *status quo* against the formation of categorical groups of peasants or workers. Without the brake provided by clientelist control, free competitive elections in fact represent a danger for the established order. When the ruling classes dare not subject themselves to the hazards of the ballot box, nor test their own capacity for hegemonic influence, institutional violence is the unavoidable resort.

3 Non-Competitive Elections in Europe

JUAN J. LINZ

For those who assume that elections are an opportunity for the citizen to express freely his preference for alternative leadership and programmes, the question tends to be, 'Why elections at all when the rulers are unlikely to give up their power whatever the outcome?'[1] Our assumption here is that if there are elections they must have some functions from the point of view of the leadership of the country, and some consequences for the political system, and the voters mut have some reason to participate in them. Any adequate analysis of elections would have to answer the following list of questions.

(1) What functions do those elections have from the point of view of the rulers, both explicitly in their statements and implicitly in their minds?

(2) What consequences do such elections actually have for the political system, whether intended or unintended, functional or dysfunctional?

(3) What motivates voters to participate in non-competitive and semi-competitive elections and plebiscites? Their motivations may or may not be in accord with the reasons why the rulers require their participation.

(4) What consequences does participation have for voters independently of their intent?

(5) What is the significance of the electoral process for the candidates in non-competitive and semi-competitive elections?

Any typology of political systems should in principle lead to different answers to these questions; the same should be true for any typology of non-competitive or semi-competitive elections.

In addition to the features of non-competitive elections emphasised by Hermet in Chapter 1, there is another dimension of importance in a European setting: the level of incorporation or universality of suffrage *versus* the restrictiveness, segmentation and indirectness of suffrage. It is important to emphasise that those three dimensions do not correlate strongly. In fact, a great variety of combinations can actually be found in non-democratic political systems.

One of the most dramatic electoral analyses we can undertake is the comparison of the results of a free election before the breakdown of democratic institutions and the results of the subsequent election helping to establish authoritarian or totalitarian rule – particularly when the new regime could not immediately dispense with elections, even though it could already severely limit the freedom of the voters through physical and moral coercion. This was the case in Germany in the March 1933 election, after the *Machtergreifung* (seizure of power) and the Reichstag fire, and in Italy in the April 1924 election, after the March on Rome. In both cases, the parties that had participated in the last fully free election could still participate, though in the Italian case under a changed electoral law that heavily favoured the majority. In Germany, the Nazis for their own good reasons still allowed the Communists (KPD) to participate.[2] The comparison allows us to analyse the capacity of the electorate of different parties in different constituencies and social settings to resist the appeal and the pressures of the fascist movements already in power and in control of the instruments of violence. A systematic study of the returns, in connection with information on the patterns of pressure, the level of penetration of the dominant party in the administration and the life of the communities, the position taken by leaders of different parties, interest groups and churches, together with information on the illegal actions of the party and the state to assure its victory, can help us better to understand the process through which coercive unanimity is achieved. This is the process that the Nazis described so well with their term, *Gleichschaltung*.

The first elections after the assumption of power by Mussolini and Hitler provide an excellent example of how to assure the outcome and at the same time still give the appearance of legal continuity with a democratic constitutional regime. The appearance of legality is highly desirable as a way of assuring the loyalty of civil servants, the armed forces, and other institutions, and of avoiding the open hostility of others before a full consolidation of power. This was certainly a consideration in allowing the Communist candidates to run even when most of them were already arrested, in exile abroad or underground and the party could not hold any electoral meetings. In addition, the maintenance of the electoral fiction facilitated the neutralisation of the growing fears of coalition partners like the Deutschnationale Volkspartei (DNVP), needed in broadening the basis of the regime and incorporating key institutional sectors, particularly when some factions in those parties begin to have cold feet about their future role.[3] Under the circumstances election day serves a dual purpose: it gives a formally legal basis within the old democratic constitution to the anti-democratic rulers and at the same time is an occasion for the plebiscitarian manifestation of a never-before-known mass declaration of faith (*Massenbekenntnis*), to use the expression of Goebbels on a day that was already officially declared *Tag der erwachenden Nation* (Day of the Reviving Nation). One might add to these three functions a more latent one – to make manifest the actual power of the party on the street and its control of the state – which, as a first lesson of prophylactic terror, can contribute to the growing passive acceptance of the regime by former opponents.

On the other hand, those last semi-free elections before the full establishment of totalitarian control provide dramatic evidence of the failure of the new rulers to achieve the same proportion of the vote that democratic parties in a free election, the Social Democrats (SPD) in 1919 and the Christian Democrats in 1953 and after, could obtain. It should not be forgotten that on 5 March 1933, after five weeks of Hitler in power, 56 per cent of the voters did not support the Nazis (NSDAP). Belying the thesis that democracy had been liquidated by the free will of the majority (with an 89 per cent participation) the NSDAP obtained 43·9 per cent of the votes and 44·5 per cent of the seats, compared to 37·2 per cent of votes in July 1932 and 33·1 per cent in November 1932. The SPD went down only from 20·7 to 18·2 per cent, and the KPD from 16·9 to 12·2 per cent, in spite of the persecution they had suffered. The Zentrum and the Bavarian party (BVP) retained 14·1 per cent of the vote, as against 15·0 per cent previously. This is not the place to review the fascinating detail that Bracher, Sauer and Schulz give of the vote in different communities, showing that in some districts (*Kreise*) and muncipalities (*Gemeinden*) the working-class parties or the Zentrum could hold on to over 60 per cent of the vote and the NSDAP remain in third place. It would be interesting to know how Nazi policy in communities like these differed in succeeding years from the party's policy in places where it already obtained plebiscitarian acclamation. It would also be interesting to know if the later manifestations of opposition to the regime reflected this solid climate of opinion in the last semi-free election. When we think of the courageous stand of Bishop Galen in Münster, as compared with the behaviour of other Catholic bishops, we perhaps should not forget that in the electoral district (*Regierungsbezirk*) of Münster the NSDAP had only 28·7 per cent of the vote and the Zentrum still obtained 39·0 per cent, and over 50 or even 60 per cent in many communities of Westphalia. It might be asked if the totalitarian regime in its process of consolidation followed a more temporising line in such areas, as Peterson's *The Limits of Hitler's Power*[4] would suggest, or if in strongly Communist and socialist districts it followed an even more repressive policy. Certainly the few studies we have on the practice of Nazi government at the community level suggests that the party and the authorities were very conscious of the climate of opinion that for the last time expressed itself semi-freely in these elections. It would also be of great interest to explain sociologically why the Catholic sub-culture in the northern and eastern German enclaves and in Westphalia was better able

to resist the Nazi tide than in many districts of southern Germany, where
the party was born but had encountered in the last years of the Weimar
Republic a limit to its expansion. Equally interesting would be to know
more about where and why the DNVP could hold on to 8 per cent of the
vote (compared to 8·3 per cent in the previous election), which, added to
the NSDAP's 44 per cent, assured the emergence of a national coalition
dominated by Hitler. The DNVP acted here under the mistaken notion
that it and the social and institutional forces linked with it could control
their more numerous and stronger allies.

It is significant for the understanding of such electoral processes to
remember that on 1 April 1933 Goebbels would say, 'It would not satisfy us
at all to work with the majority of 52 per cent; we want to embrace the
whole people and to mould it into the new form of the state.' The actions
only a week after the election and the public declarations of the
government embodied a revolution, directed from above and manipulated
from below, that was formally legitimated in the interesting plebiscitarian
mobilisations of the electorate in November 1933 and August 1934, in
which the representative component of democracy was formally abandoned in favour of the strictly plebiscitarian acclamation.

To my knowledge, no comparable study exists of the elections of 15 May
1921 in Italy and those taking place under the new electoral law of 18
November 1923 (the Acerbo law) on 6 April 1924, after the March on
Rome and the accession to power of Benito Mussolini.[5] In 1924, for the last
time until after World War II, the electorate had a semi-free choice,
though the electoral law gave an enormous advantage to the majority, to
be gained by the Fascists, in the number of seats. In contrast to Germany in
1921, the PNF (Partito Nazionale Fascista) had not been able on its own to
obtain a large representation in Parliament, and the fact that its
candidates appeared on joint lists with conservative and bourgeois parties
has made the ecological study of the Fascist vote extremely difficult. In
1924 a list under the symbol of the Fascio Littorio was able to obtain 66·3
per cent of the vote, but the parties of the left and the Populari could still
retain a considerable proportion of their former support, particularly in
northern Italy. The Communists, who in 1921 obtained 3·8 per cent of the
vote, dropped to 3·5 per cent. The socialists – in two factions, the Partito
Socialista Unitario and Partito Socialista Massimalista – were reduced
from 25·1 to 10·9 (5·9 + 4·9) per cent. The old Republican Party, with 1·5
per cent, held extremely well to its 1·6 per cent in 1921, while the Catholic
Populari dropped from 21·2 to 9·1 per cent.[6] As in the case of Germany, the
capacity of the different parties to resist the Fascist wave varied unduly,
according to social context, region and type of community, and the
differences could tell us much about the parties' own support, the support
that Mussolini was able to gain once in power, and the impact of the
coercion that made this last election with political parties semi-free. It is
certainly no accident that, while their vote in the Rome area plummeted,

the Populari were able to hold on to more than two-thirds of its vote in its greatest stronghold, the white Veneto.

The making of the *listone* – that is, the list of Fascist candidates for the whole of Italy – by the so-called *pentarchia* illustrates very well a problem that a party committed to a monopoly of power – and particularly a revolutionary party whose leadership is not drawn from the natural elites of the society and that has not penetrated a large part of the country – encounters at the first, semi-free elections after its takeover, while it cannot yet totally disregard democratic procedures. An enormous effort is made to include individual men of standing and influence, as well as opportunists from other parties, in a kind of common front or 'unity ticket'. This leaves to a later date their displacement from any position of power or influence. In the case of the Nazis, the mass electoral following that they had achieved before coming to power, the assured support of the DNVP, and the clearer commitment to totalitarian rule spared them this step. It would be interesting to analyse comparatively the process by which such fronts or unity tickets were achieved in People's Democracies under the leadership of the Communist Party in Eastern Europe,[7] and the degree to which they helped the rulers obtain the mass electoral support required to give the appearance of democratic legitimacy to the founding stages of the regimes.

De Felice[8] has analysed in some detail the political process preceding the 1924 Italian election and its consequences. Some highlights of this type of election can be derived from his work.

(1) There was a conscious decision to distinguish the parties and leaders 'to be fought with the old vigour of the Black Shirts' and those whose co-operation might still be necessary and who might be incorporated into the ruling party or at least into a unity ticket.

(2) A policy combining appeals to self-interest, complex bargaining and a variety of pressures was used to attract individuals rather than parties or organisations to the *listone*. As Mussolini said, 'We will receive in our ranks . . . all those men of populism, liberalism and the factions of social democracy who are ready to give us active and disinterested collaboration, but leaving no doubt that the majority should be reserved to our party.'[9] The appeal was made not to parties but to men in other parties, so as to profit from their influence among the electorate, their personal prestige, and their expert skills. Sometimes those who were included demanded, with limited success, the inclusion of political friends, in the hope of continuing to play a political role. While stating their support for Mussolini and the government, others attempted to present the so-called 'parallel' lists which they did not want to define as in opposition, but which the Fascists quickly defined as 'unfriendly'. This was so in the case of Giolitti, in spite of all the efforts of Mussolini to have him on the *listone*. The ambition for office of the Fascists, of the opportunists, and of

those who still hoped to control developments from the inside made nominating 357 deputies from among some 3000 aspirants a difficult task.

(3) One of the consequences of this inclusive fusion effort was the disappointment, apathy or disaffection of the old cadres of the dominant party on the local scene, who had spent many years in battle with those now to be included in the ticket at the expense of loyal leaders.

(4) The making of electoral lists of this type inevitably brought out the factional conflicts within the dominant party. The continuous bickering and compromises involved in making a *listone* led Mussolini to say in exasperation, 'This is the last time the elections are made this way. The next time I will vote for everyone.'[10]

(5) The leadership, including Mussolini himself, was torn between two contradictory goals: a desire for consensually achieved maximum support and an unwillingness to abandon the power of the myth of violence and tolerate open opposition. The confidential telegrams to the prefects and the appeals to local *ras* of the party constantly underline the need to maintain order to prevent and even repress by force the violence of his supporters. Mussolini intervened personally to assure leaders of the opposition freedom to campaign, but sometimes did so without success. At points he tolerated or closed his eyes to the violence, since he was not sure that he could ultimately dispense with it. As he said, 'The violent, the violent, I also need them.'[11]

(6) While there was an ambivalence in the use of violence against true opposition groups and a desire at least temporarily to control it against potential allies or groups linked with the social establishment, violence was fully unleashed against the tiny groups of dissidents. The repression of dissidents within Mussolini's own camp obviously could not affect the legitimacy of the electoral process, but was considered essential to prevent any risk of its spread within a party that he still did not fully control.

(7) Certain institutions, such as the freemasons and financial and business groups, had an opportunity to place their men on the *listone* and to bargain for influence under the threat of supporting parallel candidacies. Indirectly the electoral process thereby contributed to the accommodation of such institutions to the new regime.

(8) To assure for themselves a greater freedom and some chance for electoral success, the opposition parties were willing to make changes within their own leadership, withdrawing or giving a less prominent role to leaders known for their rigid opposition to the regime. This facilitated a policy of co-operation with the new regime, in the hope that the Fascist party would at least partially enter into the normal life of other parties. This process was particularly important in the case of the Populari.

(9) In the case of anti-parliamentary political movements or political forces, the electoral process poses the dilemma: should its leaders run as candidates or refuse to enter the electoral arena? Should they simultaneously occupy party and government positions with a parliamentary

mandate or avoid such accumulation of offices? It is not insignificant that
Mussolini should have been pleased that some Fascist leaders, such as
C. Rossi in Tuscany and G. Marinelli, renounced safe seats. It is no
accident that, even after becoming legally eligible, Adolf Hitler deliberately chose not to sit in parliament.

(10) While the semi-free election was claimed as an extraordinary
victory, assured through the working of the electoral law, it also made clear
that, with an unexpectedly high turn-out of 63·8 and 66·3 percent of the
valid vote, consensual unanimity was unlikely to be assured for the future.
The Fascist share of the vote varied greatly from region to region: from 54·3
per cent in the North and 69·9 percent in the Islands, to 76 per cent in the
Centre and 81·5 per cent in the South. The great electoral transformation
revealed that the Fascists had not made their greatest gains in their old
strongholds, but in the clientelistic South.

Semi-free elections, despite an assurance of victory, help convince the
anti-democratic leadership that future experiments with semi-free elections could be dangerous, so they speed up the process of transition towards
the suppression of other parties in favour of single-party monopoly and
strictly plebiscitarian elections, with a single, nationwide constituency.
The first semi-free election therefore becomes the last.

The data on electoral participation, the proportion of votes going to a
hegemonic party, and patterns of candidacies reflect the process of
consolidation of authoritarian or totalitarian rule, or, conversely, act as a
barometer of a process of limited democratisation in such regimes. These
shifts are far more likely to manifest themselves first at the lower levels of
the political system (for example, at municipal, provincial or federal-state
level elections) than at the highest levels. Electoral data of the type
mentioned can also contribute to our understanding of the limits that the
ruling group is willing to impose on the process of political change. In this
context it is particularly interesting to observe electoral trends in what may
be called post-totalitarian authoritarian regimes, such as Yugoslavia
under Tito.[12]

TOTALITARIAN ELECTIONS

This is not the place to enter into the lively polemic about the usefulness of
retaining the concept of totalitarianism as a category for the analysis, at a
relatively high level of abstraction, of the very limited number of political
systems that have emerged in the twentieth century as a model polity for
modern man. As a reality approaching an ideal type, only a few political
systems can be understood as totalitarian. There are many regimes in the
modern world that are neither totalitarian nor democratic; they are
misunderstood if they are conceived as hybrids of these polar alternatives

or models, as being only arrested totalitarianisms, pre-totalitarian, unsuccessful or failed totalitarianisms, or, as many writers in the 1950s wanted to conceive them, pre-democratic, tutelary democracies. Men in our time, particularly intellectuals, have been potentially more attracted by the totalitarian ideal than by other non-democratic types of regimes. On some value-dimensions totalitarian systems are superior in theory, and even in practice, to various regimes that can loosely be defined as authoritarian, but they also threaten to a frightening extent certain values that many hold dear.

In their philosophical and ideological assumptions, totalitarian systems are closer to some basic assumptions underlying pluralistic democracies than are authoritarian regimes.[13] A very different question is whether the social – political dynamics and the inherent instability of authoritarian regimes are not in the long run likely to make more feasible a transition to pluralistic democracy, through a, fundamental discontinuity in the legitimacy formula of the regime. Most of the literature on fascism deals with the fascist movements striving for power, but not with fascist regimes in power. Despite all the basic affinities between the regime of Mussolini and Nazism in power, their political systems and societies remained basically different. Social scientists have not developed a systematic differentiation of fascist regimes from other known non-democratic regimes, nor explained the many convergences between the political system created by Hitler and that of Stalin. One way out would be to abandon any attempt to conceptualise abstractly types of political systems and deal with each of them as *sui generis* historical realities.

In an ideal-typical definition of totalitarian political systems, I emphasised as one of three characteristic dimensions the following.

Citizen participation in an active mobilization for political and collective social tasks is encouraged, demanded, rewarded and channelled through a single party and many monopolistic secondary groups. Passive obedience and apathy, retreat into the role of parochials and subjects, characteristic of many authoritarian regimes are considered undesirable by the rulers. This characteristic brings totalitarian society closer to the ideal and even the reality of most democracies and basically differentiates it from most nontotalitarian nondemocratic systems. It is this participation and the sense of participation that democratic observers of totalitarian systems often find so admirable and that makes them think that they are faced with a democracy, even a more perfect democracy than one in which citizens get involved in public issues only or mainly at election time.

However the basic difference between participation in a mobilizational regime and in a democracy is that in the former in each realm of life for each purpose there is only one possible channel for participation and the overall purpose and direction is set by one centre which defines the legitimate goals of those organisations and ultimately controls them.[14]

It should not be surprising that elections and plebiscites should play an important role in totalitarian systems, in contrast to many authoritarian regimes which never or rarely turn to ballots. However, voting in totalitarian systems is only one of the forms of controlled participation, and is often less important than others. There are systems we might call totalitarian which have rejected the recourse to voting at the national level – for instance, Cuba for seventeen years, or China. Given the emphasis on popular participation through party and related organisations in those two societies, why did the leadership reject the idea of legitimation through plebiscitarian electoral mechanisms?[15]

Can we discover any distinctive features of electoral processes in totalitarian systems that could not be found in authoritarian regimes? To answer this question we have relatively few adequate studies, since scholars tend to perceive such electoral processes as of limited relevance.[16] But this is not the view of rulers who invest considerable effort in the preparation of elections, and propaganda about the inevitably successful outcome. The functions of such elections have to be found in the internal dynamics of those regimes.

Voting in totalitarian systems is characterised by the following dimensions.

(1) An extraordinary emphasis on participation and involvement of the voter, very often in the pre-electoral process as well as in the election.

(2) An emphasis on the public rather than private character of participation, often symbolised in public rather than secret voting and an ideological rather than pragmatic justification of this publicity.

(3) An obsessive concern for unanimity rather than a 'mere' majority in participation and in the outcome of the electoral process.

(4) The emphasis on *acclamatio* rather than on *electio*, and thus a transformation even of the elections for minor offices, such as those for local government, into plebiscites.

(5) An identity conception of representation that rejects any idea of distinction between the electorate and the rulers. The elections are conceived as an expression of the identity between the people and the rulers, of unity between *Volk* and *Führung*, with representative bodies an epitome of society.

(6) The festive, ritual, almost magical character of the election and voting.

(7) Optimism and certitude rather than hesitation, ambivalence or awareness of unanticipated consequences characterise the leadership that marshalls the electorate to vote.

(8) Elections are accompanied by a massive mobilisation of activist

supporters of the regime, requiring a single modern mass-cadre party capable of penetrating society down to the lowest levels. The party displaces the old clientelistic networks of society. Its electoral effort is based on a mixture of modern mass-persuasion techniques and personal small-group contacts and pressures and not upon the reciprocities of either clientelistic or machine politics.

(9) The electoral campaign is conceived as a mass socialisation effort, an educational process.

(10) Voting is only one of the forms of mass participation encouraged or required from the citizen. It is part of the process of continuing mobilisation of support and not an isolated event between periods of depolitisation or apathy.

(11) Elections and plebiscites tend to coincide with moments of strength consolidating the regime, rather than with crises of legitimacy.

The extraordinary emphasis on achieving total participation of the electorate, not just by faking the figures on paper but also by a real effort to bring all the voters to the polls, is well documented in studies and accounts of elections in the Soviet Union and Nazi Germany. Extraordinary facilities are granted to sick persons, persons travelling, and so on, to make sure that everyone votes.[17] That desire found its grisly expression in a Nazi effort to make sure that even the inmates of the concentration camps would vote.[18] Non-participation is defined as a public expression of opposition, inviting legal and social sanctions.

Electoral statistics show that only two Western democracies, the Netherlands and Australia, have in recent times had a turn-out rate of above 95 per cent, while all Communist countries but Yugoslavia that have reported elections have had turn-out rates exceeding this level.[19] We would not classify all Communist countries as totalitarian, but even those in Eastern Europe that today we would consider post-totalitarian had experienced a totalitarian phase. In the German Reich in 1933 the turn-out was 96·3 per cent, in 1934 95·6 per cent, and in 1938 99·5 per cent. Over the years, with increased totalitarian control, a higher turn-out was achieved or reported. While Russia in 1930–1 was content with a 79·6 per cent electoral participation in the cities and 70·4 per cent in rural areas, in 1934–5 participation reached 91·6 and 83·3 per cent, respectively. In elections to the Supreme Soviet in 1937, 96·8 per cent were reported voting; in 1946, 99·7 per cent; and in 1950, 99·98 per cent.[20] In Fascist Italy in 1929, Mussolini was content with 89·9 per cent participation, but by 1934 he was claiming a 96·5 per cent turn-out.[21]

With such levels of participation we cannot expect that different electoral units or regions will show major differences in turn-out. In other non-competitive elections, real, reported or even random variations are likely to be much greater. We should also not expect to find, in totalitarian systems, that there is a significant correlation between participation and the level of election (national, federal, local or other). In other non-competitive systems, particularly semi-competitive ones, we should expect to find major turn-out differences between plebiscitarian referenda or national elections and other kinds of elections. In totalitarian systems the meaning and function of different types of elections is the same.[22]

In some countries that are not totalitarian there have been non-competitive elections for which participation levels of above 96 per cent have been reported (for instance, in a number of new African nations in the 1960s). Competent observers would have to report whether those figures are a feat of imagination or respond to any reality. In a number of them we suspect the former. In others, a single-party mobilisational regime might account for such high participation.

In totalitarian systems political apathy and non-participation are conceived as opposition, while other non-democratic systems tend to consider anyone who is not opposed to the regime a passive supporter. Voting in totalitarian systems is not conceived as a private act. It is seen as a fundamental duty rather than as a right. It should not be an expression of self-interest of the individual or social group, but a public expression of identification with the system, an act of which the individual should be proud, and therefore ultimately a public act. There is no hiding the fact, nor any shame about voters' expressing their preference publicly rather than in secret. Although voting booths are provided in the Soviet Union, the immense majority of the voters prefer to cast their votes without using a booth. In such elections, voters often ostentatiously show their ballot. In his critique of parliamentarianism Carl Schmitt bitterly attacked the privatisation implicit in secret balloting and extolled the mainly re-sponsible public voting,[23] and during the May Days in Paris in 1968 the radicals had posters saying, 'Man does not isolate himself except to vote and to . . . .' The hostility that revolutionary movements feel towards secret balloting is based not only on a desire to exercise pressure and social control over the voter, but also on deeper ideological assumptions about the act of voting.

The most striking feature of totalitarian elections is the effort to achieve unanimity. Why should the rulers try to obtain or at least report 99·8 per cent voting Yes when they could content themselves with a two-thirds majority obtained freely without an all-out effort of mobilisation, coercion, and probably some faking? The unanimity must have a particular political, social and psychological significance difficult to understand for those committed to the notion of *pars major pars sanior* underlying majority rule in competitive political systems. Yet even in competitive systems we find strange reminiscences of an older tradition of unanimity. For example, American party conventions, after a long and bitter floor fight among nominees, agree with a few unrecognised dissenting noises to make the choice of a presidential candidate unanimous. Another manifestation of the idea is that no tally of the vote is published for the election of a Pope.

The ballots are destroyed immediately after the majority has been achieved and the cardinals voting are sworn to absolute secrecy about their vote.

In his essay on superordination and subordination Georg Simmel has written a section dealing with 'subordination under a plurality', a brilliant analysis of the search for unanimity, perfectly applicable to totalitarian elections. Simmel describes voting 'as a mechanism to avoid an immediate contest of forces and of finding out its potential result by counting votes so that the minority may convince itself that its actual resistance would be of no avail', a method to anticipate in an abstract symbol the result of concrete battle and coercion.

> In the later Middle Ages, we often find the principle that the minority ought to follow the majority. This principle evidently does not only involve the suggestion that the minority should cooperate with the majority for practical reasons: it should also accept the will of the majority; it should recognize that the majority wants what is right. Unanimity is not a fact but a moral claim. The action taken against the will of the minority is legitimated by a unity of the will, which is produced retroactively. The old-German, real requirement of unanimity thus became a pale ideal requirement. But a wholly new factor is contained in it, namely, the majority's inner right, which goes beyond the numerical proponderance of votes and the external superiority symbolized by it. The majority appears as the natural representative of the totality. It shares in the significance of its unity, which transcends the mere sum of the component individuals, and has something of a superempirical or mystical note.[24]

We might argue that totalitarian rulers are conscious that the overall levelling of all members of the society in a classless society or of a homogeneous *Volksgemeinschaft* has not been achieved and that a fully integrated community has still to be made to prevent the re-emergence of cleavages and conflicting interests of society. Therefore, even a minority expressing a different choice (though willing to abide by the decision of the majority even when insignificant) is perceived as a threat. As long as it exists it legitimately can claim a latent right at a future date to become a majority and therefore represents an intolerable challenge.

Outvoting others instead of unanimity becomes the most poignant expression of the dualism between the autonomous life of the individual and the life of a society – a dualism which is often harmonised and experienced, but which in principle is irreconcilable. Since totalitarianism aims at a fully socialised man whose individuality is only an expression of his social being, the principle of unanimity in the election returns has a deep ideological and political significance. Obviously, as a phenomenon becomes routinised, those deeper ideological roots may be forgotten and ultimately become meaningless, but we cannot ignore them. The vote is an expression of the people in its totality as a Nazi law of 14 July 1933 ('Gesetz über Volksabstimmung') formulated it: 'Das Volk in seiner Gesamtheit der Gesetzgeber ist' ('The nation in its entirety is the lawgiver').

The election in such cases is an *acclamatio* rather than an *electio*. The absence of choice is deliberate, because the voter is ultimately supposed to accept a truth about the value of which there can be no doubt. The text of the ballot in the election of the single list led by Adolf Hitler on 12 November 1933 was worded as follows: 'Do you approve, German man and you German woman, the policy of your Reich's government and are you ready to declare it as the expression of your own conception and of your own will and to confess yourselves solemnly for it?'[25] The English translation does not convey the type of identification implicit in the German wording, since it does not distinguish the familiar *du* from the formal *Sie* as a second-person form of address. The comradely form used was intended to convey a direct emotional egalitarian appeal and to make the choice a very personal one. The final word (translated 'confess') is *bekennen*, a term conveying all the emotional meaning of the Protestant 'confession of faith' (*Glaubensbekenntnis*).

Totalitarian elections are based on an identity theory of representation reflected in the Nazi phrase 'Einheit von Volk und Führung' ('unity of people and leadership'). In his speech in the Reichstag on 31 May 1935 Hitler said, 'The German people has elected with 38 million votes a single deputy as its representative.'[26] This identity theory of representation leads to the idea that the elected representatives should be a mirror image of the society. In the Soviet Union efforts are made to select candidates whose social background mirrors the social composition of the electorate.

The festive holiday atmosphere of the election day and the pre-election period is constantly emphasised in both Communist and Nazi accounts. Music, entertainment and folk dances are featured in pre-election meetings and on the streets on the day of the election. The emphasis might vary between joy and solemnity. In Germany the churches were asked to ring their bells. 'Streets are decorated with national flags and in many places there are arches with electoral slogans; polling stations are festively decorated and boxes of enormous size stand in the middle of the room, invariably wrapped in national colours and sometimes with a bunch of flowers lying across the top, as on an altar' (from a description by Pelczynski of election day in Poland in 1957).[27]

Totalitarian leaders face the electoral process with a very different spirit and mood from that of their counterparts in other types of regimes. They rightly feel fully confident about the outcome. In fact, they boast publicly of absolute success long before the returns are in. It is not just that they claim that the majority will be achieved, but that the outcome will be a proof of the unity if not the unanimity of all the people. As a result of that confidence, the electoral process can be executed according to plan. In other non-competitive elections, the leadership tends to hesitate about calling elections; it often postpones them or suspends them, and the rules and procedures to be followed are often made public only shortly before the election. They have doubts about the degree or margin of freedom they are ready to tolerate and these hesitations are reflected in the behaviour of the electoral authorities, the diversity of standards used, and sometimes last-minute efforts to change the results. Sometimes, in the course of an ongoing campaign, policy reversals take place after debates within the political elite. Totalitarian elections, on the other hand, are an expression of the self-confidence of the leadership.

The difference in attitudes reflects the very different capacity for pre-electoral and electoral mobilisation of the population. The confidence of the totalitarian system is based on the availability of a mass-cadre single party, and a large number of functional organisations subordinated to the party, that can carry on a campaign capable of reaching every voter, with social pressures ranging from personal influence to physical coercion. Because of the importance of opinion-leaders, personal influence and the social pressures of small groups in bringing the message of the candidate to the individual voter, there is a fundamental difference between elections carried out with a monopoly of the mass media, and the combination of those instruments of mass persuasion with those of personal influence.

In most regimes with non-competitive elections, the rulers cannot rely on anything comparable to the Nazi *Blockwart* and the thousands of agitators participating in Soviet-type elections. It is easy to make the analogy between those activists and the wardheelers in machine politics in democratic politics, but, unlike the latter, totalitarian activists have an absolute monopoly in their pre-election activities, are subject to effective sanctions in case of failure, and can exercise control over those in their district, particularly in the terrorist phase of totalitarian systems. Their influence has clientelistic components, but the exchange between the patron and the client in traditional non-competitive or semi-competitive elections involves greater reciprocities, however lopsided they may be. Personal influence is not exercised in a wide range of settings, like the work-place, the organisations for leisure, the educational institutions, and membership organisations providing social services.

Another of the basic functions of totalitarian elections is political socialisation – the education and the indoctrination of the voter. The educational function of the electoral process is one of the more distinctive features of elections in Communist countries, where a complex process of nomination meetings takes place and there is a formal proclamation of candidates and an account of their previous activities. (See Chapter 9.) This difference between Communist and fascist electoral processes reflects the initial democratic commitments in Communism, as against the leadership principle of fascist regimes.

Elections in totalitarian systems are not the only or even the most important form of political participation of the citizens. In this they contrast with non-competitive systems where, as Susan Kaufman Purcell has noted, 'Citizens are mobilized on a temporary basis to ratify the decisions of the authoritarian elite and to demonstrate support for the regime. Much of the time however the regime does not encourage participation. As a result, the level of political participation is low.'[28] In such regimes, characterised as a low subject mobilisation, elections occupy a unique and isolated place, for the levels of membership participation in political and para-political organisations are low and the ruling party undergoes a process of atrophy, being reduced to a skeleton organisation of second-rate bureaucrats. In contrast, in totalitarian elections the mobilisation to get out the vote is accompained, as Communist authors particularly stress, by other forms of mobilisation, such as pledges of increased productivity and campaigns to support particular policies.

A hypothesis for which we have only limited evidence is that, in totalitarian regimes, the turn to elections or plebiscites coincides with the moments of greatest consolidation and strength, when the regimes can boast of their achievements and ask for public acclamation of their success. The first Stalin election in the 1930s followed after the defeat of potential opponents and the overcoming of a crisis in the regime. It ended the exclusion from suffrage of class enemies and introduced equal, universal suffrage without the differential weighting of rural and urban votes. Similarly, the 1929 and 1934 elections in Italy took place during what De Felice calls 'the years of consensus'. The German case is somewhat less clear, particularly in the case of the November 1933 election. The August 1934 ballot came after the crisis of the 'night of the long knives' had eliminated the potential danger of a second revolution and, through a Machiavellian political design, neutralised the Reichswehr. The 1938 election was adroitly made to coincide with the plebiscite approving the incorporation of Austria into the Reich. We would argue that in many other non-competitive regimes, for example Franco's Spain, the turn to referendums and elections has tended to coincide with moments of regime incertitude about the future. In such cases, the turn to plebiscitarian legitimation can be a sign of latent crisis rather than of full confidence. Totalitarian elections involve a much greater and active participation of the citizens, the organisations of society and the candidates than most other non-competitive or semi-competitive elections. Whatever the motives of the citizen, including fear of the consequences, he is less likely to remain apathetic, uninformed or ignorant of the electoral process.

Paradoxically, the apparently incredible rates of turn-out and yes votes are more likely to be true in totalitarian regimes than the more credible figures reported for other non-competitive elections. In the absense of the mobilisational mechanisms used in totalitarian elections, rulers have to turn more often to a direct falsification of the returns and more visible forms of electoral chicanery. In authoritarian elections the citizen might not have a free choice, but many citizens will have the choice of not getting involved. The forced unanimity in totalitarian elections is real. The majorities in other non-competitive elections are often false. Visible dishonesty, like so many other policies of authoritarian regimes, makes apparent the discrepancy between ideal and reality, ideology and practice, and contributes to the delegitimation of such regimes. Perhaps outside observers are too often tempted to consider the 99·9 per cent figure endorsing totalitarian elections as delegitimising the regimes authority, but for many citizens living under such regimes its total authority can be terribly real.

ELECTIONS IN PSEUDO-CONSTITUTIONAL PARLIAMENTARY REGIMES

Authoritarian regimes of a pseudo-constitutional and pseudo-parliamentary type are more common than totalitarian regimes. They are bureaucratic military dictatorships or sometimes royal dictatorships, appearing in societies where the traditional oligarchic, clientelistic system had not consolidated itself or was in crisis and the democratic pressures began to be threatening to the social and economic order. These societies generally were not modernised enough to produce successful mobilisational and fascist movements, or movements of this type were seen, on appearance, as threatening to the traditional social order.[29]

The Danube states between the wars offer many examples. Those countries found themselves ideologically in the sphere of influence of the Western democracies because of foreign-policy alignments that guaranteed independence against their neighbours or because their intellectuals and political class were under the spell of major Western nations. Their leaders hesitated to turn away from the constitutional forms of liberal democracy in a corporativist or in a single-party direction.

While such regimes were not democratic in the Western sense of the word, they were often anti-fascist in the 1930s, repressing, outlawing or persecuting fascist movements and exiling fascist leaders. In Romania, the Iron Guard was suppressed and its leader, Codreanu, assassinated ('while trying to escape') by agents of the dictator, King Carol, after the Iron Guard had registered 15·6 per cent of the total vote in the relatively free Romanian election of December 1937. In Baltic states such as Estonia and Lithuania, the desire to prevent the rise of fascist parties brought about the establishment of authoritarian regimes with semi-competitive elections.[30]

Such countries maintained on paper a liberal democratic constitutional framework and consequently held elections with more or less regularity. At the same time, they made sure that the government party or coalition would win a safe majority. This was not difficult to accomplish, given a predominantly rural and provincial society, in a permanent state of dependency upon the cities; some capacity for coercion, on the part of the representatives of the government; clientelistic connections of landlords and professionals; and a modicum of pork-barrel benefits to offer in return for a reasonable turn-out for the government-sponsored candidates. If necessary, electoral coercion and corruption, including false counting of the ballots, could assure the result. Political groups that intended to interfere with such arrangements could be excluded and persecuted, either legally or illegally. Foreign observers interested in such regimes as allies against a Communist or fascist danger were often willing to close their eyes to those fictions.

Elections in such shame-faced authoritarian regimes show the following characteristics.

(1) There is no official ideological position against competitive electoral processes, there are no apparent changes in the electoral laws, and there is an acceptance in principle of the electoral mechanism to produce legislatures and local governments with functions in theory identical to those of competitive democracies.

(2) In principle all parties except a few labelled as extremist or anti-constitutional are legally allowed to participate in the electoral process.

(3) The legal tolerance for political parties opposing the government is violated *de facto* through a wide variety of governmental actions, such as incorporating parties and their leaders into the government party through a variety of appeals, including corruption.[31]

(4) There is a wide disparity in the electoral process between coercion in the countryside and relative freedom in the cities, particularly the capital city.

(5) The government does not conceive of the elections as a plebiscitarian process of approval of a leader, a party or a policy, but as a mechanism to produce a formal majority in the legislature to assure its formal control.

(6) Only a limited effort is made to produce a large turn-out, and the authorities are willing to allow at least some of the opposition parties to obtain votes and seats, as long as the government majority is assured.

(7) Opposition parties can protest some of the most outrageous electoral frauds, and an occasional concession is made in such matters.

(8) There is relatively less use of plebiscites and referenda to legitimate the system than in other types of authoritarian and in totalitarian regimes.

We have no systematic studies of elections in pseudo-democratic authoritarian regimes; the evidence must be buried in contemporary accounts in the press and to some extent in parliamentary debates on the outcome. Statistical data and impressionistic evidence suggests the plausibility of the following empirical generalisations.

(1) Elections do not have the acclamatory plebiscitarian character of totalitarian systems and certain single-party authoritarian regimes. Therefore the tolerated and reported rates of abstention are likely to be relatively high.[32] We would hypothesise that abstention might be greater in the cities and more developed parts of the country than in many rural districts, where governmental and clientelistic pressures as well as outright false reports are likely to exaggerate the number voting.

(2) Government pressures are likely to be particularly great in the pre-electoral period, discouraging and even forcefully preventing opposition candidates from presenting themselves or campaigning, particularly in rural areas.

(3) Voting in rural settings is likely to be heavily controlled; there might be greater electoral freedom and more honest counting of returns in the cities.

(4) The government has two main goals: to assure a comfortable majority to the government party and its allies, and to prevent the election of representatives of the more radical or principled opposition. The election of non-governmental candidates willing to participate in the established political process and parliamentary activities is tolerated or even desirable.

(5) The Government is not likely to attach great symbolic importance to the electoral outcome, but to consider it as necessary to maintain the fiction of constitutional government, for reasons of international respectability and as a price that vice has to pay to virtue.

The system has many of the characteristics of nineteenth-century notable and clientelistic politics, but government intervention is likely to be more blatant and the reciprocities between government and local notables weaker than under late nineteenth-century constitutional or semi-constitutional Western-type regimes.

VOTING IN ORGANIC-STATIST AUTHORITARIAN REGIMES

Regimes we have called organic-statist present a pattern of great complexity in their electoral processes. They are based on a rejection of what they call inorganic suffrage, unable or unwilling to build a mobilisational single party capable of penetrating the whole of society and of organising nationwide plebiscitarian elections, but unwilling to forgo some form of popular electoral legitimation. Their response is thus to create a representation system based on fragmented constituencies defined and created by the ruling groups. This disenfranchises large segments of the population, without introducing suffrage restrictions that would run counter to the egalitarian values of the twentieth century.

Organic-statist regimes have been inspired in catholic, conservative and fascist ideologies. Through a variety of corporative channels they establish a multi-level electoral process that allows the filtering of candidates and outcomes by the ruling group, particularly at the higher levels.[33] It is a system more adapted to urban and industrial societies than clientelistic politics and electoral corruption, particularly after periods of democratic mass politics.

Organic democracy rejects political alignments on a nationwide basis both in principle and through the use of the state power. It is easy in the repressive atmosphere of authoritarian regimes, to prevent the formation of cross-constituency political alignments based on the organisation of a common programme and solidarity among candidates. The fragmentation of the electorate in the multi-level process assures that the election does not produce a challenge to the ruling group, but it also makes it very difficult to use voting as a mechanism of political integration. The proclamation of candidates, the electoral campaign, the election itself, and its outcome cannot be used effectively as a plebiscitarian endorsement of the regime, as single-party elections tend to be. The fragmentation of the process among multiple and different types of constituencies, and the duration of the multiple-level elections are obstacles for plebiscitarianism; as a result, the pressures for massive participation and propaganda about the outcome are not the same. Elections in such systems are likely to have high rates of abstention and even the participation rates are more often than not false or left unreported. Voting is unlikely to acquire the festive symbolic characteristics of many single-party elections.

It is significant that in Franco's Spain an effort was made to reach a high reported turn-out in referendums, while the fact of widespread apathy in the corporative type of elections in the *sindicatos*, the professional associations, and in the elections for one-third of the members of muncipal councils was accepted.[34] In referendums such as those of 1947 and 1968, a plebiscitarian, pseudo-democratic legitimation of the regime was at stake, while in the organic type of elections the issue was to confirm particular candidates representing a variety of oligarchic interests and factions within the system. It is no accident that the election for family-head representatives to the Spanish Cortes after 1968, which represented the first attempt of the regime to turn to something closer to a universal direct suffrage for the legislature, should occupy an intermediate position.

Confidence is high in the ultimate control of the outcome at the national level, thanks to the fragmentation of the constituencies, the multi-level filtering of votes, the enormous difficulties in organising partisan alignments at a national level, and the relative weakness of the political machine of the rulers at the grass-root level, due to the absence or apathy of the single party and the desire to give an appearance of a relatively free choice at the lowest unit level. This has important unintended consequences from the point of view of the rulers. In relatively advanced sectors of the society in a period of liberalisation or pseudo-liberalisation, elections can lead to unintended and undesired results. Apathy can reach levels that tend to delegitimise the system. Individual opposition candidates willing to make the effort and to take risks are able to win votes and become opinion-leaders and a nuisance for the system. At the lowest level, a legal or illegal groups and activists can assure the election of their man or stand-in, forcing the rulers to void the election or to take coercive measures against representatives duly elected. This has been the case with the elections for shop stewards and enterprise committees in the Spanish *sindicatos*, with the emergence of Catholic workers' organisations and the *comisiones obreras*. It has also allowed, in some muncipalities and even among the direct elected *procuradores familiares* in the Cortes, the election of individual candidates with a semi-opposition or even opposition character, and the same electoral system has permitted the politicisation of professional associations, such as those representing the legal profession and architects.

It is probably no accident that regimes with a corporativist ideological component but also a single mass party have soon opted for the political mobilisation of plebiscitarian elections when the leadership has wanted to embark on a dynamic and potentially totalitarian transformation of society. The rejection by the Nazis of anything resembling *ständisch* corporativist ideologies like those of Othmar Spann, advocated by some currents within the Nazi movement, is typical.[35] Even Mussolini did not develop the corporative electoral process but preferred a plebiscitarian election of the Chamber of *Corporazioni* with a single national list. Even the turning away, in the Soviet Union in the Stalin constitution of 1936 and in other Communist countries, from representation through Soviets or *Räte* based on class categories reflects a shift to the more plebiscitarian model of nationwide campaigns through a single cadre and mass party. In all these cases we find a return to the principle of representation on a territorial rather than a functional basis.

In regimes committed to a corporative type of representation but with a strong single party, the party is assigned a leadership position leaving for a future date the development of the theoretically democratic character. The more developed the previous political ideological mobilisation of their members, the more cautious the development of electoral procedures within such bodies. Significantly, in the Franco *sindicatos*, the appointed leaders (*línea política*) coexisted with formally elected leaders. Those appointed members had to be by law members of the party and subject to party discipline. In the arrested totalitarian phase of the Franco regime, the electoral processes required by its organic democratic ideology remained undeveloped. In the presence of a single party, those structures were conceived as political instruments, as transmission belts. By contrast, the weakness of the União Nacional in Portugal allowed for a formally more autonomous development of the corporative structures. It also made for a much slower institutionalisation of nationwide corporative structures and proably accounted for the persistence throughout the Salazar regime

of a territorially elected National Assembly with universal suffrage,
retaining some of the former characteristics of a liberal democratic
legislature. Control was achieved by more traditional methods of electoral
manipulation, combined with the suppression of independent political
parties.[36]

We have few empirical studies of electoral processes in organic-statist
authoritarian regimes. Attention has been focused almost exclusively on
the working-class electorate in such systems, neglecting the electoral
behaviour and participation of the employers. Evidence from the early
1960s suggests that Spanish employers did not find themselves legitimately
and adequately represented by their formally elected representatives.[37]
The question of how the Spanish political leadership managed to maintain
control and why a growing and to some extent dissatisfied entrepreneurial
and managerial class submitted to that control will probably remain
unanswered. The same is true for the distortion of the electoral process in
the organisations of the liberal professions – for instance, the patterns of
cleavage within bar associations, the medical profession, and so on, based
on professional self-interest, clientelistic ties, and ideological alignments
within such organisations. They are of great importance in understanding
the process whereby important sectors of society become alienated from
the regime, and certain leaders of the non-legal opposition become
increasingly visible and prestigious. Also of importance in this connection
is the way that official monopolistic student organisations created as a
politically conscious elite and transmission belt were later transformed into
an apolitical professional mass organisation, which was then slowly forced
to democratise itself, finally disintegrating as a result of the ideological
consciousness and polarisation of the student body.[38]

Organic statism, contrary to the intended purpose of those establishing
the fragmented and controlled institutions of representation, has turned
into a troublesome problem. It has not been able to serve as a legitimating
mechanism for the rulers, nor allowed the emergence of genuinely
competitive national politics. It is an arena for the expression of discontent
of politically conscious activist minorities, which despite repressive
measures could gain positions of leadership useful for an alegal or even
illegal opposition.

Organic-statist elections are therefore quite different from the plebiscitarian consensus elections of totalitarian systems or of mobilisational
single-party regimes. They are also different from the semi-coerced, semi-
free, semi-falsified elections of the pseudo-parliamentary, bureaucratic
military or royal dictatorships of the East European variety, or some of the
pseudo-democratic, oligarchic, caudillistic regimes in Latin America.

Organic elections do not formally legitimise the ruler and/or his
government. The ruler can have a sovereign magistracy for life, without
requiring any formal electoral legitimation. The government derives its
power from that magistracy, as in the pre-constitutional or semi-

constitutional monarchies, and not from a vote of confidence of an elected legislature. The tolerance of widespread abstention is another indication that plebiscitarian unanimity is not pursued by the rulers.

The question might then be asked, 'What functions do the rulers assign to such elections?' One that cannot be ignored but should not be considered primary is that of gaining international legitimacy in their relations with competitive democracies and in international bodies, such as the International Labour Organisation. Probably the most important function is the creation of some semblance of representation at the lower levels of social organisation, so as to be able to negotiate about certain types of social conflict and obtain information on the variety of interests in socety, to prevent more anomic forms of conflict. Initially at least, the election of factory stewards (*enlaces sindicales*) and factory committees (*jurados de empresa*) in Spain was intended to provide channels for minor grievances of the employees, and minimally legitimate workers' representatives through whom employers and the official political *sindicatos* could communicate their directives. In cases of professional associations, such as the *colegios profesionales*, that had traditionally had an elective and representative leadership, appointment from above inevitably created too much discontent.

A policy of filling by appointment all leadership positions in the multitude of social institutions of a complex society was probably too cumbersome for those who had to find suitable persons for all those offices, particularly in the absence of a mass-cadre type of single party. To create fragmented, controlled and unco-ordinated constituencies in such a situation might well have seemed a more efficient way to provide leadership that would have only limited power but be capable of dealing with many specific and tiresome conflicts that higher officials were unable to manage. Once the idea of centrally and bureaucratically regulating many potential conflict situations was abandoned, elections at the lowest level became desirable. Slowly the idea of collective bargaining, so central in the trade-union experience of other advanced industrial societies, would substitute for enacted labour regulations, the *reglamentaciones de trabajo*, dictated by the Ministry of Labour with practically no participation by the interested parties.

Another function of fragmented and limited-scale elections is the need to draw into the politico-administrative process persons who might have been reluctant to accept strictly appointive positions. In the Spanish case, the hope was that persons identified with the regime, civic-minded and with a certain prestige in their constituency, might be drawn into public office. In a sense elections would serve to increase the pool of civic-minded persons, if not of those with political ambitions. In a context of low politisation at the base, owing to limited penetration by the single party, the self-presentation of candidates, the pressures from the community on some people to run, and the appeal of the authorities to local notables or younger persons with some ideas of what to do in the community might well make it easier to pull into local government some people who would not otherwise come to the attention of those higher up.[39]

Another function is the convenience of giving some institutionalised representation to the limited pluralism of ideological tendencies, organisations, interests and factions, within a regime supporting coalition. The records of the Spanish Ministry of the Interior and the Secretaría General del Movimiento, including computer print-outs, show that such a policy was consciously pursued in Spain even at the highest level. The manoeuvring preceding even controlled elections would allow a better fit with the reality of leadership in different constituencies.

Whatever the functions pursued by those in power, institutionalising organic elections also had unanticipated consequences, such as the need to revitalise the dormant, single-party organisation. It would be interesting to know more about the life of the Movimiento in the years after the failure of the totalitarian ambitions of the Falange and the earliest electoral experiments.[40] At the level of the small and medium-size community, the electoral process probably led to a revitalisation of the Movimiento and its various subsidiary organisations, above all the farmers' organisation, the Hermandad de Labradores y Ganaderos.

More important and largely undesired was the fact that the authorities at the provincial level and the political class at the national level had to pay a little more attention to aspirations and demands at the periphery. They were not forced to listen to the people, but they had to listen to some of the local officials they themselves had appointed, the local notables and to persons representing local interests, since for the first time they came asking for something rather than to give orders and receive homage and gratitude for what they had done for the community. The government was not seeking the vote of all the people, but a minimum of support and activity on the part of those who could influence the few who would bother to vote or could be pressured into voting.

In a few cases in Spain, within the limits provided by the law and the social constraints, multiple candidacies could appear in the pre-electoral stage, and in a few cases on election day. The authorities wanting to control the outcome had to turn to a mixture of pressures and bargaining to assure the election of their friends and, in extreme cases, mobilise supporters of the regime or one of the factions within it to turn out to vote. Voting did not make the ruling political class dependent upon the local notables or the surviving organisational structures of the single party, but at least it obliged it to listen to their demands and, like the old politicians they had so long vituperated, make some promises and begin to act as intermediaries between the constituencies and the central adminitration.

The elections in organic-statist regimes pose serious problems for the surviving members of the defeated opposition, the exiled leaders and their friends, and the citizen with some political ambition who is unwilling to identify with the regime. Two basic positions can be outlined under such circumstances, the first of them based on a principled, moral outlook: to participate is to be co-opted into legitimising a system that is unfree and a ruling structure which ultimately will be unaffected by whatever critical and independent position those elected might take. The other is that, without accepting those institutions as legitimate, without making more than verbal concessions with mental reservations to the system, every opportunity to gain positions of some influence and leadership in the society will be an advantage for the opposition, on account of the influence in a particular constituency, the visibility and the opportunities for protest that those opposition leaders might gain. Participation does not express confidence in the representative function. It is assumed that the regime will not tolerate the performance of that function, that it will void the elections, isolate and discredit those elected, and ultimately persecute and arrest them. The reaction of the authorities is expected, and is renewed evidence to the opposition that there is no possibility for real representation through the fundamentally false and illegitimate institutions of the regime.

Principled rejection and abstention is the immediate response of an opposition denying legitimacy to an authoritarian regime. It excludes any ambiguity, the risk of co-optation of leadership and of strengthening the international credibility of the regime. A principled opposition after defeat, with the repression recent and ongoing, finds it morally difficult to defend even a limited, pragmatic or cynical participation. Participation is also difficult to defend for those without strong ideological and organisational commitments to an illegal activity that does not exclude subversive or infiltration tactics. It is difficult to believe that participation does not represent compromise with the regime. How is anyone to distinguish those who participate without committing themselves to the regime from those ready to participate and commit themselves? In the absence of organised slates, party labels, and public campaigning, individuals who consider themselves in the opposition cannot communicate their position to a wider constituency. Inevitably the regime can claim a large turn-out, and even freedom granted to those not originally identified with the regime or belonging to the single party. Abstention from presenting candidates and from voting is the obvious choice of a disorganised opposition whose legitimacy is derived mainly from its principled stand.

The fragmented, partial, low-level constituency elections of organic-statist regimes can be seen in a very different light by other opposition forces. They do not represent participation in the political process at the national level, since in the conception of the rulers themselves they do not legitimise those in power. They can therefore be defined as an opportunity to represent within narrow limits the interests of a constituency against the arbitrariness of authoritarian rule. Groups can claim to participate only with that narrow goal – articulating specific interests, effectively channelling the grievances of the people, making explicit the lack of responsiveness of those in power and the arbitrary curtailment of the freedoms formally granted. In their appeals to participation, candidates and elected representatives can claim that they represent the interests of the people within the limits allowed. They can claim to unmask the real power structure and to make people conscious of their rights and the oppression they suffer. They formally non-political character of many of those elections in the ideology of corporativism makes it possible for a grass-roots opposition with a clear identity to participate without appearing to legitimise the regime. This would be much more difficult in a nationwide election under controlled conditions.

The alternative of conditional participation presents serious difficulties and dangers for those in opposition to the regime but without strong ideological positions and organisational linkages. The risk of being co-opted or misunderstood encourages abstention. Paradoxically, the pseudo-freedom of authoritarian regimes tends to exclude the participation of moderate opponents and makes it attractive for well-organised underground movements or organisations. It is no accident that Spanish liberals and social-democrats were for a long time extremely reluctant to use such opportunities, while the Communist Party, once it had abandoned any hope of armed insurrection, did make use of them.[41] Anti-Communist, authoritarian regimes have in an unintended and unanticipated way made possible the rise, at grass-roots level, of Communist-controlled organisations or Communist-supported leaders, while socialists and other democratic opposition groups have disintegrated owing to a lack of visibility and activity.

At the time when the initial decisions to use the very limited and treacherous opportunities offered by the electoral process at the grass-roots level are taken, the leadership probably is far from conscious of the long-range implications of that choice. Any study of the electoral process within authoritarian regimes has to include an analysis of the functions and dysfunctions of participation for the opposition as well as for the rulers and the voters.[42]

ELECTIONS WITH CONTROLLED OR LICENSED PARTIES IN AUTHORITARIAN REGIMES

The dilemma of abstention or participation confronts the opposition in authoritarian regimes which opt for the creation of a controlled party system with a licensed or tolerated opposition allowed to participate in elections. A principled opposition cannot claim as in a corporative-type election that it participates only to represent specific interests and to gain visibility. Participation in elections defined as overtly political inevitably contributes to the legitimation of the system, and the benefits for the constituency are dubious. On the other hand, the prospect of contributing to a peaceful transition to a less authoritarian and perhaps ultimately to a democratic, competitive, or semi-competitive system is meaningful and tempting. The total rejection of the opportunities offered and the principled isolation of a ruling party well entrenched in power is a costly choice for those wanting a return to competitive politics. The dilemma is particularly acute for those advocating a moderate alternative, not identified strongly with the predecessor regime, rejecting the apocalyptic hopes of an extremist opposition, or sharing many goals and values with those in power while rejecting specific policies and the mistakes of the group in power. The dilemma does not confront the persecuted, underground opposition as much as the moderate alegal or semi-legal opposition sectors, or the leaders of non-partisan interest groups dependent on the government and the younger generations that have grown up under the regime.

This situation is more typical of regimes where a military, bureaucratic, technocratic elite has taken power, creating from above a government or privileged party rather than coming to power with the support of a movement-type party. A ruling group that does not espouse an ideology rejecting moderate competition between parties and that has not formally abolished the institutions of direct representation would like to see the emergence of controlled and limited political competition, to help it to gain international legitimacy. Competition within a limited range of the political spectrum and an agreement to share power between the non-democratic components of the political system and the more representative ones are a desirable alternative to strict hegemonic rule for those in power.

Authoritarian regimes born without the help of a mobilisational, 'anti-party' party in societies in which the previous party system had only limited penetration will be tempted to try to license and control parties. The model of a hegemonic or dominant party capable of an inclusionary policy that would assure it even under semi-competitive or competitive conditions a large majority is tempting. It is, however, a model that cannot be tried successfully in most societies. Using the Latin American experience, Alfred Stepan has analysed the complex conditions for such an inclusionary attempt.[43] Many rulers in the world can dream about creating a situation like the Mexican 'revolutionary family' within the Partido Revolucionario Institucional, but few are likely to succeed.

The creation of a licensed party system in an authoritarian regime results in a number of constraining conditions for the electoral process.

(1) One of the parties inevitably occupies a privileged position, as the party supporting the government. It will enjoy more or less shameless favourable treatment by the authorities. Electoral laws are likely to be interpreted on behalf of the government party.

(2) The leadership and organisation of other parties is likely to encounter many difficulties and the licensing process itself will exclude possible

parties. Whatever commitment the leadership might have to challenge the authoritarian regime, the laws regulating the licensing of political parties will demand a public commitment to that institutional order, and the substantive acts of the regime. In addition, the ruling group can and very often does exercise a veto against the participation of certain categories of persons or individual personalities. In this respect the exclusion from politics of those who have held public office under a previous regime (as in the case of the *casados* in Brazil) represents a basic break with the conditions for free competitive politics.[44]

The institutionalisation of a party system with licensed parties confronts the society and its voters with a difficult dilemma: whether to accept the system, even with the hope of ultimately transforming it, or to reject it as a mockery of competitive politics and democracy. Some will argue that the recognition of the principle if not the reality of competitive politics, the opportunity to develop some opposition leadership and organisation, and the hope of winning at least some contests is preferable to continuing one-party or no-party rule. Others will argue that such a controlled, pseudo-competitive system will deceive the people, reduce the pressures for real democratisation, co-opt part of the opposition, and give a false in-ternational legitimation to an authoritarian regime. It could be argued that rejection of such an opportunity makes sense in the case of an authoritarian regime that has not consolidated its power and finds iself in crisis and is internationally isolated. The situation is quite different when the regime is relatively consolidated, confronts no crisis that might lead immediately to its breakdown, and does not demand total subservience of the tolerated opposition.

Confronted with such a choice, the opposition is likely to divide on the strategy and tactics to be pursued, which benefits the regime in power. Those who have an opportunity to participate in the creation of a semi-competitive system might be mistaken about the stability of the existing regime or the commitments to liberalisation of at least a faction within the authoritarian ruling group.

The voter confronted with such a semi-competitive or pseudo-competitive political system has the choice to abstain or to give his support to either the government party or the tamed opposition. Abstention is less likely to have the symbolic value it can have in single-party regimes. Voting for the tamed opposition could serve as an expression of discontent, an instrument of pressure on the ruling group or even of political change. This mixture of motivations, together with the organisational weakness of the government party and the limited appeal that it can have, owing to its dependency upon the state, might lead to an unanticipated success of the opposition, as was the case with the Movimento Democràtico Brasileiro (MDB) in its contest with the Arena party in Brazil.[45]

The key question confronting the political elites of the country is whether the creation of a licensed, semi-competitive party system within a liberalised authoritarian regime can lead to its transformation into a competitive political system. Unfortunately, the number of cases in which authoritarian rulers have opted for such a controlled transition to competitive politics is too small to make any generalisations. Much depends on the degree to which the ruling group believes in the value of competitive politics and perceives the opposition challenging its future role in politics and in the society, or the degree to which the opposition appears as a threat to the existing nation-state, socio-economic order or values considered essential – for instance, in Ataturk's Turkey, secularism.[46]

The opposition can make it less difficult to establish mutual confidence. The one successful case of peaceful and constitutional transition from a single-party authoritarian regime to a competitive Western type of democracy, the Turkish experience after World War II, is particularly interesting. The authoritarian regime had not been born as a result of civil war, but as a modernising nationalist movement opposing foreign threats in a period in which the ideological models available were dominantly democratic. Turkey was a relatively underdeveloped, agrarian country whose proletariat had not developed a radical class consciousness and which did not retain ethnic or linguistic minorities threatening the unity of the nation-state. In addition, the strong man founding the regime, Ataturk, had died. His successor, who enjoyed considerable legitimacy among the regime-supporting forces, became committed to the transformation and many of the leaders of the opposition were dissidents from the ruling party rather than political outsiders.

It remains to be seen if other authoritarian regimes that are not based on a single-party movement and that have a sense of historical mission will be willing and able to take the risk of such a controlled transformation toward competitive politics. The Spanish situation after Franco has been characterised by the mobilisation of a variety of opposition forces, including the Communist Party and regional nationalisms, visible under Franco. This has excluded a system with a government party and licensed and controlled opposition parties.

From all that we know, the transition from pseudo- or semi-competitive politics to competitive politics and pluralistic democracy is not a slow, evolutionary process; generally it has been accompanied by an unconstitutional and fundamental discontinuity. This basic discontinuity should not blind us to the contribution that pseudo- or semi-competitive elections may have made to the emergence of leaders or parties that play an important role in competitive, democratic politics after the breakdown of an authoritarian regime. A number of leaders of the democratic parties in Portugal today, such as Pereira da Moura and Sa Carneiro, were at one time elected to the chambers of the Caetano regime.

To what extent does the creation of a licensed and controlled multi-party system offer greater or lesser opportunities for real political

participation and transition to competitive politics than the institutionalisation of greater pluralism and freedom along the lines of internal
party democracy within a single party? This important question cannot be
answered on the basis of empirical data, since true inner-party democracy
has not been realised in monopolistic, single-party regimes. It might be
argued that Yugoslavia and Tanzania represent such efforts. In Yugoslavia it is debatable whether the process of democratisation has taken
place within the single party or, rather, on its periphery, through mass
organisations offering greater opportunities for political participation at
the factory and community level to non party members. The case of
Tanzania is in some respects different from that of other single-party
regimes, since the party in question does not have an ideologically
disciplined membership. I am inclined to think that the limited pluralism
of licensed parties might be a better avenue to competitive politics than the
internal democratisation of a single party. Thus, I do not share the
optimism of many observers about what the Czech spring of 1968 would
have led to, had the Czechs been left alone.

Semi-competitive elections with licensed or controlled parties are
unlikely to have the festive and revivalist character of elections in
totalitarian systems. The rulers are less likely to encourage this, because
they are uncertain about the turn-out and the outcome. Without being
assured of a turn-out that would give symbolic expression to the willingness
of the people to participate within the regime, and fearful, despite all the
manipulations, of the number of votes that the opposition might gain, they
are unlikely to attach much symbolic and legitimising significance to the
elections. Otherwise, they might be forced to recognise a setback in terms
of turn-out or losses in those districts where the electoral results are more
likely to be considered reasonably honest. The rural and provincial vote is
likely to be discounted by most observers, even when it may be more or less
honestly gained by the regime-supporting party. This type of election is not
a great opportunity for political indoctrination and propaganda for the
regime. Very often, the government party is not formed by men skilled in
mass agitation but by officials drafted as candidates, quite often without
any previous electoral experience, and with little popular appeal of any
kind. While they can enjoy the support of the administrative machinery of
the state and municipal governments, the large number of activists needed
to reach every household and organise meetings in every neighbourhood or
work-place is not there. Civil servants are not good propagandists, even
when they serve as election agents.

In relatively modernised societies we can expect that the mass media
will carry a glib and relatively effective public-relations campaign that will
remind the readers more of advertising campaigns for consumer products
than of a political debate. We would not deny the effectiveness of such a
campaign in getting out the vote for the government party, but we doubt
that it can have the mobilising effect of participation through primary

groups and personal involvement in election rallies. Much of the energies of the government party will go into complex manoeuvres in setting up the election tickets and convincing notables to give their support. The government party itself is likely to be a conglomerate of personalities, factions and interests without common ideological or programmatic positions. It is therefore likely to turn to relatively simple, uncontroversial slogans, such as 'peace', 'order', 'economic progress', 'social justice', 'patriotism', or 'nationalism', rather than commit itself on divisive issues. In many cases it might be reduced to extolling and defending the achievements of those public officials who themselves might take little or no part in the campaign. Real power is likely to be in the hands of government officials, military men or technocrats who do not campaign but have a decisive part in shaping the slates and setting limits to the independent expression of political alternatives by the candidates. Ultimately, the government party runs on the record of the administration, the desire for stability of the political system, and the uncertainties that might result from a victory of the opposition.

Within the narrow limits in which it has to operate, the opposition is unlikely to contribute to a lively and hot campaign. Its leaders have to be careful to stay within the more or less visible boundaries that the government sets to their activity. Whatever their feelings about the political system, they cannot publicly question its legitimacy. The normal and natural demagoguery of the electoral process has to be subdued. Under conditions of semi-freedom or scepticism about the future, the public identification of the voters with the opposition parties would be limited. The real issues are not likely to be discussed but remain underneath. This does not mean that the voters might not know why they make their choice. As the Brazilians put it so succinctly, 'Vote for the MDB – you know why.'[47] The opposition also faces difficulties in obtaining financial resources, because of laws the manifest purpose of which is to assure the independence of parties from wealthy donors or interest groups. Elections will not have a profound and visible politicising effect except in localised settings. Semi-competitive elections can thus only to a limited extent serve the legitimising or political-education functions of plebiscitarian elections in mobilising single-party regimes. The transition from an authoritarian regime with no popular voting or a monopolistic single party to a licensed and controlled party system makes sense to a ruling group unwilling to consider the possibility of losing power only if social and economic conditions and the inclusionary politics allow the government party to maintain a hegemonic position. In this respect, the Mexican Partido Revolucionario Institucional occupies a unique position. If a controlled party system and semi-competitive elections are not conceived as a step towards competitive pluralistic democracy, in the long run they are likely to lead to the destabilisation of authoritarian rule, whatever they might contribute in the short run to its legitimation.

4 Clientelism, Elections and Systems of Inequality and Domination in Cameroun: A Reconsideration of the Notion of Political and Social Control

JEAN-FRANÇOIS BAYART

For the observer of African political life, the importance of clientelist phenomena is not in doubt – from the employee who spontaneously offers his boss some small present in anticipation of a favour in return, to the political class which, in full force, religiously accompanies the president of the republic to the airport on each of his trips and is there on his return. The behaviour characteristic of clientele relations is found at every level of social reality.

The most frequent explanation of the prevalence of the clientelist phenomenon is cultural in nature: clientelist ties are a heritage from former societies and constitute an integral part of the African political culture. To some extent, this type of assertion reflects reality, but it neglects the essence of the question. For our part, we think that the different clientelisms in Africa can be understood only in relation to the historical evolution of the structure of systems of inequality and domination in the societies of that continent.[1] *Structure* because the processes of social-class formation (in the strict sense of the term) and the reality of the class struggle seem to us undeniable aspects of contemporary African life; *historical evolution* because one cannot, in our sense, dissociate the study of this process of change from the historical analysis of traditional social forms: very early – often well before the nineteenth century – the penetration of the capitalist mode of production began to erode indigenous economic and political processes.

Social relationships internal to the pre-capitalist societies and the relations of these societies and capitalist economic transformation quickly became part of the same reality; they must be considered simultaneously.

This infrastructural interpretation generally emphasises the social control function of clientelism, an approach illustrated by Alain Rouquié in Chapter 2 of this volume. Other authors think, like R. Lemarchand, that 'the model of authority that proceeds from the institution of clientelism can be adapted to ends totally different from that of maintaining the social order from which it emanates'.[2] It is this relationship between clientelist phenomena and the structure of systems of inequality and domination that we shall now consider with reference to the example of Cameroun and, in a more general way, the relationship of any political structure to the social struggle. Political scientists, and especially Marxists, always tend to relate institutional or ideological means of domination to the political practices of single dominant groups, to reduce them to means of alienation and to abolish the intervention of the masses in the social system. We consider this approach too simplistic. No political process, be it as manifestly oppressive or conservative as the clientelist relations or one-candidate elections studied here, escapes completely the political influence of lower social groups; nor is the process outside the social struggle.

THE DIFFERENTIATION OF SYSTEMS OF CLIENTELISM[3]

Pre-colonial political systems in what was soon to become Cameroun (for a brief background account, see appendix to this chapter) could not be reduced to the notion of clientelism. But, whether it be in the lineage societies of the central south, of the littoral or non-Foulbé north, in the meta-lineage chiefdoms of the west or in the pseudo-feudal system of the Peul in the north, clientelist relations constituted a fundamental feature of political life. While unable to describe these systems of clientelism in the limits of this paper, it is advisable to underline an important characteristic of all of them. In societies of this type, power, kinship and relationships to the means of production stood (and stand) in a dialectical relationship to each other, and familial relations are intrinsic elements of the dynamics of clientelism.[4] It is therefore legitimate to extend the strict meaning of the concept of client[5] to include wives, junior members of the family (in a status sense) and offspring, in so far as they fill this social role. In the following pages, we shall see how the historical evolution and the contemporary dynamics of clientelism justify this decision.

In the first half of the nineteenth century, trade by treaty with Europe replaced the slave trade; by 1868, at Duala, it had reached the stage of continual exchanges with English and German merchants. European goods penetrated even further into the interior. This commercial insinuation of capitalism had a considerable effect on the social structure of the indigenous societies. Along the littoral and in the south, its initial effect seems to have been to reinforce the position of the leaders of the established clientele systems, who could monopolise to their own profit the use of imported goods and the new sources of wealth. The resulting differentiation of wealth and extension of large-scale polygamy channelled new dependants to the most powerful chiefs. Faced with an acute shortage of women, to become a client of a rich man became one of the few means of obtaining a wife for oneself.[6]

But this intensification of inequalities at the same time aggravated the tensions inherent in these societies. Tensions arose first of all among chiefs, who were becoming more and more unequal: the power that some acquired from the treaty trade meant relative pauperisation for others, and aroused their resentment. Secondly, tensions arose between chiefs and their dependents. The chiefs' monopolistic polygamy angered those social inferiors (*cadets sociaux*[7]) whom it deprived of wives. Women saw their position as mere objects accentuated by trading. Customary subtle procedures of exchange were upset. The collective and religious dimension of the clientele systems changed, with chiefs (at least on the coast) more and more openly using their dependants for personal ends.[8]

The intensification of trading ended up destroying the indigenous monopolies that benefited the most powerful chiefs, and multiplying opportunities for the accumulation of wealth.[9] It was not until colonisation that this trend was confirmed in the hinterland, but it crystalled very early on the coast. Numerous lesser Duala men came to trade with the Europeans and were thus able to convert subsistence goods (which were subject to no customary control on the part of the more important elders) into prestige goods of Western origin. The elite of the great chiefs began to fear losing their exclusive control over the allocation of these prestige goods and, by virtue of this fact, losing control of their clienteles. For A. Wirz,[10] there is no doubt that it was this confrontation with their dependants, together with the fear of losing in it, that in 1851 prompted the Duala chiefs, in a reflex action that one cannot help but compare, *mutatis mutandis*, with the recourse of the French bourgeoisie to Bonaparte, to demand that England, then Germany, sign a protectorate treaty.

The treaty trade, which had initially reinforced the domination of the southern chiefs over their clienteles, was not long in undermining it from within, and exacerbating the contradictions of the established clientele systems. Colonisation and the direct penetration of capitalist production were gradually to transform this social unrest into a genuine organic crisis throughout the country by creating new clientele networks, most often to the benefit of former dependants.

The almost immediate effect of colonisation was to change the scale and nature of domination in these societies: leaders of formerly powerful clientele systems, who based their authority on supernatural sanctions, became intermediaries between a transcendent political and economic system and their dependants.[11] Beyond this, colonisation did not affect clientele structures equally or simultaneously across the whole country.

Three main scenarios can be distinguished, according to the tempo of social transformation (capitalist economic growth, the spread of primary education, and Christianisation) and the capacity of established clientele leaders to channel it to their advantage. In the lineage societies of the south, where modernisation was rapid, colonisation radically altered the control exercised by elders over their dependants. On the one hand, the remarkably congruent processes of colonisation, evangelisation, acculturation and capitalist production favoured the emancipation of dependants from traditional clientele relations and their integration into new clientele systems based on economic enrichment and jobs as cultural intermediaries (religious catechists or teachers of lay subjects) or administrative intermediaries (interpreters, village, canton or higher chiefs). On the other hand, the aristocracy of the great chiefs declined while losing the power and wealth that their monopoly of trade with the Europeans had procured for them. Also contributing to this decline were the active role of intermediate chiefs during the German military occupation, the undermining of the very foundations of their prosperity (slavery and polygamy) and their increasing inability to maintain their own status in the subtle test of *bilabi* (Potlatch), all of which caused them to lose their pre-eminence.

The two processes were contradictory: it was inevitable that there should be at least a partial confrontation between these two ideal types of clientelism or, more exactly, between these multiple overlapping clientele systems. The colonial administration exiled recalcitrant traditional chiefs and repressed tradition-inspired revolts; it also executed conspirators opposed to the new political hierarchy – which finally proved decisive. But the old aristocracy did not disappear completely: it kept its prestige to some extent, notably in rural milieux, where the administration-appointed chiefs were quickly discredited by the unpopularity of the duties delegated to them (collecting taxes and recruiting forced labour).[12]

In the north of the country, by contrast, the effect of colonisation and slow modernisation was to extend and reinforce existing clientele systems. The German military occupation succeeded in destroying the Nigerian emirates' suzerainty over the Peul chiefdoms of Cameroun, but confirmed the domination that the *lamidats* exercised over the indigeneous pagan population and, very often, extended it to ethnic groups that had until then safeguarded their independence. The ensuing unrest prompted the French authorities to renounce this system and to place under their direct administration those groups that did not have a historical dependence on the Peul.[13] The Peul's authority over their traditionally vassal populations was nonetheless maintained and given financial backing to the extent that the administrative tax levied by the French was not without benefits for the *lamibé* (Peul elders) who were responsible for collecting it.

In the west, with the exception of the Bamoun sultanate, the colonising power, without seeking to intervene in their internal functioning, structured its rule around the traditional chiefdoms and introduced a system of quasi-indirect administration that worked to the chiefs' benefit. This was especially true in Bamiléké country. The *fo* (chiefs) took advantage of the situation to increase their powers: they tended to turn away from the traditional religious societies that placed so many constraints of custom on their personal powers, and to embrace exclusively the secular modern societies founded and completely controlled by themselves. But this trend exacerbated tensions between the *fo*, on the one hand, and the *nkem* (notables) and dependants, on the other – more especially as the *fo* were obliged to fulfil regularly such unpopular administrative duties as collecting taxes or recruiting forced labour. In other respects, too, capitalist penetration made itself particularly felt in this region. It did not draw people away from established clientele systems, because for the Bamiléké it was inconceivable, even when exiled in towns, that they should not belong to a chiefdom. But coffee-growing spread and enriched the *nkem* in addition to the *fo*. Moreover, trade, which increased remarkably after the end of the First World War, brought new sources of wealth. At length, the educated and Christianised elite gained in confidence and tended to oppose the chiefs. In 1944 the Bamiléké country found itself in a paradoxical situation: the reinforcement of traditional clientele systems was progressing hand in hand with the development of social forces largely antagonistic to these systems.[14]

Whatever the peculiarities from one region to the next, colonisation and the economic and social changes that it brought tended generally to undermine the legitimacy of traditional clientele systems by differentiating social elites and relations of dependance. This trend manifested itself in the social and economic advancement of people who had been dependants in traditional clientele systems. It became evident that a major problem for the emerging Cameroun political system was the relationship between these elites and between clientele systems. Various possible outcomes were taking shape: a scenario of conservative modernisation in which elites controlled and channelled social change to their own advantage; a scenario of bourgeois revolution, in which new social strata gained the advantage over the traditional aristocracy; an intermediate scenario involving the reciprocal assimilation of new and old elites. But already more serious questions were being posed, especially in the west and north. Were not dependants in established clientele systems, new and old, going to revolt against their domination and question the direction of political change itself?

MULTI-PARTYISM ELECTIONS AND CLIENTELISM

The liberalisation of the colonial state started in 1945; representative institutions were grafted onto the layers of clientele systems. To analyse these innovations we must isolate the significance of electoral procedures in the decolonisation process.

From the standpoint of the colonial power, elections defined and delimited the legal and legitimate political arena outside of which no political gains were to be made. The administration controlled this arena of political contest. It alone made the rules, it determined at its own discretion who was to be included on electoral lists, and it manipulated the results. It was thus that it could deprive the Union des Populations du Cameroun (UPC), a nationalist and revolutionary movement, of all parliamentary representation.[15] In short, elections were one of the cornerstones of peaceful decolonisation, a strategy of insinuating capitalist production and its superstructures throughout the Cameroun social structure.

Elections equally coincided with cultural structures and with political and economic rivalries rooted in the indigeneous social system. On the whole, the cultural ethos equated wealth with numbers of men, and subordinated economic to political power. The logic of elections, we might even say of electoral clientelism, could be found in this ethos. Furthermore, at least in the south, elections offered a new arena for the competition that had characterised relations among different ethnic communities for more than a century. Some groups saw in elections a chance for revenge, others an opportunity to better their position, or a threat to established status. In most cases, Cameroun politicians were able to take advantage of these feelings to maximise local support and to unite their native groups around their person.

The power conferred by elections immediately became a primordial political resource, and the introduction of representative institutions had great relevance for the dynamics of clientele systems. By introducing a new source of political power, elections aggravated the hegemonic crisis started in the nineteenth century with the intensification of trade by treaty and the direct implantation of the capitalist mode of production by adding a younger and more modernist third segment to the social elite – and a third generation of clientele systems. This was true even in those regions (the north and west) where the leaders of the oldest clientele systems or those born in the wake of colonisation had been able to use the 'clientelist control of the suffrage'[16] to their own advantage. In the north and Bamoun country, for example, where the sultan, Peul *lamibé* and canton chiefs of pagan origin managed the conduct of elections, most of the local educated elite organised themselves into modernist associations, which competed with the traditional chiefdoms, and succeeded in gaining representation in the territorial assembly, thanks to the support of a section of the French administration.

But elections, parliamentary representation and the formation of political parties above all provided the colonial power and indigeneous governing strata with the means of devising a response to the hegemonic crisis of clientele systems in conflict, by insuring the amalgamation of the different elites and the integration of their dependants into common political institutions. Conflicts provoked by elections, especially at the village level, were themselves no more than constituent parts of this process.[17] It was the responsibility of the 'more advanced' persons engaged in political competition, as circumscribed by the colonial authorities, to guide this change and channel its dynamics through the expedient of modern clientele organisations and networks or, alternatively, to oppose it, the political game that it supported and the dependent role reserved for the subordinate masses.

The crisis of clientele systems was the crucial question facing the territory's political elite shortly after the Second World War, although, because of different positions taken on the issue of Cameroun independence, it was not defined in that manner. .In 1938 the French administration had managed to group almost the whole of the modernist and traditional elites into a single association under its auspices, the Jeucafra, which was charged with opposing German annexionist propaganda. In 1945 the Jeucafra became Unicafra, so as to perpetuate the amalgamation and serve the process of colonial liberalisation. However, in 1947 Cameroun political life became cleanly polarised between moderate and nationalist elements. What is interesting is that the cleavage materialised first of all between nationalist and moderate positions and not between segments of the elite. Members of the old aristocracy, administrative chiefs and the new modernist generation could be found in either camp. The nationalist movement, even in its early stages, seemed to gain the upper hand in the old aristocracy and to benefit from its clientele networks. The Ngondo, a Duala assembly run by the old families of the region, appeared to subscribe to nationalist arguments; and the first president of the UPC, Mathias Djoumessi, was a powerful Bamiléké *fon*, who started a council similar to the Ngondo, the Kumsze. But the colonial authorities put their full strength behind the notables, both traditional and administrative, and succeeded in reversing the situation to the advantage of colonialism. The Ngondo and Kumsze broke away from the UPC in 1949–50. The nationalist instincts of the southern notables had never been very strong. As for the northern *lamibé*, sultan and canton chiefs, they had always been unconditionally committed to the French presence, because it constituted the best guarantee of their domination.[18]

It is at the regional and local level that the dynamics of the new clientelism are best seen. The Union Tribale Ntem-Kribi (UTNK or Efoula-Meyong) and the Union Camerounaise (UC), offer two good examples of reciprocal accomodation and assimilation on the part of the different elite segments in a neo-colonial setting. Both played a critically important role in the country's evolution.

In the south, Fang country was in full ferment in the period following 1945. The tribes who lived there had managed to conserve their traditional clan structure by giving them the appearance of a modern association. They had kept up the periodic reunions (*bisulan*) affirming clan solidarity and had obtained from the French authorities recognition of clan chiefs within administrative units. Genuinely traditional chiefs had therefore managed to regain part of the ground lost following colonisation and, to some extent, to perpetuate their authority despite the relative emancipation of their dependants. The Fang soon showed their concern to realise their unity, and founded the UTNK in July 1948. The supreme organ of the Union was the tribal assembly, which divided into a number of clan councils and committees, representing the traditional political units, and of local councils and committees, representing the administrative units created by the colonial authorities. Each clan association, being directed by an elected general committee and built upon a structure of local committees, was further subdivided into a number of societies (women, youth, work, and so on).[19] The UTNK was thus used to restructure Fang society and to unite partially antagonistic clientele networks: traditional chiefs, administrative chiefs, associations of the inferior strata (young people, women). It remained to articulate these processes in national political life. According to general opinion, the Fang movement was at first quite anti-colonial.[20] But it is possible that the reticence of the French administration in opposing it was more apparent than real.[21] The fact remains that Charles Assalé, co-founder of the UPC, joined the Efoula-Meyong in 1948, at the time of its second meeting, gained control of it in a few years and, after his break with the nationalist movement, had himself elected to the territorial assembly by 'an almost plebscite majority',[22] thanks to its support. He was to transform it into a remarkably homogeneous political and electoral instrument.

The Union Camerounaise parliamentary group, for its part, included elected representatives from the north and from Bamoun country: the sultans, Peul *lamibé* and canton chiefs who took over electoral operations, and the leaders of the modernist associations who tended to question the former's political monopoly. The Foulbé elite progressively lost its political supremacy. In contrast to the Bamiléké *fo*, it had withdrawn into a restricted conservatism, sulking over the new socio-economic rationality. What is more, by rejecting the principle of independence and remaining attached to the political forms of an outdated imperialist period, the traditional northern elite betrayed an inability to take charge of the conservative modernisation movement implied by peaceful decolonisation. This was a role that its privileged position in the political scene seemed to reserve for it. Its clientelist control of elections in the north and in

Bamoun country had given the UC – which the aristocracy largely controlled in its initial period – nearly half the seats in the territorial assembly elected in 1956 and had made it the premier legal political force in the country.

Within the UC parliamentary group, the balance gradually swung in favour of the Young Turks: one of them, Mr Ahidjo, was named Deputy Prime Minister and given the Ministry of the Interior in the Mbida cabinet (1957), and then became Prime Minister (February 1958). They also carried off the presidency of the parliamentary group. In April – May 1958 they were able to impose on the most traditionalist section of the old elite the formation of a political party, the UC, that was to transcend the chiefdoms for good. The rapid creation of local party organisations throughout the region, the manipulation of electoral succession procedures, the reduction of the traditional elite's representation in the UC parliamentary group under cover of the 1960 legislative elections, the suppression of particular laws and certain customary taxes, and, as a last recourse, the deposition of hostile *lamibé* and sultans, all led to the definitive pre-eminence of the modernist elite within the political apparatus.[23] In exchange, the reigning traditional elite was conceded superficial corporate privileges (the local survival of their institutions, a policy of Islamisation) and had the chance to become part of the new elite. The youngest and most dynamic members of the Foulbé aristocracy were integrated into the modern structures of the political system.

The organic conciliation of the different generations of clientele systems could occur because the antagonism between the traditional and modern segments of the elite was in fact less profound than is usually thought. Certainly, disagreements were numerous and often intensely felt, particularly at the village level. But the tactic of matrimonial alliances, kinship ties, a certain community of interests, and the concern to promote the welfare of the collectivity all appear to me to have created and maintained solid bonds between traditionalists and modernists in each ethnic group and to have helped hide from the colonial power the subtlety of various political strategies.[24]

However, in 1958 the process of fusion was far from being completed at the national level. The political system had a quasi-indirect structure. It was propelled, under the aegis of the colonial administration, by powerful *caciques* (leaders) or regional federations of *caciques* who, for the most part, had encouraged the vertical integration of their native country around their own political machine. They opposed or allied themselves with each other according to the interests of the social strata that they represented and the satisfaction of their own personal ambitions. Within this political elite the tendency was toward the exacerbation of antagonisms. Mr Mbida, invested in 1957 as the first governmental leader of the autonomous Cameroun state, soon showed his inability to surmount fundamental problems. He claimed to reject independence, publicly displayed his indifference to the question of reunifying territory, depended exclusively on his own ethnic group, successively fell out with all other political leaders, and, finally, let slip his intention to abolish the northern chiefdoms. He thus disqualified himself from carrying out the reciprocal assimilation of different segments of the social elite at the national level, and from insuring the autonomy of the new dominant class from the colonial power. His failure resulted in a serious governmental crisis in February 1958, which emphasised the clientelist state's instability and its powerlessness to come up with a political response to the spread of an organic structural crisis.[25]

Instability occurred in a context which made it still more dangerous. The UPC, forced to radicalise its stance because of electoral frauds and political repression on the part of the colonial authorities, abandoned in 1950 by the Duala and Bamiléké aristocracies, and prey to the hostility of the indigeneous administrative chiefs, became more and more extremist. It relied upon the dependants of the established clientele systems for its support, and even on some social groups that these systems in future tended to make marginal: in particular on women organised in the very active Union Democratique des Femmes du Cameroun and on younger people disadvantaged by prevailing social norms (notably the Bamiléké non-heirs, who were forced into exile in ever greater numbers by the decline of marriage under *nkap* in favour of dowry marriage and who hoped in exile to become rich enough to pay the entrance fee into the prestigious traditional societies and buy a wife). What it is crucial to see, allowing us to understand the historical evolution of the clientele systems, is the combination of modern, capitalist exploitation and traditional patterns of domination: wage-earning labourers and the unemployed scorned by the new economic order were social inferiors (*cadets sociaux*) naturally from the point of view of custom. It is true that colonisation and the clientele systems that it created had ensured the economic and political advancement of a small number of these social inferiors by opening up unprecedented positions of power and channels for enrichment. It had even emancipated entire social groups, such as women and slaves. But in most cases it was only a question of individual advancement or relative emancipation. The ruling circles might have grown larger and domination grown milder, but the sphere of dependence remained the same.

The UPC, which tied its domestic political struggle to an international struggle against imperialism, pursued another political plan: more or less consciously, it aimed to establish political control of the social inferiors as such, particularly by asserting the pre-eminence of the party over traditional and administrative hierarchies in the areas that it controlled.[26] However, it did not systematically attack the structures of the established clientele systems.[27] It sought rather to subordinate them to its influence, even liquidating those chiefs who opposed it. In Bassa country, the usufruct of the territories indispensable to the development of the party organisation and the conduct of the guerilla warfare depended on the lineage chiefs. Um Nyobé was himself part of a secret society, through which he obtained the support of numerous clans. But the most prestigious Bassa society was the Um Nkoda Nton, within which the Ndog-Njoué clan, led by the Matip family, had the greatest influence. The grandson of the last chief of the Ndog-Njoué clan, Matip Ma Mbondol – who was to be succeeded only by administrative chiefs – was Mayi Matip, Um Nyobé's assistant and president of the Jeunesses Démocratiques du Caméroun (JDC).[28] The UPC's National Organisation Committee in Bassa country therefore wove itself into the oldest clientele networks. Presiding over an alliance between the social inferiors and an aristocracy deprived of real power by colonisation, it blamed the plight of both groups upon the clientele systems run by village and canton chiefs under the French administration.

In Bamiléké country, another UPC stronghold, the majority of the big *fo*, grouped in Mr Djoumessi's Kumsze and represented in the territorial assembly by the Paysans Indépendants (PI), broke with the nationalist movement very early. The important Baham chief, Kandem Ninyim, remained faithful to it, for which he was deposed in 1956 and placed under house arrest at Yokadouma, from where he commanded underground forces. Furthermore, the UPC strove to make use of the hostile relations between the chiefdoms, to profit from the conflicts between *nkem* and *fo* caused by the latter's autocratic evolution, and to take advantage of the ties that the emigré social inferiors had kept with their chiefdoms of origin. Moreover, the UPC did not despair of rallying the *fo* to its cause; they were attacked only in the case of refusal to collaborate, and the party did not establish a republican or communal organisation.[29]

Thus it appears that the superimposed complex of clientelist networks was the particular object of political conflict during the years 1945–62. The electoral scene, which was itself closely bound up with the clientelist dynamic, represented a basic element in the reciprocal assimilation of the different segments of the elite. The recognition of multi-partyism, which in its own way registered the relationships of strength inside the structure of clientelism, expressed the legitimacy of this process of assimilation and competition in the eyes of the colonial administration, so long as it remained confined to the ruling social groups. The administration, by manipulating them in different ways to the detriment of the UPC, sought to protect elections from the autonomous intervention of lesser orders. The manoeuvre succeeded. But the elections manipulated by colonial authorities were not unmarked by the political actions of social inferiors; the latter, by exerting continual pressure on the badly elected and by abstaining at the territorial elections in 1956, weighed heavily on the elections and, more generally, on the political evolution of the country.

CLIENTELISM, ELECTIONS AND THE ONE-PARTY REGIME

To the degree that it was confronted by a truly revolutionary threat, the clientelist state which linked the French presence to the indigenous ruling classes was born dead.

The nomination of Mr Ahidjo as Prime Minister in February 1958 started a process that in the years 1962–6 was to end in the establishment of a one-party presidential regime. Such a regime constitutes a coherent response, Bonapartist in nature, to the organic crisis begun in the nineteenth century by the penetration of capitalism and aggravated by colonisation.[30]

The acceleration of the process of organic conciliation between the different elite segments and its extension to the national plane – made necessary by rivalries within the political class and by the fragility of a clientelist state faced with the revolutionary threat embodied by the UPC – occurred in the melting pot that was the UC. For its part, this organisation had realised the structural integration of half the country (the north and Bamoun country) and seemed the best placed to safeguard national unity. Moreover, a far from negligible fact in a clientelist context, its chief had become the first person in the state.[31] From 1958 onwards, the front-ranking persons in the southern clientele systems joined the UC, and the numbers rallying to it became even greater after the 1960 legislative elections. In the same period, the revolutionary UPC lost hope of subordinating the pre-colonial clientele systems. With Um Nyobé killed by the *gendarmerie* in September 1958, Mayi Matip forsook clandestine activity and, taking his clientele with him, created a legal UPC, the machinery of which assumed a quasi-monopoly on political representation and organisation in the Bassa country. Likewise, in the west, the Bamiléké *fo* turned their backs firmly on the UPC and supported instead the neocolonial state through the intermediary of Kandem-Ninyim's Front Populaire pour l'Unité et la Paix (FPUP). The situation was ripe for the UC to absorb the other clientelist organisations into its bosom: in 1961 the Efoula-Meyong and the FPUP; in 1962 almost all the eastern Cameroun's other political organisations, with the notable exceptions of the 'Bassa' UPC and Mr Mbida's Démocrates Camerounais (DC); and in 1966, the year in which the principle of a single party covering the whole federation was realised, the western Cameroun parties. This principle worked to the benefit of an ostensibly new formation, the Union Nationale Camerounaise (UNC). However, it required several years more for certain non-institutionalised regional clientele systems to become integrated into the UNC (Mbida's rally in 1967, Matip's in 1968 and Ngondo's in 1972–4).

The absorption in so short a period of different clientelist networks into a single party gave it a structure of amalgamated groups; it did not have individual members. While the clientelist state could accommodate itself to a monolithic face, the means at the disposal of Mr Ahidjo to combat such enclaves were limited. To attempt to eliminate systematically the most influential local personalities would be to compromise the establishment of the single party.

However, the political personnel of the clientelist state have today lost the essence of real power, under the impact of the presidentialisation of authority, the institutionalisation of the party and the ascent of a new generation of middle-level cadres through the single departmental sections (*sections départementales*) and, at the national level, of the bureaucratic elite. Nevertheless, the political personnel of the clientelist state remains associated with the political mechanisms of a regime which has undertaken the task that the local political machines of the preceding epoch had set themselves: to bring together throughout the country the various generations of the social elite and the various kinds of clientele systems by transcending them.

A priori, one might think that a single party is best placed to fulfil this function. But at the national level the balance of power is relatively unfavourable to it, and at the local level the party is only one of a number of political forces. It is in a situation of dependence in relation to the territorial administration and competes with other clientelist channels, such as the notables of the truly traditional aristocracy, the chiefs recognised by the administration, religious notables, and organisations, employers and family heads. It is the territorial administration that supervises and ensures the local articulation of the different clientele networks – including the UNC. However, it does not really bring about their organic fusion.

In reality, the monolithic façade of the single-party presidential regime hides a very complex dynamic relating three positions, each different in nature from the others and of a type to control a clientele network:

(1) *class* (belonging to the traditional aristocracy or to the category of the *nouveaux riches* created by colonisation or the post-colonial era);
(2) *power* (a chief associated with the administration, a municipal notable, a deputy, a party official, a member of the territorial or central bureaucracy, a minister); and
(3) *wealth* (in agriculture, transport, trade, real estate, public or private administration or, more rarely, industry).

These positions combine or contradict within the person of individual claimants to authority. To take an example, a position of power is often a means of enrichment and it is not unusual for it to be held by an heir of the traditional aristocracy. But that is far from being automatic and, above all, all power positions are not equal in value. Village by village and region by region, conflicts between these positions flare up and are immediately translated into terms of clienteles and struggles for influence. 'These small quarrels end up in the formation of antagonistic blocs, each of which tries to recruit partisans among political, administrative, municipal or traditional officials, and even among the population at large.'[32]

At the level of the Cameroun social formation, a new system of inequality and domination is in gestation. This is propelled by micro-conflicts. The political regime, to the extent that it creates new relationships among the positions of power, enrichment and class, brings forth change. What is at stake is the transformation of the various segments of the national elite into an homogeneous and dominant social class, according to that process of reciprocal assimilation that has been at work in Cameroun for some thirty years. The authoritarian state in its totality (and not in the form of its isolated institutions) is the active agent of this transformation. The clientelist system, which largely remains open, is both the product and a constituent element in this hegemonic quest.

While acquiring notable autonomy as regards the clientelist dynamic, because of the general evolution of the regime and of the growing control by the centre of the political system, elections have been important in the emergence of a new ruling class. While certain elements of political pluralism have remained, chiefly by the help of federalism and regional feeling, elections have been able to provide many opportunities for bargaining for sections of the elite with reservations about the regime's orientation. On the occasion of the first federal election, on 26 April 1964, the law could not compel a single national list, flourishing now in most of the French-speaking African states. The two dominant parties of the federated states (the UC for eastern Cameroun, the KNDP for western Cameroun) had made hardly any progress in the process of fusion adopted in principle in 1962. Now, opposition parties are allowed to contest seats, by nominating lists of candidates for multi-member constituencies. But the opposition has no assurance of winning any seats, for each constituency is fought on a winner-take-all basis; the party whose list secures the most votes sweeps all the seats.

In western Cameroun, the CPNC party, in opposition to the Cabinet of Mr Foncha, gained none of the ten seats reserved for the English-speaking state in the National Assembly, but, by winning 24·7 per cent of the votes cast, gave fresh proof of the continuing vigour of its support. This comparative success made it almost impossible for its leaders to be arrested, and brought about a certain 'decompression' of regional political life. It also underlined the fact that the KNDP, contrary to its hopes, had not been able to eliminate the opposition before setting up a unified party and would not be alone in representing the English-speaking state. On the other hand, in eastern Cameroun, the election results brought a renewal of tension. The UC did carry the forty vacant seats, but the Démocrates Camerounais entered a list in the centre – south federal province and gained 129,000 votes (6·5 per cent of the votes at national level), despite the manipulations and police operations which accompanied the election; on the other hand, in the same region, the percentage of abstentions seems to have been higher than elsewhere. There followed a taking in hand of the region which led the general staff of the Démocrates Camerounais to support the Ahidjo – Foncha ticket at the presidential election the next year, and not to present candidates in the eastern-state elections which took place two months later.

The regime's increasingly monolithic development (in which the birth of the single party in 1966, the suppression of federalism by referendum in 1972, and the setting up of a single national constituency for the legislature in 1973 were the three most important stages) did not end the contribution of elections to the process of forming a new ruling class. Competition did not entirely disappear from elections, other than presidential elections and referendums. On the one hand, there is multiple candidacy for the renewing of the basic organs of the UNC and (if one excepts the case of some personalities of the first rank, whose clientelist resources Mr Ahidjo was seeking to decrease) it seems that the central authority means to play the game and guarantee the freedom of these elections. On the other hand, even when the principle of the single candidacy is retained (as for municipal elections or legislative elections), there is very lively competition at a local level to gain endorsement by the political bureaux of the party in the case of legislatures, or by the *bureau de la section départementale* (UNC) in the case of municipal elections: for example, 2699 nomination papers were entered at the 1970 legislative elections for 150 seats, and 2650 in 1973 for 120 seats.

This political competition is of essential interest to prominent people of all sorts – those who hold one or more of the positions of power, wealth or class, as mentioned earlier. At stake is the internal ordering of the future ruling class. Thus we see that elections give rise to the exacerbation of local conflicts, particularly between cadres of the party and administrative authorities, in a way that is regularly deplored by the political secretariat of the UNC.

Thus, from this point of view, it appears that the various electoral processes always work to the advantage of the bureaucracy, whatever may be the degree of control by the central authority that they establish. The freedom to replace the local and departmental cadres of the party is largely responsible for their effacement in the face of the power of the territorial administration. In a regime where power emanates from the top of the institutional pyramid, a democratic-type legitimacy is not enough to give the foundation of an autonomous power. It also takes away the strength conferred by a presidential choice. The president of the Wouri section was not mistaken in requesting the Political Bureau to choose the candidates at internal elections. It is also noteworthy that the mobility of local officials of the UNC is constantly growing, while prefects and provincial governors tend to keep their positions for a longer and longer time. The control of legislative, municipal and union elections by the centre of the political system also comforts the bureaucracy. The territorial administration plays a decisive role in the selection of the candidates finally appointed by the party and, in 1973, it even presided for the first time as electoral officials on election day. Finally, elections show the evolving strength of the ruling class which is in process of formation in a system of bureaucratic power.

If the morphology of the future dominant class and the outcome of the struggle for control over clientelist structures that the various elites carry on among themselves are still relatively uncertain, the place of the subordinate social strata in this emerging system of inequality has been clear since the revolutionary UPC's final defeat. The mass of the population is as much dependent on the new order as it was on the former one.

In particular, the organisation of the party perpetuates the old clientele and dependence relationship between chiefs and social inferiors (essentially the young and women). Each clientelist machine from the preceding period supervised associated organs that helped it mobilise women and the young. As in former times, social inferiors reinforced the chiefs' power; and more often than formerly, doubtless, that was never done without a minimum of tensions within the clientele systems.[33] The single party did not delay in demanding the dissolution of these associations to the benefit of movements that it would control directly: the Jeunesse de l'Union Camerounaise (JUC) was created in 1960, the Organisation des Femmes de l'Union Camerounaise (OFUC) in 1965 (transformed into the JUNC and the OFUNC respectively in 1966). It was planned that the JUNC's and OFUNC's organs corresponding to the different echelons of the UNC would be placed under the tutelage of party officials. In a cultural context in which wealth was still usually calculated on the basis of the number of people the chief had at his disposal, and in a political climate that valued to the extreme the recruitment of party members and electoral participation, section and sub-section presidents frequently wanted to see the young and women placed under their authority only as a mass of manpower swelling the numbers in demonstrations, membership figures, and electoral results. However, contemporary clientele systems have not escaped political action on the part of social inferiors. The weight of the subordinate classes makes itself felt even within political machines endowed with a Bonapartist autonomy.[34] OFUNC officials especially quickly deemed the tutelage of UNC local officials overbearing: at this level, the conflicts between the two organisations seem very numerous. Strengthened by the support of an important fraction of the UNC's Political Bureau, who think it necessary to stop 'treating women as eternal minors',[35] those who run OFUNC have acquired a greater freedom of action. In 1966 it was planned that their militants (as well as those of the JUNC) would no longer pay their associated organism's subscription and would disappear from the UNC's books.[36] In 1969 the organisation was endowed with a national bureau and a national council. The relationships between OFUNC and UNC will continue to evolve.

It thus appears that the systems of inequality and domination prevailing before colonisation have clearly not been eliminated. They still pursue today their historical practices under the cover of neocolonial institutions. Ancestral relationships between elders and social inferiors, enriched by an unprecedented dimension and a new content, find themselves transposed within the political mechanisms of the authoritarian, capitalist state and mediated by these mechanisms in a specific fashion. If it is obvious that the capitalist mode of production and its political expression, the authoritarian state, have subordinated pre-existing modes of production and organisation in order to function,[37] it is no less true that historical systems of inequality and domination have in turn assimilated to the capitalist mode of production and its political expressions, and through them have been reproduced in renovated and widened forms.

In this context, the control of elections by the central authority appears chiefly directed against the social inferiors of yesterday and today. The manipulation of results during the multi-party period was used to the detriment of the political forces representing best the lower social strata: the UPC and also, in the centre – south, the alliance of Démocrates Camerounais and the Catholic Church. The Church, despite its conservative political standpoints, had a distinctly popular foundation, on account of the historic role of Christianity in relation to the liberation of social inferiors, and of the place it gave to women's and young people's associations. As soon as a one-party regime was established, it became obvious that the principle of unanimous elections was essentially what the subordinate masses were accustomed to.

While (as we have seen) electoral rule and practices permit a certain amount of competition at the level of locally important people in the selection of candidates, the emphasis is put on massive, monolithic participation in the ballot by the population, abstention being a *de facto* offence. This is true not only of national elections (presidential, legislative, referendums), but also, and much more significantly, of municipal and categorical elections, the issues of which are more directly popular. It is noteworthy in the case of the municipal that the 1966 and 1967 laws lessened the representative nature of the communal councils, by substituting a proportional ballot for a first-past-the-post ballot and by abolishing constituencies (*sections electorales*) which had only one seat to fill, and that UNC cells are kept out of the selection of candidates. Again, the new central union, L'Union Nationale des Travailleurs du Cameroun (UNTC) has also adopted the single-candidate principle for delegate posts. Nominations are put forward by the regional offices of unions, the national union and regional sections of the national union under the control of regional committees composed of people from the UNTC, the UNC, the Inspection of Works and the territorial administration.

However, by trying to use the clientelist dynamic, or by means of practices, often full of challenging implications, introduced into the party on the initiative of the OFUNC militants, inferior social classes manage to a certain extent to take over the means of electoral domination, particularly through the JUNC and the OFUNC, when the basic party organs are renewed and the legislative elections take place. The social inferior can also try to get round these control mechanisms in a variety of ways: by abstention, as in the centre – south in 1964; or, as in the west and on the coast, under cover of the Jehovah's Witnesses, who form a substitute opposition movement and seem to resist the repression they have been subject to since 1970, just because of their orders to abstain;[38] by direct action aimed at palliating the unrepresentative nature of the electoral process, among which a certain amount of diffusion may be prefigured by the distribution of leaflets, the writing of slogans, or more commonly, the unofficial strikes that one sees at the present time; or, much more frequently, by an unexpressed, unconscious attitude of reserve regarding the ideological speeches which carry one-party elections, and the global system of political and economic development which the regime promotes.

CLIENTELISM, ELECTIONS AND SOCIAL STRUGGLE

Analysis of elections and clientelism in Cameroun in a historical and structural perspective appears to confirm our original hypothesis; no political organisation escapes the action of subordinate social groups or is capable of interpretation in simple terms of social control.

It seems doubly insufficient to reduce the clientelist phenomenon to its function of social and political control, although in Cameroun as elsewhere the failure of the clientelist state has led to the establishment of an 'emergency bureaucratic regime' and clientele systems have historically been the principal *factors* in domination.

The assimilation of clientelism to the notion of 'clientelist' control obliterates in the first place the active – one might say, creative – role of clientele systems: their organic, constituent dimension of inequality and domination. The institution of clientele systems, whether they be traditional, colonial or neocolonial in origin, can be a seedbed for a dominant class. Political power, aristocratic, electoral or bureaucratic in foundation and immediately ramified into clientelist structures, has always constituted the privileged axis for the primitive accumulation of capital in the indigeneous social system. The clientele provides cheap labour that generates surplus values.[39] The purely economic aspect of the question demands more thorough analysis: it is possible that the terms of the exchange have altered considerably with time and that today the profit-earning capacity of dependants is less. Above all, according to the clientelist ethic, the gains thus realised have been widely redistributed. This process of redistribution adds to the control of the 'patron' over his clientele. Now, political power is more important in the medium term than strictly economic wealth accumulation when the political society is the organising principle of the dominant class, the mode of production and the civil society. From this point of view, the setting aside of personnel managing the clientelist state had, I believe, decisive consequences in preventing the southern rural bourgeoisie from becoming the pivot of the bloc in power, as in the Ivory Coast, leaving the door open for a clearly bureaucratic political and economic course of action.

In the second place, the notion of clientelist control makes one forget that clientele systems have constantly borne burdens on behalf of their dependants. In traditional societies, social inferiors placed chiefs under very great pressure to fulfil their redistribution duty,[40] and the behaviour of contemporary clienteles is identical. This does not mean that the terms of the unequal exchange have remained unaltered. The differentiation of clientele systems and, when they take place, the holding of competitive elections have probably not worked to dependants' advantage, contrary to what Scott found in South-East Asia.[41]

Furthermore, vertical integration of the clientelist type has not really been an 'obstacle to the outbreak of social revolutions', nor even always a 'conservative response to change'.[42] In certain regions, clientelist structures have constituted the axis of a revolution that, with a slightly facile analogy, may be called bourgeois to the extent that it has established the supremacy of a new mode of production and of a new elite over the traditional aristocracy and economic organisation, considerably modifying the condition of dependants without so much establishing political management. In other societies, the chiefs of established clientele systems have controlled to their own profit a more or less full process of conservative modernisation. Finally, the UPC has with some success used the oldest clientelist solidarities to attempt to realise truly revolutionary change. At the level of the Cameroun social structure, a social revolution has occurred which tends to the emergence of a new dominant class and which was carried through by adapting to the clientelist dynamics. Or, to be more precise, the historical systems of inequality and domination have not been *perpetuated* thanks to clientelist control: they have, in contrast, been *reproduced* in a widened form by taking advantage of the clientelist dynamic. If this is kept in mind when studying electoral phenomena, our two observations are confirmed. The clientelist vote had a *creative* role in the transformation of Cameroun social arrangements: if it is true that it has exercised a conservative effect by contributing to the UPC's defeat, it has on the other hand been the driving force behind the amalgamation of the different clientele systems to the advantage of the new dominant class. Today, elections in one-party regimes continue to contribute to their organisation without, however, escaping pressure from lower social orders. Clientages and controlled elections, even if at first they appear as mechanisms for domination, are in the last instance arenas of social struggle. This is what should make their study so fecund. The heterogeneity of most African, Asian, Latin American and even southern European political systems is now recognised, whether the conceptualisation be in terms of tradition and modernity, periphery and centre, dominant and dominated, or capitalism and pre-capitalism. Clientele systems and elections ensure the precise specification of these composite elements and constitute for this reason fundamental structures in political systems: their analysis recalls us to our awareness of the unity of social action.

APPENDIX TO CHAPTER

Extreme geographic and cultural heterogeneity, together with bilingualism, is characteristic of Cameroun, which is often called 'the microcosm of Africa'. The German protectorate of Kamerun was occupied by a Franco-British expeditionary force during the First World War. When peace came it became a League of Nations mandate territory, the administration of which was entrusted to France in large part and to Britain to a smaller degree. In 1945, the mandate was transferred to United Nations control.

France and Britain prepared, more or less separately, for the autonomy and, latterly, independence of the territories in their charge. In English-speaking Cameroun this change-over was dominated by the choice between becoming attached to Nigeria and becoming attached to French-speaking Cameroun. In the French area, the chief theme was the struggle against the revolutionary nationalist movement, the UPC (Union des Populations du Cameroun), which went underground in 1955. French-speaking Cameroun gained its autonomy in 1957, and independence in 1960, under the leadership of Mr Ahidjo and his party, l'Union Camerounaise, originally established chiefly in the north. In 1961 the greater part of the English-speaking Cameroun opted by a referendum to join the French-speaking Cameroun in a federal system, following the course extolled by its prime minister, Mr Foncha, leader of the KNDP (Kamerun National Democratic Party).

In 1966, the UC (Union Camerounaise), a party which had a strong lead in French-speaking Cameroun, the KNDP and two opposition parties in English-speaking Cameroun were fused into what was in fact a single party at national level, the UNC (Union Nationale Camerounaise). This opened the way to the abolition of federalism in 1972, as had become inevitable, owing to the growing centralisation of the country administratively and economically, and the superior weight of the French-speaking community. At the same time, the regime experienced a great degree of presidentialisation, allied to great stability, to the benefit of Mr Ahidjo, the head of state since 1960 and prime minister of French-speaking Cameroun from 1958 to 1960.

The United Republic of Cameroun, 470,000 square km in area, stretches from Lake Chad to slightly north of the equator. It is bordered by Nigeria on the west, the Republic of Chad on the north-east, the Central African Republic on the east, the Republic of the Congo on the south-east, the Gabon Republic and equatorial Guinea on the south, and the Gulf of Guinea, or, more precisely, the Bay of Biafra, on the south-west. The total population is approximately 6 million, of which about 20 per cent are English-speaking.

From a geographical and cultural point of view, several regions may be roughly defined:

(a) the north (consisting of the Adamawa plateau, the Benoué valley and a fraction of the Chad basin), which is mostly savannah where the Moslem Peul have established supremacy over the pagan aboriginal peoples by means of pseudo-feudal institutions;

(b) the forested southern plateau, inhabited by a mosaic of non-centralised societies based on kinship, of which many have been converted to Christianity;

(c) the forested coastal region, lower and wetter, with ethnic societies of the same type as in (b); and

(d) the western mountains, largely clear of trees, divided into a large number of centralised chiefdoms, where the impact of Christian missions, though more superficial than in the south, is nevertheless predominant, except in the sultanate of Bamoun, which converted to Islam.

Several cross-cutting divisions can be distinguished: the opposition between the predominantly Islamic north and the more developed and westernised south (b + c + d); the sometimes violent reactions provoked by the expansion of the Bamiléké, who are the largest and most dynamic tribe of the western mountains; and the cleavage between French and English speakers, on the coast and in the western mountains.

PARTIES AND GROUPS IN CAMEROUN

BPN: Bureau Politique National du Parti Unique.
CPNC: Cameroon Peoples National Congress (English-speaking Cameroun; led by Dr Endeley, 1960–6).
CUC: Cameroon United Congress (English-speaking Cameroon; led by Muna Tandeng, 1965–66).
DC: Démocrates Camerounais (eastern Cameroun, led by Mr Mbida, 1956–6).
FPUP: Front Populaire pour l'Unité et la Paix (eastern Cameroun; led by Kandem Ninyim, 1960–1).

Jeucafra: Jeunesse Camerounaise-Française (eastern Cameroun; led by Aujoulat, Fouda and Soppo Priso, 1938).

JUC: Jeunesse de l'Union Camerounaise (1960–6).

JUNC: Jeunesse de l'Union Nationale Camerounaise (from 1966).

KNDP: Kamerun National Democratic Party (English-speaking Cameroun; led by Mr Foncha, 1955–66).

OFUC: Organisation des Femmes de l'Union Camerounaise (1965–6).

OFUNC: Organisation des Femmes de l'Union Nationale Camerounaise (from 1966).

UC: Union Camerounaise (eastern Cameroun, from 1956 to 1958 as a parliamentary group elected by the French-speaking north, and from 1958 to 1966 as a party led by Mr Ahidjo).

UNC: Union Nationale Camerounaise (single party resulting from the fusion of the UC, the KNDP, the CPNC and the CUC in 1966).

UNTC: Union Nationale des Travailleurs Camerounais (formed in 1972; a single union close to the UNC).

UPC: Union des Populations du Cameroun (eastern Cameroun; formed in 1948, banned in 1955, multiple tendencies since then).

UTNK: Union Tribale Ntem-Kribi, or Efoula-Meyong (eastern Cameroun; led by Mr Assalé, 1948–1962).

5 'Semi-Competitive' Elections, Clientelism, and Political Recruitment in a No-Party State: The Kenyan Experience[1]

JOEL D. BARKAN with JOHN J. OKUMU

INTRODUCTION

On 12 October 1974 Kenya held her second 'semi-competitive' elections to the National Assembly within the framework of a one-party state. The elections marked the seventh time Kenyans had chosen representatives for a national legislature since the British colonial government initiated the process in 1957 to commence the transition of the country to independent rule. Though the elections of 1974 produced no significant changes in either the composition of Kenya's governing elite or government policy, the exercise was of considerable significance in terms of the evolution and routinisation of the procedural and structural mechanisms employed by President Jomo Kenyatta and his government to maintain their authority *vis-à-vis* the Kenyan public, particularly in rural areas.

As in most single-party systems in the developing world,[2] the primary purpose of elections in Kenya is *not* to provide voters with a choice of policy alternatives or governing elites, but to recruit new individuals into the present ruling elite, promote other individuals within that elite, and to renew the legitimacy of the elite and its mode of governance in the minds of the electorate. To assess such elections in terms of whether they provide the electorate with a set of policy choices is to misconstrue the nature and significance of the exercise.[3]

The most salient feature of political change during the past decade in many Third World countries, and especially those of Africa south of the Sahara, has not been the development of strong political institutions, and the integration of these typically plural societies into viable national political systems, but the process of political decay.[4] The attempt by departing colonial regimes to transplant Western democratic institutions, including multi-party electoral systems, to African soil usually failed to take root. Overloaded by a ceaseless flow of demands by the members of impoverished and ethnically divided societies, these nascent political institutions have been shoved aside by revolutionary parties, military juntas and, especially, approximations of the former colonial administrative state.

Viewed in this context the Kenyan electoral experience is both atypical and perhaps prototypical, for it provides a possible model for the establishment and maintenance of popularly elected civilian governments within the constraints of weak one-party or no-party systems. On a continent where fewer than half of the states ruled by civilian regimes a decade ago are so governed today, and where fewer than half of these regimes continue to hold elections at regular intervals, the Kenyan experience is hardly representative of the African norm. The underlying socio-economic structure of Kenya, however, is very similar to that of most other African countries.

Like virtually every other former colonial dependency in Africa south of the Sahara, Kenya is a plural society marked by deep cleavages among a diversity of ethnic groups, the largest and most economically developed of which dominate the political system. 89 per cent of Kenya's population resides in the rural areas, engaged in smallholder agriculture, though, as in other developing countries, the rate of migration into the capital city, Nairobi, has steadily increased. Kenya also exhibits all the major features of the typical post-colonial economy. Cash-crop agriculture consists basically of commodities for export (coffee, tea, pyrethrum), while the country's commercial – industrial sector (including tourism, Kenya's second-largest earner of foreign exchange) is dominated by foreign firms. Notwithstanding the legacy of Kenya's European settler community, a legacy which has made Kenya the focal point of foreign investment in East Africa and hence stimulated a faster rate of commercial and industrial growth than that found in most other African states, the fundamental structure of Kenya's economy and the sources of social cleavage within the society are the same as in every other independent African state. Indeed, if Kenya is at all atypical in respect of any of these factors, it is because the degree of social cleavage in the country, on both a horizontal and a vertical dimension, is greater than that in most other African countries. Ethnic rivalries, particularly among the Kikuyu, Luo, and Kalenjin peoples, and between sections of the Kikuyu, are intense. The extent of class formation, and the potential for class conflict arising out of inequities in the distribution of wealth are also more pronounced because of the more rapid economic growth of the commercial – industrial sector, and the growth of the central city on which this sector is based.[5]

The stress that these cleavages generate on Kenya's political institutions is at least equal to and most likely greater than the stress generated by similar cleavages on the political institutions of other African states. If Kenya has succeeded in institutionalising a 'semi-competitive' electoral system in a context where most other African states have failed, the questions are: *why* is this so, and what inferences may students of political development – both academic observers and practioners – draw from this experience?

This essay tries to answer these questions and several subsidiary queries by examining the process and outcomes of the Kenyan electoral system since 1969, when Kenya held 'semi-competitive' elections for the first time. We shall be particularly concerned with the nature of the voting decisions by Kenyans residing in the rural areas, and what their participation in the electoral process suggests for the pattern of authority relations, and organisational links between those who control central government institutions, and the general public residing on the periphery of the political system. Although we shall consider the question of 'who won' and 'who lost' these elections, we shall not dwell on the fact that elections in political systems like Kenya do not present voters with a choice of alternative programmes or of governing elites. Rather, we shall consider the extent to which elections are 'feed-back' mechanisms which provide members of the governing elite with the information and support they need to maintain their regime. Put differently, do elections in a polity like Kenya engender a relatively closed and authoritarian governing elite with the flexibility it needs to maintain its capacity to govern?

Before turning directly to a consideration of these questions, it is useful to define just what we mean by 'semi-competitive' electoral systems and provide a brief historical review of the evolution of electoral politics in Kenya from 1957, when Africans elected representatives to the national legislature for the first time, to 1974, the country's second exercise in 'semi-competitive' electoral politics.

SOME BASIC FEATURES OF 'SEMI-COMPETITIVE' ELECTORAL SYSTEMS

By referring to Kenya's electoral system as 'semi-competitive', we wish to place the Kenyan experience in a category which falls somewhere in between that for the pluralistic electoral systems of the West, and that for the single-party and revolutionary systems of the socialist bloc and parts of the Third World. Whereas these two types of electoral systems are invariably described as 'competitive' and 'non-competitive', by virtue of the extent of inter-party competition found in each, *both* exhibit relatively little *intra*-party competition when it comes to choosing party nominees for legislative office, especially that form of intra-party competition where members of the general public participate in the nomination process. In 'semi-competitive' electoral systems, such as Kenya's, however, inter-party competition is non-existent, while intra-party competition is high, and involves the participation of the general public. The extent to which central political authorities can manipulate electoral outcomes in 'semi-competitive' systems is significant but never total. 'Semi-competitive' electoral systems are few, and are most often found in non-revolutionary political systems in the Third World and one-party electoral districts of the United States. Kenya, Zambia and, to a lesser extent, Tanzania constitute the main examples of 'semi-competitive' systems in black Africa.

Three other features distinguish 'semi-competitive' electoral systems from those classified as 'competitive' or 'non-competitive'. First, party organisation in 'semi-competitive' systems is extremely weak in terms of the capacity of central party authorities to impose their policies and discipline upon subordinate officials, and the party rank and file. Second, in the absence of a highly disciplined party organisation, clientelist relations between central party leaders and local leaders are the norm. Although 'semi-competitive' electoral systems are thus 'one-party' systems in terms of inter-party competition, they are 'no-party' systems in terms of virtually every other facet of party and electoral activity. Third, in 'semi-competitive' systems, political discourse and electoral competition rarely revolve around ideological considerations, because the protagonists in such systems usually represent territorial or ethnic interests, as distinct from those of religion or class. These distinguishing features of 'semi-competitive' electoral systems are summarised in Table V.1. Most are

TABLE V. 1

Distinguishing Characteristics of 'Semi-Competitive' Electoral Systems

	Type of electoral system		
	'Competitive'	*'Semi-competitive'*	*'Non-competitive'*
Level of inter-party competition	High	None	None
Level of public participation in intra-party competition	None/moderate	High	None
Extent to which central authorities determine electoral outcomes	Low	Medium	High
Party organisation	Moderate/strong	Weak/non-existent	Strong
Extent to which ideology shapes campaigns and political debate	Moderate	None/low	High

analogous to those distinguished by Alain Rouquié in Chapter 2, but, whereas, Rouquié makes these distinctions to delineate different types of non-competitive electoral systems, we prefer to divide the non-competitive category in two.

In contrast to the highly disciplined party organisations found in revolutionary single-party systems, party organisation in 'semi-competitive' electoral systems takes the form of highly decentralised coalitions of local political machines, devoid of any ideological coherence, and dominated by local political entrepreneurs, or bosses, skilled at creating patronage networks within their local communities, and between these communities and central government institutions. Elections in these systems are thus contests between rival entrepreneurs who compete for votes on the basis of their claimed and demonstrated potential for servicing the local community and promoting its development. In such systems, political debate is invariably dominated by local issues to the virtual exclusion of discussions of 'national policy'.[6] Voter turnout is also lower than in 'non-competitive' mobilisation systems, but, as will be demonstrated below, those citizens who do participate in the electoral process do so on a highly rational basis in so far as their voting decisions appear to be based on a careful calculation of how their interests will best be served. In 'semi-competitive' systems, voters may not express a choice between alternative government policies, but they do make significant decisions regarding who will represent them at the centre of the political system. Though such decisions may not result in a circulation of governing elites, they do affect the composition of the governing elite, with substantial impact on the evolution of elite behaviour and the overall structure of political conflict in these societies.

THE EVOLUTION OF THE KENYAN PARTY AND THE ELECTORAL SYSTEM PRIOR TO 1969

Although Kenya's electoral system is less than two decades old, its basic structure, the nature of voter participation, and the outcomes it yields have become valued and perhaps institutionalised features of Kenyan political life. The first parliamentary elections in which Africans participated were held six years before independence, in March 1957. Approximately 127,000 voters from a total African population of almost 6 million elected to the Legislative Council eight representatives from eight large single-member districts. The elections of 1957 were carried out on a restricted franchise which required Africans to meet one of seven criteria to be eligible to vote (ten years of education, an annual income of more than £120, and so on), and also involved the election of sixteen representatives by Kenya's European and Asian communities.[7]

The 1957 elections occurred nearly two years after the British colonial government had legalised African political organisations for the first time following the banning of all such groups at the height of the *Mau Mau* Emergency in 1953. However, the legalisation of African political organisations was limited to groups operating within Kenya's administrative districts, as a ban on national organisations was continued until 1960. This policy, combined with the longstanding British colonial practice of creating administrative districts with boundaries that were more or less coterminous with the historical boundaries between ethnic groups, resulted in the establishment of political organisations that were fundamentally tribal and sub-national in character. These organisations quickly became the main political parties in the 1957 elections and in the process made an indelible mark on the character of Kenyan electoral politics at its formative stage. Their impact was particularly pronounced because the elections were held in eight large single-member constituencies. Although these constituencies encompassed several administrative districts, the boundaries between them also conformed to the boundaries between Kenya's major ethnic groups. In the course of Kenya's transition to independence in December 1963, this pattern was repeated and entrenched with each increment in the number of elected parliamentary seats, culminating in the creation of the present 158 single-member constituencies in late 1966.[8] Thus, as the structure of Kenya's electoral system was put into place, constituencies became smaller and more homogeneous in terms of the ethnic composition of their residents.

The leaders of the district political organisations which contested the 1957 elections all came from a new group of educated Africans, most of whom had some experience in local government, in teaching, or in both. The organisations that they created, however, were often grafted onto existing voluntary associations, which in turn were built upon the traditional clan and lineage structures of the respective tribes. Their local power base was rooted in the support given the organisation by powerful clan, lineage and family heads, who wielded influence in the local communities. It was customary for the leaders of the new political organisations to attempt first to win the confidence of these elders rather than to build their organisations on a mass base. The elders controlled lineage and family votes which could be exchanged for material goods to which the leaders had access. A system of exchange relationships soon developed very much along the classical lines of machine politics,[9] as each district developed its political activities around a district 'native son' who established himself as the boss of a local clientelist network.

Right from the start, electoral politics in Kenya developed on a highly parochial basis emphasising ethnic ties and the personal qualities of the individual leaders attempting to organise district machines on their own behalf. The Kenyan electoral system was organised 'from the bottom up' rather than 'from the top down', with local rather than national issues the focus of political debate, and questions of ideology and social class largely irrelevant.

The full impact of these developments became evident in 1960, when Africans were permitted to form political parties on a nationwide basis. In March and May two conferences were held among the leaders of the district organisations at Kiambu to found the Kenya African National Union (KANU). Each district party represented at these conferences sought to project its leader into the executive of the new party, despite the fact that there were only six posts to be filled. Competition and bargaining among the district leaders who attended the Kiambu meetings was intense. Those who were successful in becoming part of a winning coalition survived to form and control the new party. Those who did not so succeed split off and founded a rival, the Kenyan African Democratic Union (KADU).

After the Kiambu meetings, the district political organisations were not dissolved, but merely converted into district branches of the national parties. This enabled the district organisations and their leaders to retain most of their former autonomy within the larger political organisations with which they were now affiliated. KANU and KADU were thus cartels composed of district organisations over which the national leadership had little influence. The two parties had remarkably similar structures, which differed only in respect of the particular regions and ethnic groups from which they drew their support. On this dimension, KANU was a coalition of the largest and most politicised groups, including the Kikuyu, who comprised 20 per cent of Kenya's population and had been the base of nationalist politics in the country since the 1920s; the Luo, who were the second largest group (14 per cent) and dominated the trade-union movement in Nairobi and Mombasa; and the Kamba, the fourth largest, with 11 per cent. By contrast, KADU was a coalition of district organisations representing smaller and less-developed tribes whose entry into the political arena had not begun until the middle and late 1950s. Fearful of being placed in a permanently subordinate position by the leaders of the larger groups who dominated in the founding of KANU, the leaders of the smaller groups, with the active encouragement of the colonial government, founded KADU. In both KANU and KADU, however, the first loyalty of the leaders of the district branches was to other local notables in their areas rather than to the party leaders at the national level. To gain access to the rank and file, the national leaders had to pass through the district bosses and the local notables around whom they built their district machines. This process depended almost entirely on the kind of personal relationships existing between the national and district leaders.

This decentralised pattern of political organisation became more pronounced with the elections of 1961, the first to be conducted on the basis of universal suffrage, and the elections of 1963, the last prior to the granting of independent rule. To create a more representative legislature, the number of seats and constituencies was first increased to 33, and then to 117. This opened up new opportunities for a younger, urban-based and better-educated generation of leaders to enter politics. These elections, both of which were won by KANU, produced many new faces who were not part of the old district political machines, and who were therefore not indebted to the bosses who controlled them.

This phenomenon did not affect all districts equally. In some, such as Central Nyanza, which had a well-organised machine and, in Oginga-Odinga, a powerful boss, candidates had to get a public endorsement from the district boss before they could be elected. More typically, however, the district machines declined in significance as they were displaced by constituency machines created by the candidates running for office, or by those who sought to develop such machines during their term of office. Another pattern was the displacement of the district organisations by several constituency machines, followed by the decline of some of the latter owing to the failure of those elected to the legislature to maintain their personal organisation once in office. Whatever the particular pattern that evolved in each district, the national parties were little more than fragmented confederations of autonomous organisations at the grass-roots. The only differences were the form and extent to which this fragmentation developed.

Thus, while KANU 'won' the elections of 1961 and 1963, it did not do so as a unified party which offered voters a clear set of policies alternative to those of KADU. Rather it did so as a coalition of local organisations which represented the largest proportion of the Kenyan electorate, primarily because it appealed to the largest and politically most sophisticated ethnic groups for its support. In both elections the major unifying force within the KANU coalition was provided by Jomo Kenyatta. Detained at the beginning of the *Mau Mau* Emergency in 1953, Kenyatta was still in gaol in 1961, and the demand to the colonial government for his release was virtually the only common issue on which KANU candidates based their campaigns.[10] Released to his home at Gatundu six months after the elections, Kenyatta attempted to bring about a merger of the two coalitions into a single party, but, having failed in this, accepted the presidency of KANU. After the elections of May 1963, Kenyatta became Prime Minister at the head of a KANU government. Independence followed in December, and in the space of a year Kenya quickly evolved into a *de facto* one-party state, as members of the minority coalition were one by one co-opted into the ruling group. KADU formally dissolved itself in November 1964, but KANU remained a fundamentally weak and faction-ridden party.

Though KANU has been Kenya's ruling party since 1964, and has experienced only one serious challenge to its status as the country's sole party, the developments described above have meant that for all practical purposes KANU as an organisation does not exist outside the chamber of the National Assembly. A few party branches remain active at the district level, as in Nakuru, but these hardly constitute a viable apparatus for linking the central government with the grass-roots of Kenyan society. For this reason, Kenya is often referred to as a 'no-party' state.

ELECTIONS AND CLIENTELIST LINKAGE STRUCTURES

Cognisant of this situation from the start, Kenyatta has relied on two, alternative linkage structures – one bureaucratic, the other clientelist – to govern the country and, particularly in the rural areas, maintain the authority of his regime. The bureaucratic structure consists of the provincial administration (a creation of the colonial government), through which the President seeks to transmit central-government policy to the grass-roots of Kenyan society in the same way as colonial governors before him.[11] As an instrument for extending central government activities into the rural areas, the provincial administration is not our prime concern. Clientelist linkage structures, however, are of special interest because they constitute the most important outcome of the electoral process, *and* depend on the institutionalisation of that process for their regeneration and survival.

In developing countries such as Kenya, clientelist structures exist primarily for representing rural interests on the periphery of the political system at the centre. Given the absence of party organisation in these societies, and the concentration of well-organised interest groups in the urban areas, clientelist structures are frequently the sole mechanisms through which the residents on the periphery can penetrate the centre – not only to make demands on central government institutions, but also to provide support for those institutions.

In choosing to foster the development of linkages from the periphery to the centre of Kenya's political system out of clientelist structures instead of continuing a futile effort to transform KANU into a well-organised and disciplined party, Kenyatta cleverly turned a liability into an asset. Rather than attempting to control the plethora of constituency machines that emerged during and after the 1963 elections, he positioned himself above the political fray as the *Mzee*, the Swahili term for wise elder or patriarch, which he adopted as his official title soon after independence. In this role, Kenyatta sought to establish what Henry Bienen has described as 'court politics'.[12]

With Kenyatta, the acknowledged 'father of the nation', in control of the central government, local political entrepreneurs were to be given free rein to organise constituency and district-wide ethnic machines, campaign for election, and then pay homage to the President and appeal to 'his' government for assistance to their home areas. By virtue of his un-challengeable position, Kenyatta thus installed himself as the premier

patron in a clientelist network consisting of roughly four tiers. At the apex
was the President, who awarded government ministries (and the resources
at their disposal) to senior politicians of longstanding reputation who,
despite the fissiparous proliferation of constituency machines, wielded
power beyond their own constituencies by influencing election outcomes in
neighbouring electoral districts. Ministries were thus awarded to regional
leaders who demonstrated their ability at election time to 'bring in their
ethnic base' in support of the government. These regional leaders are
simultaneously clients of the President and patrons to aspiring younger
politicians. If elected, the latter become backbenchers in the National
Assembly, and are in turn patrons to local notables in their constituencies.
These notables, some of whom might hold elective office themselves as
members of town councils, are in turn patrons to small segments of the
general public. The structure of this four-tiered pyramidal system of
patron – client linkages is summarised in Figure V.1.[13]

While this four-tiered system of linkages between centre and periphery
has become the model for political development in Kenya, it does *not* exist
on a uniform basis in all areas of the country, and in some areas scarcely
exists at all. On the one hand, these linkage chains are based on a series of
informal personal relationships, which periodically break down or fail to
develop at one or more of the four levels. On the other hand, some chains
consist of fewer than four tiers, as when a minister appeals directly to the
local notables in his own constituency rather than via a member of
parliament or local notable, or when a backbencher bypasses the local
notables to make direct contact with the people at the grass-roots.

Another significant variation is the linkage network involving roughly
thirty-five members of the National Assembly who are assistant ministers.
Comprising almost a quarter of the legislature, this group consists mainly
of energetic young organisers of constituency machines who have been
elected by substantial majorities, or easily re-elected to a second term.
Most assistant ministers occupy a somewhat ambiguous position in the
linkage networks in that they are frequently not clients of ministers, nor
particularly close to the President. As effective organisers of their
constituencies, they are simultaneously regarded as potential regional (i.e.
ethnic) leaders, and a possible source of opposition to the centre. Their
appointments as assistant ministers by the President may thus be construed
as both a promotion acknowledging their performance to date, and an
attempt to co-opt them into his clientelist network to thwart any tendency
to challenge his rule.[14]

The main function of elections in Kenya is to recruit talented political
entrepreneurs into a national system of clientelist networks which link the
periphery to the centre, *and* contain their activities so that the entrepreneurs pose no challenge to the regime.[15] Election to the National
Assembly does not confer the opportunity to participate in the formulation
nor, increasingly, the deliberation[16] of public policy. Election confers the

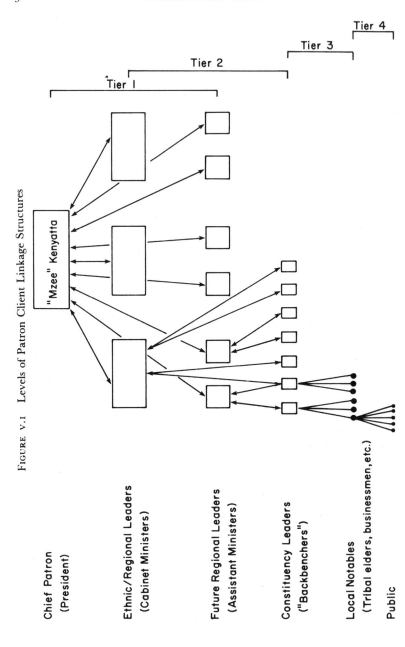

FIGURE v.1   Levels of Patron Client Linkage Structures

opportunity to join a national patriarchy and gain access to a share of the resources that the patriarchy commands. Re-elected members of these clientelist structures are rewarded by being promoted to a higher tier within the system, while those who repeatedly organise a region become members of the President's cabinet and occasionally his inner circle of advisers. Through this process, elections also legitimise the regime in the minds of the mass population, because they provide members of the public with a relatively free hand at choosing their representatives to this clientelist structure, and in so doing provide their communities with a link to the centre.

Elections, in the context of the 'no-party' state, may also institutionalise the roles of which these clientelist linkage structures are composed, because the public and each tier of patrons develop a fairly stable set of expectations regarding the content of these roles each time they are called upon to evaluate the performance of the occupants of these 'offices'. Were it not for the periodic articulation of these expectations which elections provide, the survival of these clientelist linkage structures would depend solely on the personal relationships among the members of these structures. Put differently, elections in the no-party context rejuvenate clientelist linkage structures because the roles played by members of the linkage chains and the interrelationships of these roles, are *not* determined by the occupants of these roles alone. To the extent that elections force a distinction to be made between the patron – client role or 'office' at each tier of each clientelist structure, and the occupants of these roles, the fusing of clientelist linkage structures with the electoral process constitutes a significant step towards maintaining regime authority in developing societies where party organisation does not or cannot exist. It is perhaps for this reason that, despite the weakness of the ruling party, and the fact that the Kenyan system depends so heavily on the political skills of an astute but ageing President, Kenya remains under civilian rule thirteen years after independence. Indeed, the Kenyan political system has been sufficiently resilient to survive several crises similar to those that have brought down other African regimes.[17]

The basis of this resilience would appear to be Kenya's electoral process. Whereas party organisations have declined in virtually every African state,[18] and been displaced by clientelist linkage structures similar to that found in Kenya, the latter has been able to use elections to recruit members into these linkage structures and define the roles they are to play. Contrary to Huntington's thesis, political order in changing societies may not be dependent on the existence of a strong national party organisation to bind the periphery to the centre.[19] In plural societies where the prospects of creating such parties are remote, clientelist structures might well be the only feasible means of accomplishing this task, provided that a 'semi-competitive' electoral process is part of the system.

VOTING BEHAVIOUR IN KENYA: THE ELECTIONS OF 1969 AND 1974

Having suggested the systemic functions of 'semi-competitive' elections in a no-party state, it behoves us to describe what the dynamics of this type of the electoral process are in Kenya. Our data consist of selected voting returns from the Kenyan parliamentary elections of 1969 and 1974, and data from a series of surveys, involving 3828 adult respondents, that we conducted in thirteen rural constituencies during April and May 1974.[20]

Kenya's first nationwide election after independence occurred in December 1969 and was followed in October 1974 by a second. In contrast to the elections of May 1963, when KANU and KADU confronted each other in a conventional competitive contest, and the 'Little General Election' of 1966, when KANU was challenged by candidates of the Kenya Peoples Union in twenty-nine constituencies, the elections of 1969 and 1974 were 'semi-competitive' contests in that they were intra-party contests limited to KANU candidates who had sworn their allegiance to the party and *Mzee*.

The 1969 elections followed a three-year period of political turbulence, which began with the formation of KPU by twenty-nine dissident KANU MPs in 1966, and ended with the banning of the opposition party in October 1969.[21] Four months before the ban, Kenyatta declared that KANU would hold primary elections to select its nominees for the final contest with KPU.

Following the ban the President announced that the primary elections would go ahead as scheduled in December. The primaries were consequently the general elections as well, for, after the results were in, KANU nominees were declared elected to the National Assembly in view of the fact that there were no nominees from an opposition party to challenge them in a second round at the polls.

As the first elections limited to intra-party competition, the 1969 elections were also the first explicit attempt by the President to utilise the electoral process as a mechanism to allocate and define positions in his clientelist machine. In marked contrast to the government's continuous harassment of KPU, Kenyatta adopted a 'hands-off' posture towards all but a handful of contests where some of his close associates faced serious challenge.[22] In contrast, too, to the pattern of political recruitment in one-party states where elections are no longer a regular feature of political life, or where the outcomes of elections are manipulated by central authorities, the Kenyan elections produced a high turn-over and reshuffling of personnel within the clientelist structures which tie centre and periphery together.

The elections facilitated a highly 'open' process of recruitment, in so far as any adult over twenty-five years of age who was literate in English and prepared to pay a £50 deposit was eligible to run; 611 individuals ultimately did so in 150 constituencies after being certified by the KANU Executive Committee as loyal to the 'Party'. Of these, 143 were incumbent MPs seeking re-election.[23]

Apart from certifying prospective candidates, KANU as an organisation played no role in the elections. At the constituency level, the elections were usually contests between rival politicians who spent most of their time organising constituency machines with the assistance of selcted local notables, in the hope of mobilising an electoral majority from the dominant clan(s) in the constituency, or a coalition of small ones.[24] As in the competitive elections of the early 1960s, this method of campaigning caused political debate to become focused almost exclusively on local issues, particularly on the question of which candidate would be most effective at fostering economic and social development in the area. The parochial focus of political debate was also compounded by the 'semi-competitive' nature of the contests and the President's increasing rhetorical emphasis, beginning in 1969, on achieving rural development via 'self-help'. Given the organisational weakness of KANU, on the one hand, and the absence of opposition parties, on the other, discussion of alternative government programmes for the nation as a whole rarely occurred. The President's policy of self-help – or *harambee*, as it is commonly known in Swahili – specifically called on local leaders, particularly MPs, to play active roles in organising such community development projects as the building of schools, health clinics, feeder roads, and so on. Indeed, participation in self-help efforts was to become the main activity in which MPs should engage. Instead of concentrating their efforts on debating government policy in the National Assembly, legislators were to spend more time directly serving their constituencies and be judged by their constituents accordingly.

By emphasising self-help, Kenyatta was partially responding to complaints by MPs during this period that their positions as leaders in their home areas were often undermined by representatives of the provincial administration, and to criticism within the National Assembly of government policy in general. Official sanction of MP's participation in self-help simultaneously legitimised the positions of MPs *vis-à-vis* the provincial administration and reduced the level of debate within the National Assembly, by suggesting to MPs that their political futures would be determined outside the legislative chamber. Official sanction of self-help also encouraged local leaders to engage in activities which provided a natural base for the establishment of personal constituency machines. And, perhaps most important of all, the President's official definition of the role MPs should play was highly consistent, if not identical, with public expectations.

In view of these expectations and the local orientation of campaign oratory, the primary elections of 1969 became referendums on the adequacy of constituency service by incumbent MPs. Many incumbents who had preferred legislative debate to constituency service lost. The results (see Table V.2) indicate that, although losses among incumbents were substantial, their rate of success was at least double that of the challengers as a group. More significant for our purposes, the rate of electoral success rises at each tier of the clientelist chain, as assistant ministers had a higher rate of victories than backbenchers, while ministers had the highest rate of all next to Kenyatta himself, who was unopposed in his constituency.

TABLE V. 2

Winners and Losers in the 1969 Election by Type of Candidate

	Challengers	Backbenchers	Assistant ministers	Ministers	All incumbents
Winners (%)	20	37	63	74	46
Losers (%)	80	63	37	26	54
No.	(468)	(86)	(38)	(19)	(143)

Sources: *Daily Nation*, 8 Dec 1969; Goran Hyden and Colin Leys, 'Elections and Politics in Single-Party Systems', *British Journal of Political Science*, II, no. 4 (Oct 1972) 396, 399.

Assuming that Kenyan voters cast their ballots after assessing the quality of their MP's service to his constituency – an assumption that will be partially confirmed below – it would appear that Kenyan voters tend to view incumbents, especially those at the highest rungs of the clientelist ladder, as the leaders most likely to have access to the central-government resources their communities need. This pattern of voting, moreover, articulated, to an extent that is rare in clientelist systems which recruit their members through non-competitive elections or no elections at all, public sentiments regarding the roles that members of clientelist structures are expected to play. The high turn-over of backbenchers also confirms the extent to which elections in 'semi-competitive' electoral systems do not result in a change of the governing elite, but, rather, in the circulation of individuals on the periphery of that elite.

The results of the 1974 elections are virtually identical to those of 1969, suggesting that Kenya's electoral system may be in the process of becoming an institutionalised aspect of political life that will outlive its creator, Jomo Kenyatta, who is now in his late eighties. As in 1969, the elections consisted of a series of KANU primaries in which several candidates contested seats in single-member districts but the party played no role other than certifying those eligible to run.[25] Once again the elections were mainly referendums on the performance of incumbent MPs, with rival campaigns focusing on local issues. As indicated by Table V.3, the rate of electoral success was again highest among incumbents who occupied positions at the highest tiers of the clientelist ladders.

TABLE V. 3
Winners and Losers in the 1974 Election by Type of Candidate

	Challengers	Backbenchers	Assistant ministers	Ministers	All incumbents
Winners (%)	15	35	64	79	49
Losers (%)	85	65	36	21	51
No.	(496)	(78)	(36)	(19)	(133)

Source: *Daily Nation* and *East African Standard*, 19 Oct 1974.
Note: The results presented in this table are for 140 districts of a total of 158.

The function of Kenyan elections – to allocate and define roles within a series of clientelist structures linking periphery and centre – is underscored by an examination of the relationship between the role expectations Kenyans hold of elected representatives and the way they vote. Contrary to conventional wisdom, members of peasant societies frequently have a much higher knowledge of political events, including who their elected leaders are and what they do, than members of the public in polities presumed to be more developed.[26] While this knowledge tends to be limited to events in their local communities, peasants are not unaware of the parameters of the larger political system in which they live. Thus 89 per cent of our sample could accurately volunteer the name of their MP when asked who he was, a third could distinguish his duties from those of civil servants and judges, and 86 per cent correctly stated that President Kenyatta exerted more influence on government decisions than any other individual or institution.

When asked to state the most important activity to which members of the National Assembly should devote their time, 84 per cent of the respondents expressed an opinion. Their responses (see Table V.4) suggest that most Kenyans are aware of the MP's role in clientelist linkage structures; 71 per cent of the entire sample and 85 per cent of those responding to the question said that linkage activities constituted the most appropriate role an MP could play, particularly when the MP represented the needs of the local community at the centre, or obtained resources from the centre for *harambee* development projects in the constituency. In contrast, only 5 per cent of the sample felt that debating national policy in the National Assembly should be the activity on which MPs should spend most of their time.

These role expectations closely resemble those articulated by the President. The most interesting point about these expectations, however, is

TABLE V. 4
Most Important Activity which Kenyan MPs Should Perform

	%
Linkage activities	
Tell government what people in district want	29
Obtain projects and benefits for the district	25
Visit district frequently	11
Explain government policies to constituents	7
Total linkage	72
Non-linkage activities	
Help constituents with their personal problems	6
Take active part in the debates of the National Assembly and pass bills	5
Help solve conflicts in the community	2
Total non-linkage	13
No answer and don't know	16

(No. in sample: 3828)

that they are also *the basis on which Kenyan voters evaluate incumbent members of the National Assembly* at the polls. It is for this reason that Kenya's 'semi-competitive' electoral system is so significant for the operation of the political system as a whole.

The relationship between the respondents' role expectations and their voting decisions is presented in Figure V.2 in the form of a causal model[27] explaining the vote received by the eleven MPs of the thirteen representing our sample constituencies who stood for re-election. To construct the model, the percentage of the vote received by these incumbent legislators was regressed on the number of candidates who stood for election in their districts in October 1974, and on an aggregate evaluation score (derived from the district surveys) of the MP's performance. The evaluation scores were computed by taking the rating each respondent accorded his MP for the activity that he had said was the most important. These activities were rated on a three-point scale of 'very active', 'somewhat active', and 'not active'. The aggregate evaluation score for each district is thus the percentage of respondents in the district who rated their MP as 'very active' on the activity they regarded as most important.

Upon computing the correlations and path coefficients for the model, we found support for the expectation that the respondents' ability to evaluate MPs according to their role expectations would be related to their voting decisions. Low evaluations of MP performance result in an increased

FIGURE V.2   Regression Model Explaining Vote Received by Incumbent Kenyan MPs in Election of 1974[a]

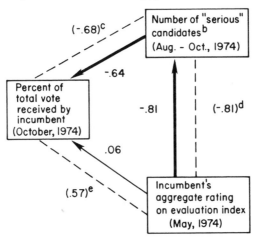

Coefficient of indirect effect of evaluation index on		
vote	0·52	$(-0·81 \times -0·64)$
Multiple correlation	0·68	
Multiple correlation, adjusted for small no.[f]	0·64	
No. in sample	11	
Significance	0·09	

[a]Beta weights for model appear without parentheses, while correlation coefficients (Pearson r) appear with parentheses.

[b]'Serious' candidates are those who ultimately received at least 5 per cent of the vote.

[c]Significant at 0·011.

[d]Significant at 0·001.

[e]Significant at 0·034.

[f]J. P. Guilford, *Fundamental Statistics of Psychology and Education* (New York: McGraw-Hill, 1965) pp. 400 – 1.

number of candidates, as more and more would-be challengers jump into the race. Virtually all the challengers are local notables who are in a position to discern voter sentiment accurately, albeit unsystematically. The message to incumbent MPs is clear: either they carry out their duties in conformity with the role expectations of their constituents, or they face a stiff challenge at the next election.[28]

The apparent ability of rural Kenyans to make their voting decisions on the basis of their expectations of the roles their representatives should play is also interesting in view of the common belief that members of peasant societies are bound by traditional norms, and are therefore incapable of engaging in 'rational' political behaviour. While it is true that political organisation at the grass-roots of Kenyan society is based on ethnic, clan and family ties, election outcomes are not necessarily determined by these ascriptive considerations. Since all major candidates in a constituency must pass these ascriptive tests to qualify as serious contenders, the variable on which they are most likely to be distinguished is their record in 'delivering the goods' to the local community – that is, their assistance to self-help development projects. When ascriptive criteria are held constant, considerations of achievement usually determine the voting decision.

The results of the model also suggest that the 'rules of the game' of Kenya's 'semi-competitive' electoral process have been internalised by the public at large, and are not merely an exhortation by the national leader who articulated them. While President Kenyatta and his close associates may have defined the purpose for which elections are held, and to this extent determined the outcome of the exercise, it is important to remember that the system they have devised is consistent with both public expectations and the structure of political organisation existing at the grass-roots of Kenyan society.

CONCLUSION

In conclusion, let us return to our original question of whether a 'semi-competitive' electoral process contributes to regime stability in plural societies where the authority of central government institutions is not firmly established in the public mind. The Kenyan experience would suggest that the answer to this question is probably 'yes'. By using the electoral process to facilitate public definition of the roles which members of clientelist linkage structures are supposed to play, the government of President Jomo Kenyatta has created a more durable set of linkages between the periphery and centre of the Kenyan political system than would otherwise exist.

To the extent that this fusion of clientelist structures and electoral process constitutes a unique blend of 'traditional' and 'modern' procedures through which central government authority can be maintained in the context of a 'no-party' state, the Kenyan experience may indeed be a prototype for other polities to follow. The real tests for the Kenyan system, however, have yet to be passed. While the 'semi-competitive' electoral process has provided President Kenyatta with a means for readily recruiting new members into clientelist linkage structures and promoting others, it remains to be seen whether the electoral process is itself sufficiently institutionalised to survive Kenyatta's passing from the political scene, and whether it can facilitate the choosing a new chief patron to succeed him.

Second, and perhaps more serious, is the test of what Scott has termed the problem of 'inflationary democracy'.[29] Given the nature of the Kenyan system, the electoral process has already begun to place on central government authorities pressures new to them and with which they may not always have the capacity to deal. As a greater proportion of those winning elections in Kenya actually seek to fulfil their constituents' expectations, the total sum of demands which these political entrepreneurs will make on the centre, and on the clientelist linkage structures themselves, may be more than these nascent institutions can bear. It is therefore possible that, while a 'semi-competitive' electoral process has provided Kenya with a measure of political authority unique for polities of this type, this process may also result in an undermining of political authority in the long term.

6 The 1975 Tanzanian Elections: the Disturbing 6 per cent

DENIS MARTIN*

> The figure of 6 per cent is nevertheless disquieting. It should call for serious thinking in the party, for it does raise important issues about its ability to implement its own decisions.[1]

In Western elections analysts would normally concentrate on the majority of votes, rather than on the actions of 6 per cent. In the Tanzanian presidential election of 1975, the 6 per cent of votes cast against Julius K. Nyerere, the President and only candidate nominated by the Tanganyika African National Union (TANU) and the Afro-Shirazi Party (ASP), was a disquieting result leading the ruling party to think seriously about its political mobilisation capability. One might laugh at a seemingly partisan exaggeration of dissent, but it would be preferable to follow the advice of Bismarck Mwansasu and try to discover the reasons for these six percentage points of dissent – as well as for the total results of the October 1975 Tanzanian election.

DECIPHERING THE ELECTIONS

Presidential elections in Tanzania operate on a single candidate system: TANU and ASP conference meet in joint session to designate their joint candidate. Once officially nominated, the candidate must not campaign personally. It is the two vice-presidents (named by the President at the

* Part of the information used in this paper was gathered during a trip to Tanzania financed by the Fondation Nationale des Sciences Politiques, Paris. I should particularly like to thank Anthony Rweyemamu, Goran Hyden, John Okumu, Katabaro Miti, all of the Department of Political Science, University of Dar es Salaam, and Liliane Lacherez for the help that they gave me in preparing this work.

same time as the Cabinet, with the First Vice-President being the President of Zanzibar) who appeal to the electorate to vote for him. The procedure for voting for the Presidency is simple in the extreme. Each ballot paper gives the name of the single candidate – Julius K. Nyerere. A voter has the choice of marking a box saying Yes or of marking one saying No to Nyerere as President. If the sole candidate were not to obtain 50 per cent of the votes cast, the leaders of the parties nominating him would need to meet again to choose another candidate, and a second ballot would be required.

Elections to the National Assembly operate differently. There are no parliamentary elections in the Zanzibar part of the country. In Tanganyika, to be a candidate in a constituency (since 1975, constituencies and administrative districts have coincided), it is necessary to have been nominated by TANU. To be considered as a candidate, one must be a party member, at least twenty-five years old (the minimum voting age is eighteen) and submit a request to the local party organisation. The aspiring candidates in a constituency are summoned before the annual district conference, where they are heard speak and are questioned. At the end of this conference, the delegates are called upon to choose the individual whom they consider the best possible candidate: a list is then drawn up in which the competitors are ranked according to the number of votes that they received in the annual district conference. These lists are then submitted to the district executive committees, which examine them and send them in turn to the regional directorates of the party. From there, they progress upwards to subcommittees of the Central Committee and finally to TANU's National Executive Committee, which makes the final decision and announces the names of the party's two official candidates in each constituency. Once chosen, the two constituency candidates must campaign together for a month, speaking from the same platform as they make their electoral rounds. Unofficial campaigns, whether conducted by the candidates or by their supporters, are in theory forbidden.

On 26 October 1975, therefore, each Tanzanian citizen had to vote for one of the two parliamentary candidates in his constituency, and say whether he wanted Julius K. Nyerere to continue in supreme command as President of the Tanzanian state.[2]

The parliamentary elections

In each district TANU had nominated two candidates by means of a procedure which takes account of the would-be candidates' political commitments and also their moral qualities. The procedures implemented decisions taken by TANU's National Executive Committee meeting at Musoma in November 1974; these decisions stipulated that the Leadership Code concerning ethical as well as political standards should henceforth apply to all party members and no longer just to its leaders; moreover, to keep their positions of responsibility or accede to new ones, leaders should display an unimpeachable morality in their actions. These extra constraints did not discourage parliamentary aspirants, since there were more than 1050 would-be candidates for the ninety-six directly elected seats in the parliament.[3] There was an increase in the number of intellectuals who aspired to candidacies, and this was reflected in an appreciable rise in the level of education of candidates.

As in previous years, turn-out was huge, especially in the countryside, where voter registration had been carried out in a particularly dynamic fashion and the number of polling booths had almost doubled since 1970, to more than 30,000. The number of registered voters in 1975 corresponded to about 70 per cent of potential voters. For the first time in a Tanzanian election, the number of people who actually voted exceeded half the potential electorate.[4] The number of registered voters, each of whom was given a voter's card (previously lists had been drawn up at each election), was 5,577,566, of which 4,557,595 voted – a turn-out of 82 per cent.

In four districts, the ballot was a simple formality, since the party had decided to present only a single candidate: Rashidi Kawawa in Liwale, Isael Elinewinga in Hai, Joseph Mungai in Mufindi and Leonsi Ngalai in Rombo. In all the other constituencies, two candidates competed, each having been given a symbol (either a hoe or a house) which was printed on the ballot sheets to allow illiterates to distinguish them more easily.[5]

Of the 120 members elected to the preceding parliament, twenty-two decided not to run in 1975, one presented himself as a candidate for a national seat, and fifteen presented themselves as candidates for regional seats. Eighty-two sought re-election, but sixteen of these were not endorsed by the district conferences and six others were rejected by the party's National Executive Committee. Sixty outgoing MPs therefore remained in the race for the ninety-six constituency seats; this was a reduction of twenty-four from the previous total, owing to a reform adjusting the number of constituencies to the number of administrative districts. Four members were re-elected without opposition; thirty-one beat their competitor (who, given the decreased number of constituencies, might himself well have been an outgoing MP); and twenty-five lost their seats. If one adds those members *appointed* to the 1970 parliament and contesting a constituency in 1975, the number of outgoing members returned in 1975 rises to forty-three. Of the ninety-six members elected by direct, universal suffrage, fifty-three entered the National Assembly for the first time.[6] Although twelve members of the outgoing Cabinet were re-elected, two ministers and a junior minister were beaten. Five military figures (including the Minister of National Culture and Youth, Major-General Sarakikya) won the constituencies that they contested.

At this level, it would seem premature to seek in the parliamentary election results a trend indicative of how Tanzanian political life is evolving, or permitting an authoritative deduction about the masses' adherence to or disaffection from the regime. At the very most, one can consider the renewal of political personnel through the elections. Such renewal is a constant feature of Tanzanian elections, owing to (a) the bitter competition between candidates for a position that carries both prestige and material advantage, and (b) the attitudes of voters, feel it right that the privileges of office should change hands fairly frequently, and that one who has defended their interests badly should be punished, whatever his standing.[7]

The presidential elections

Examining the presidential election results allows us to see the evolution of Tanzanian political life more clearly. Julius K. Nyerere won the election by a very large majority, receiving 4, 168, 457 Yes votes (91·5 per cent of all votes cast and 74·8 per cent of the registered electorate) as against 302, 578 No votes (6·7 per cent of the votes cast) and 83,327 blank ballots (1·8 per cent of the votes cast). Taken as a whole, these results evidently give no cause for alarm, but Bismarck Mwansasu noted that the percentage of votes hostile to the 'father of the nation' was about twice as many as at the 1965 and 1970 elections (approximately 3 per cent in each case). In absolute terms, this figure is certainly not large, but, after taking account of the structure of Tanzanian political life, one is immediately inclined to interpret it as the sign of muted discontent.

The incentive to accord this 6 per cent of the vote a political significance out of proportion to what the figures seem to represent is still greater when the results are analysed by region (see Table VI. 1). In all regions except Zanzibar, Arusha and Tanga the percentage of Yes votes in 1975 decreased relative to 1970, and in almost all regions except Zanzibar and Arusha the percentage of No votes increased, even in the regions holding the record for Yes votes. The percentage of No votes varies considerably from region to region, and so does the difference between the 1970 and 1975 results. For example, Mara went from 3·0 per cent to 5·5 per cent, staying very close to the national average, while Shinyanga, not far removed from Mara geographically, went from 3·7 to 18·8 per cent No.

When one combines the four regions giving the highest percentage of negative votes (Mwanza, Shinyanga, Tabora and West Lake) one finds that these regions accounted for 46·6 per cent of all the No votes. When the four regions giving the largest number of negative votes in absolute terms are combined (Mwanza, Shinyanga, Tabora and Dodoma), the percentage of No votes covered rises to 48·3 per cent. There is therefore a marked regional concentration in the distribution of No votes. Dodoma excepted, these regions are adjacent to each other, and form a wide band covering the western fringe of the central Tanganyikan plateau. In the 1970 and 1965 elections there were similar, though less heavy, concentrations of No votes. The Mwanza region figures in all the groupings.

TABLE VI. 1

The Results of Tanzanian Presidential Elections, by Regions, 1965–75

	Votes			Yes (%)			No (%)			Spoilt (%)		
	1965	1970	1975	1965	1970	1975	1965	1970	1975	1965	1970	1975
Arusha	91,847	170,457	223,500	97·6	92·6	93·7	1·8	5·7	5·1	0·6	1·7	1·8
Coast	228,264	320,622	165,488	94·7	95·9	92·7	4·5	3·1	5·7	0·8	1·0	1·6
Dar es Salaam*			276,079			94·3			4·3			1·4
Dodoma	155,809	178,350	302,334	88·2	90·6	90·3	10·6	4·7	7·5	1·2	4·7	2·2
Iringa	108,518	167,299	233,800	96·8	96·9	95·0	2·3	1·7	3·1	0·9	1·4	1·8
Kigoma	121,330	122,251	168,140	98·3	90·9	90·0	1·1	2·7	5·9	0·6	6·4	4·1
Kilimanjaro	135,865	189,695	235,980	97·6	98·0	95·8	0·7	1·7	2·6	1·6	0·3	1·6
Lindi*			161,594			93·4			4·8			1·8
Mara	91,544	135,021	193,281	92·9	93·6	91·2	5·5	2·9	5·5	1·6	3·5	3·3
Mbeya	143,013	249,659	255,139	84·6	97·9	97·1	2·1	1·6	1·7	13·3	0·5	1·2
Morogoro	124,691	185,044	244,778	96·0	96·1	95·3	3·3	2·4	3·0	0·7	1·5	1·7
Mtwara	252,817	377,722	272,708	96·0	93·8	92·7	2·5	3·5	4·7	1·6	2·7	2·6
Mwanza	160,276	255,641	296,433	91·0	90·7	79·0	8·0	6·9	18·1	1·0	2·4	2·9
Rukwa*			100,226			91·6			5·3			3·1
Ruvuma	78,520	114,454	142,675	98·2	96·2	93·3	0·6	1·8	4·8	1·2	2·0	1·9
Shinyanga	178,954	273,355	238,260	95·8	94·0	80·4	3·1	3·7	18·8	1·1	2·2	0·8
Singida	136,443	166,145	166,757	96·6	94·0	93·3	2·9	2·1	5·4	0·5	3·8	1·3
Tabora	133,402	136,234	178,500	94·6	95·2	85·0	5·0	3·0	13·9	0·4	1·8	1·1
Tanga	184,805	227,176	259,290	95·8	95·2	95·6	2·1	2·1	3·1	2·1	2·7	1·3
West Lake	134,216	194,871	229,472	97·7	96·1	90·3	1·8	1·8	7·7	0·5	2·1	2·0
Zanzibar	184,102	185,693	200,928	99·0	98·9	99·2	0·8	0·5	0·4	0·2	0·6	0·4
TOTAL	2,636,040	3,649,689	4,554,362	95·6	94·9	91·5	3·4	3·0	6·7	1·0	2·0	1·8

* Regions created in 1975.

Moreover, the MPs who appeared particularly critical of governmental policies during the 1968 parliamentary crisis came from regions where the number of negative votes was higher than average.[8]

What in fact is the significance of these negative votes, which stand out starkly against the unanimity reigning generally in the united republic? Where they are higher than average, do they signify tiredness of the man who has headed the national liberation movement and then the state since 1954; hostility towards the regime; tiredness of the incessant political upheaval into which Tanzania has been drawn since 1967; or a reaction by members of social strata particularly affected or upset by the country's advance along the road to socialism?

The hypothesis of a vote directed against Julius K. Nyerere personally is unlikely, at least when presented in this form. Everything in fact works to make a respected personage of the man,[9] and the criticisms that can be heard against him as an individual come from such restricted milieux that they could not possibly acquire so great an electoral expression. More to the point, perhaps, the negative vote in a presidential election is one of the few channels that the political system allows for expressing discontent – be it general political discontent (hostility to socialist policies) or a more limited discontent (opposition to a particular measure, to party and state representatives in a region, or to the way that certain central directives are carried out in the regions). Whatever the motive, a vote hostile to Julius K. Nyerere is seen as a transgression (opposing the 'father of the nation'), so much does this man seem to personify the nation and its history, the regime and its policies and socialism (or Ujamaa, the Tanzanian brand of socialism, as defined by the Arusha declaration of 1967; *ujamaa* is a Swahili word referring to the extended family and the organisation of traditional communities).

If the rise in the negative vote is accepted as the expression of a degree of discontent, what are the reasons for this discontent? President Nyerere is the first to admit that not all is well in the best of all possible African socialist worlds.[10]

Drought, dependence and development

The Tanzanian economy has been very seriously affected by the drought that afflicted a large part of the country in 1971, 1973 and 1974, causing a drop in agricultural production and hence in the export of commercial crops, and by the increased price of oil, directly affecting the import costs of oil and indirectly the costs of importing machinery manufactured in the industrialised countries.[11]

The most serious consequences are those affecting agriculture. Faced with the possibility of famine, the government had to import 1000 million shillings worth of foodstuffs in 1974, and, it is estimated, 551 million in 1975. (Approximately eight Tanzanian shillings equal one US dollar.) In

concrete terms, this means that choices have been made that bring into
question, if not the previously elaborated development strategy, at least its
timetable. Thus the third development plan was to have been launched in
June 1975; it was delayed until July 1977. The funds spent on foodstuffs
have limited the machine imports of a country still totally dependent on
outside industry for much equipment.[12] This situation has inevitably been
followed by a relatively high rate of inflation, a deterioration in the balance
of payments and a drop in currency reserves.[13]

The clear result has been a general weakening of the Tanzanian
economy, which is especially dangerous because it brings into question the
government's often reaffirmed need for self-reliance.[14] As President
Nyerere notes, 'in the very immediate future our food suppliers could, if
they wished, impose conditions on their sales which we would be forced to
accept or starve'.[15] More generally, during these dark years Tanzania finds
itself once again placed in a position of structural dependence that could
have grave consequences both on its development policy and on its
national independence. In addition, the frequent intervention of firms of
foreign consultants not knowing very well the realities of the country's
situation, and the decision to finance 55 per cent of the country's 1975/6
development investments with external funds (from Sweden, Norway,
Denmark, the United States' AID and the World Bank) could be
interpreted as a failure of the strategy to encourage development through
the reinvestment of internal surpluses and therefore as the collapse of the
economic policy applied since 1967.[16] Such conditions constitute for many
a solid foundation for opposition to TANU policies: an opposition of
principle, denying that Tanzanian socialism, Ujamaa, has any real
development potential; or a more radical opposition, accusing Ujamaa of
not having really broken with neocolonialism; and of favouring the
emergence of a bureaucratic bourgeoisie.

Voyage to the heart of the bureaucracy

In 1971, in reaction to the Ugandan *coup d'état* of General Amin, the
TANU Guidelines were published. These specified Tanzania's political
goals, announced the creation of a popular militia and unambiguously
confirmed the party's supremacy over all other institutions in the state.[17]
In 1972 a policy of decentralisation was implemented the aim of which was
to reduce the powers of the bureaucracy by giving more powers to the local
authorities and involving the population more actively in the planning
process.[18] In 1974 the Leadership Code, which since 1967 had restricted
the extra-curricular earnings and activities of Tanzanian politicians, once
again became a prominent item on the party's agenda. At the beginning of
the year a committee overseeing the application of the code met in the
regions and districts to check the behaviour of local leaders, and in
November TANU's National Executive Commission promulgated stricter

conditions for leaders and extended the application of the code to all party members. In the same year elections within the party took place, with a particular emphasis upon choosing honest cadres committed to Ujamaa.[19] Finally, in 1975, TANU's national executive Commission, meeting in Shinyanga, decided to modify the composition of the National Assembly, and thus on 13 June the parliament adopted a constitutional reform solemnly sanctifying the supremacy of the party ('all political activity in Tanzania shall be conducted by or under the auspices of the party; and the functions of all the organs of State of the United Republic shall be performed under the auspices of the party') and ratifying the new composition of the National Assembly.[20]

The common thread in the political evolution of Tanzania during the five years separating the 1970 and 1975 elections is insistence upon party supremacy. This institutionalises a state of affairs implicit since the adoption of the Arusha Declaration and the parliamentary crisis of 1968 and, despite these, constitutes in fact a small political revolution. That the leadership role of the party should have been confirmed and juridically codified would not in itself have been astonishing had this enterprise been no more than a modification of vocabulary and of the distribution of powers in the machinery of state. But it was a struggle of a fundamentally new kind that began in 1971: a struggle pitting dedicated builders of socialism against those giving lip service to socialist ideals in a situation of permanent neocolonial dependency. And it is in the context of this subtle confrontation that the elections must be placed and their results interpreted.[21]

The first element to be considered underscores the contradictions running through Tanzanian society, concealing antagonistic objectives behind an apparent leadership consensus. From 1971 to 1974, the Tanzanian government continued a policy of bringing under state control the country's principal sources of wealth: 1971 saw the nationalisation of precious-jewel mines and the societies trading in them, and of all real estate valued at more than 100,000 Tanzanian shillings; 1973–4 saw the nationalisation of agricultural lands and plantations, belonging for the most part to British citizens; and 1974 also saw the government-owned National Insurance Corporation increase its insurance monopoly. Almost all these measures were aimed against either foreigners (companies exploiting the diamond mines; British planters) or Tanzanians of Indian or Pakistani origin (real-estate owners). These measures increased the Tanzanian government's economic power, and thus may be considered socialist. At the same time, they can also serve to consolidate the social base of what some people call the bureaucratic bourgeoisie, or the parasitic bureaucracy.

The second indicator of radicalisation seems unequivocal, although it is still too early to judge the real success of the undertaking. It is the struggle against the bureaucracy. The political aspect is concerned with removing those whom President Nyerere calls 'the village tyrants and insensitive bureaucrats',[22] and the economic aspect, under a 'struggle against corruption' banner, attacks job privileges, including the bribes derived from them. This reinforcement of party powers has been insolubly coupled with an appeal 'to revolutionise the leadership of TANU'.[23] The denunciation of growing corruption in the army and police force has effectively produced some very important changes in the officers of these two forces, especially through the integration of National Service personnel into the army, giving the leadership a greater political control over the army. Yet elections within the party themselves leave a peculiar impression when, after the bureaucracy is stigmatised and the emergence of new revolutionary leaders called for, factory directors are re-elected to the presidency of the party branches in some firms, as happened at Ubungo Farm Implements and the Friendship Textile Mill.[24] The bureaucracy could well be a two-headed creature: one head clamouring 'Down with the bureaucracy', the other whispering 'Pass the money.' The imprecision of the concept *bureaucracy* in official Tanzanian phraseology, blessed by what one might call the 'left', bears witness to the fact that the factional struggle, although it has become appreciably more severe since 1971, still has not reached the breaking point of ties uniting the holders of power.

This antagonistic complicity manifests itself in two instances in which political and economic issues are intimately mixed and in which the two trends came, one after the other, to occupy the political limelight: the desire for change shown by certain leaders, and the conservatism of many when faced with a radical questioning of the power structure in which they play leading roles; and the aspiration of a part of the population for new forms of participation in the decision-making process, and their rejection of measures imposed upon them without consultation. This kind of hesitation waltz can be illustrated with reference to the 'villagisation' campaigns of 1973 and 1974 and the industrial disputes of 1971–3.

Rural and urban workers

The often-voiced objective of President Nyerere and other Tanzanian leaders is to establish in the countryside, where traditionally dwellings have for the most part been dispersed, a network of villages to consolidate essential services (the water supply, schools, medical services, and so on) and to serve as bases for the growth of mutual-aid groups and co-operatives, leading to the foundation of genuine Ujamaa villages. The idea dates from before independence, but it really began to take shape after the failure of the settlement schemes that were launched at the beginning of the 1960s with the help of the World Bank. The failure of these schemes, which were based upon heavy technical and capital concentration, caused the formulators of agricultural policy to gamble thereafter on self-help schemes. The first villages sprang up under the impetus of the party youth organisation in 1965, and very slowly the movement then developed. The 1969 Presidential Circular no. 1 urged that the tempo of the consolidation be accelerated. 'All efforts and decisions on the part of governmental officials must henceforth stress the advantages of community life and work for the good of all.' In 1970, setting an example, President Nyerere himself participated in the pilot operation organised in the Dodoma region: in a year, close to 30,000 families had been grouped into 190 villages. The grouping of villagers was to be on a voluntary basis, after detailed study of the sites for the new villages. However, on 6 November 1973 it was reported, 'President Nyerere said that living together in villages is now an order. And that it should be implemented in the next three years . . . . That people who refused to accept development changes were stupid, if not ignorant or stubborn.'[25] This speech, an astonishingly violent one from the President, in fact marked the eruption into the political field of discontents arising from the drought. An editorial in the official daily newspaper shortly afterwards explained that it was not possible to offer suitable help to rural inhabitants whose dwellings were dispersed, still less to improve their living standards, if they did not form village settlements.[26]

On 15 October 1973 the *Daily News* announced that there were 5556 Ujamaa villages, with more than 2 million inhabitants, or 15 per cent of the population. By 17 September 1974 this figure had doubled, and by 21 December of the same year Prime Minister Rashidi Kawawa spoke of 90 per cent of the population having been grouped into villages. This was an exorbitant and probably exaggerated claim, since by 5 July 1975 the reported number of 'villagised' people had dropped to 9 million. Official statistics gave the number as 65 per cent of the rural population on 9 October 1975, with the remaining 35 per cent to be grouped at the end of 1976.

It appears likely that 50 per cent of the rural population, between about 7 and 8 million people, changed their place of domicile in just two years. These hundreds of thousands of small migrations constitute a movement of a size barely equalled in Africa. Despite all the reservations that may be made about the conditions under which they were carried out, they denote an uncommon political mobilisation capacity.

But there was more than a capacity to convince and to carry people along. In some regions grouping occurred spontaneously and there were few problems. In others, groupings were achieved by force. It is difficult to disentangle the effects of tactlessness, the abuse of power or sabotage, or to resolve the contradiction between ends and means and wonder, once again, whether it does not reflect the antagonism which divides the different factions in the highest leadership stratum.

One is especially inclined to think this since the villagisation movement had to be altered in the course of its implementation and some leaders were denounced. To quote the *Daily News* at some length,

There are reports from a number of places where these operations are currently underway which give rise to some concern. The reports almost invariably tell of people being moved with very little, if any, prior planning of the kind which had been envisaged by the Party Conference. They tell of people being moved almost 'en masse'[27] without due care and regard as to how they are going to be able to manage in their new areas. Some correspondence has come to us to the effect that in certain cases, people have been transplanted from villages into the bush where planned villages are to be established and left there to fend for themselves under conditions which even the most ardent would find difficult to cope with. There are even reports of property being destroyed as the hurriedly arranged movements are being conducted.

First let us reiterate that it is the party's policy to move people into the villages. Many millions have moved and where proper planning was carried out first, the results have been very encouraging. There are still many people who must and will be moved, for the advantages of living together as opposed to the isolation are very well known.

What we feel has gone wrong in some cases is that enthusiastic leaders have overplayed their hand. They have not undertaken the necessary precautions to make the moving smooth.

The result is that they have made many people suffer unnecessary inconvenience. They have used the name of the party or even of its leaders to hide their shortcomings in carrying out the party's directive. They have even caused a dislocation in food production, by failing to determine when moving would not interfere with farming and food production. Such leaders, whether in the party or government hierarchy, will no doubt be strongly cautioned for these mistakes.[28]

Praising those in charge of forced villagisation as 'enthusiastic' and impersonally denouncing their faults shows that one cannot easily question power-holders at any level in the hierarchy. Their faults nonetheless left wounds in certain sections of the population that were extremely easy to exploit politically.

Concurrently, in the towns, a series of industrial disputes brought to light identical problems. In a few private firms the workers, justifying their actions by article 15 of TANU's *Mwongozo* Guidelines,[29] embarked on a series of protests, varying in form from slowdowns to sit-ins, downing tools and locking out the management and foremen. The objectives of these actions concerned not only wages and working conditions, but also the relationship between management and workers. Workers and white-collar employees in two firms succeeded in obtaining the eviction of the bosses and the formation of co-operatives. In a third case, similar efforts failed because of intervention by the government, which, it seems, was frightened by the idea of the extension of the movement, a likely outcome had this third take-over been successful. While just a few days previously take-overs had been hailed as 'revolutionary and historic' (the *Daily News*, 9 June 1973), it was now said that the fact that workers at two other firms were allowed to take over their firms 'did not mean and shall not mean that TANU and the government have now permitted anew the workers to invade industries or that it should now be the method of nationalizing. (*Uhuru*, 21 June 1973.)'[30]

Problems of power

These two crises undoubtedly allow us to see a little more clearly the nature of the confrontations that have been taking place in Tanzania. What is at stake is power, especially since power can greatly influence the distribution of the meagre national wealth. But the political stature of President Nyerere, and the supremacy of the party, as written into the Constitution, are there to prevent the question of power from being posed in such a stark fashion. As it is impossible to question at the top, the political struggle therefore focuses on the use of power in particular cases. In this respect, 'villagisation' and the industrial disputes exemplify both the kinds of struggle in progress and the strategies through which they are managed. Both involve those sections of the population that play the most important role in the country's economic development, and occurred after minority attempts at 'destabilisation' had failed.

On 25 December 1971 one of the party's most prominent members, Wilbert Kleruu, the TANU regional secretary for Iringa (and therefore also a regional commissioner) was assassinated by a well-to-do peasant opposed to the politics of the Ujamaa villages. On 1 June 1972 some unidentified aircraft released anti-government leaflets over the towns of Dar es Salaam, Iringa, Arusha and Moshi. Twelve days later there were several explosions in the centre of Dar es Salaam, as well as an attempt to destroy Salender Bridge.[31] During the same period, anxiety was caused by frontier incidents between Tanzania and Uganda, and then Burundi, and a persistent undercurrent of military grumbling.

This picture – albeit incomplete – of five years of change should lead us to wonder why *no more than 6 per cent* of the votes were negative in the presidential elections. But too black a picture should not be painted: if problems rather than successes are presented here, it is because they undoubtedly show the contradictions in Tanzanian society more clearly.[32] A fairer perspective would include the remarkable performances in the popular mobilisation of the rural peasantry for purposes of improving adult education, improving health (*Mtu ni afya*: 'man is health') and increasing agricultural production despite the drought (*Kilimo cha kufa na kupona*: 'agriculture is a life or death matter').

Sections of the Tanzanian population found themselves disappointed with their living conditions; in their wish to participate in making the decisions affecting them; with the relative deterioration in the economic

situation; and with a politics that in practice contradicated the ends that it
had set for itself. At the same time, the increased emphasis on the regime's
socialist ambitions affected more harshly than before those who thought
that they could learn to live with a policy, whatever its rhetoric, of which
the first stage was to build a truly national economy from next to nothing.
Consequently, they sought to reassert themselves and put a brake on
socialist progress by trying to gain the support of a population whose latent
discontent could, to some extent, be exploited. The doubling of the
percentage of negative votes, and, less obviously, the large-scale turn-over
in parliamentary personnel, including an appreciable increase in the
number of educated representatives, can be interpreted in contradictory
ways: as a clue to a slight weakening in the popular support for the régime;
or as an indication of a largely shared anxiety about the future, leading a
fraction of the citizenry to adopt a wait-and-see attitude. These possibilities were what caused Tanzanian leaders to become so preoccupied with
the significance of the 6 per cent No votes. But the outcome can also be
seen as the failure of the adversaries of socialist politics to turn popular
disillusion to their advantage during the elections.

ELECTIONS AS A MULTI-DIMENSIONAL PHENOMENON

One might conclude that elections in Tanzania have a 'stabilising' or
'anaesthetising' effect.[33] It is true that the country's future will not be
decided by elections, but in the villages and farms. However, an analysis of
the elections has to go a little further than this: it should take into account
the regional grouping of the votes.

The regions giving the highest percentage of negative votes in the
presidential elections were also ones where the villagisation campaign was
carried out in an authoritarian and brutal fashion: West Lake, Mwanza,
Shinyanga and Tabora. Undoubtedly this factor is not a negligible one,
but it does not provide a complete explanation: in Mara or the Rufiji delta
(Coast region), the villagisation campaign was no better conducted,[34] but
the increase in No votes was only from 2·9 per cent (1970) to 5·5 per cent
(1975) in Mara and from 3·0 to 8·5 per cent in the Rufiji district. In
contrast, in the Dodoma region, where villagisation was begun very early
and posed no great probelms, the increase in the No votes was of similar
proportions: from 4·7 to 7·5 per cent.[35]

Mwanza, or intolerable authority

Delving more deeply into elections in the Mwanza region, which shares in
most of the problems already discussed, shows electoral attitudes more
complex than national-level analysis would lead one to suspect. Mwanza is
not poor, but its inhabitants resent an imbalance that works to their

detriment: whereas the region generates about 7·5 per cent of the Tanzanian gross national product, and its cotton production is responsible for about 10 per cent of the country's currency resources, the annual average income per inhabitant is lower than that for the country as a whole – 600, as against 900, Tanzanian shillings. The region also possesses some characteristics peculiar to itself. Electorally, it is among the most turbulent regions, rarely re-electing even its most prestigious outgoing MPs,[36] and always casting one of the highest proportions of No votes in presidential elections.

In the Mwanza region there is in fact a sort of endemic opposition to all forms of centralised authority. The 'traditional' social organisation of the Sukuma (who also people a large part of the Shinyanga region) knew no such authority. They organised themselves around some fifty small, autonomous kingdoms, whose chiefs had powers that were more magico-religious than political, in the European sense of the term. The chief's powers were strictly limited by councils, whose disapproval might lead him to renounce his position, and by youth organisations, which could unseat him by demonstrating publicly against him. His 'rule was in a sense only legitimate as long as it remained effective'.[37] This was particularly true with regard to rain, for the chief was also the rainmaker and the reality of his powers was expressed in the rain that fell. If no rain fell, or not enough, he was deemed to have failed in his task and to have lost his authority, and the consequence was usually the segmentation of the community. 'The Sukuma outlook seems to have been the independent, egalitarian one of dispersed homesteaders balanced with a theme of association in the performance of certain agricultural, ritual and entertainment activities. There was no tradition of penetration from the Chiefdom's centre into its periphery for the extraction of any significant amounts of tribute or labour or for the regulation of behaviour.'[38]

In these circumstances, it is hardly surprising that the Sukuma bore colonial rule only with difficulty. Broadly speaking, such rule had two consequences. It reinforced Sukuma hostility to all centralised power, especially when it claimed the right to levy taxes, to oblige peasants to treat their cattle, which were of high symbolic value, according to 'healthy' veterinary standards, or to cultivate their fields according to certain techniques. It also devalued the chiefs, since the Germans, as well as the English, made them part of the colonial administration by totally subverting their traditional role, making the position almost hereditary and ridding traditional groups of their means of control.

Therefore, in the post-1945 period, Sukumaland was one of the centres of nationalist agitation in Tanzania. The Tanganyika African Association (TAA), and then TANU, rapidly became very popular there – so much so that from 1954 to 1958, and beginning only a few months after its creation, TANU was outlawed there. Political action went on none the less, but more informally – through co-operatives (which were very powerful and

long-established), trade unions (run at that time by Rashidi Kawawa) and
a clandestine, embryonic party organisation. The result was a paradox: on
the eve of independence, Sukuma country was one of TANU's greatest
strongholds, although formally the party had never really been organised
there.

    Once the enthusiasm of the independence celebrations had passed and
TANU came to power, it, in its turn, became suspect.[39] The skirmishes
between the central authorities, or their representatives, and the region's
inhabitants multiplied. The peasants refused, as they had always done,
spontaneously to adopt modern agricultural methods, and only with
difficulty paid their taxes.[40] In 1967, so as better to control agricultural
production, especially of cotton for export, the government decided to
reorganise the state within the state that was the Victoria Federation of Co-
operative Unions; renaming it as the Nyanza Co-operative Union, that
government took the prerogative of appointing its managing director and
decided that its officials would have to obey the leadership code. There was
a gnashing of teeth. The following year saw one of the region's MPs in the
front line during the attack on the party that was launched by some
parliamentarians; he represented the Geita East constituency, which 'has
traditionally been a problem spot for both colonial and independent
governments'.[41] He was expelled from the party and, as a result, lost his
seat. In the by-elections that followed, the turn-out of registered voters
there was 15·5 per cent and the elected candidate was not the district
conference's first choice.

    In this atmosphere, 'to the people, Ujamaa villages came to appear as
another one in a succession of government agriculture programmes'.[42] At
best, some modernist farmers forced themselves to establish more or less
functioning organisation which, once they had been called Ujamaa
villages, hoped to get state subsidies. But for the common man there was no
wish to abandon, at the command of a central power seeking to reform a
whole way of life but incapable even of making it rain regularly, the
traditional system of dispersed dwellings.[43]

Electoral behaviour

There is no question of arguing that the Mwanza region's presidential vote
can be solely and entirely explained by the persistence of 'traditonal'
attitudes, or of claiming that, in all the regions where the percentage of
negative votes increased, this stemmed from behaviour dating back to
'ancestral times'. The Mwanza example illustrates that in Tanzania
elections are perceived at several levels. The circumstances under which
villagisation was conducted played some role in bringing about the
increase in No votes. The discontent that came to the surface added to, and
notably reinforced, feelings of prejudice against central authority, which
feelings had their roots in pre-colonial modes of socio-political organisation

and changes in life-style experienced during colonisation and persisting, in principle if not in form, in the independent state. The problems posed by the behaviour of members of the 'bureaucracy', for instance in the co-operative movement, or during the villagisation campaign, influenced by the factional struggles discussed earlier, acquired a very great importance and reinforced pre-existing attitudes.[44]

One finds in elections, therefore, the combination of a 'modern' manifestation of 'traditional' behaviours (hostility to the central power) mixed with reactions 'appropriate' to the stimuli giving rise to them (hostility to a policy of socialism and to the means by which it is implemented).

THE MANIFESTO AND ITS POLITICS

A scarcely electoral manifesto

The evidence points to a greater politicisation of the elections than in the past. The institutionalisation of the party's supremacy was the first guaranteed indication of this. The reform of parliament and TANU's adoption of an election manifesto are further indications.

To an unprecedented extent, Tanzanian elections have been characterised by intensive political mobilisation and education campaigns. In this respect, the text of the election manifesto itself is enlightening. No line in it glorifies the party or its leaders; it is above all a didactic document. Institutional mechanisms are explained first of all; then the party's objectives are set forth, at length and in detail; finally, the 'important qualities' that need to be possessed by leaders are reiterated. The manifesto was written as if it were addressed directly to the voters: 'The purpose of issuing this Manifesto is to make available to all the voters relevant information regarding the party's aims and objectives during the coming five years.'[45] It was intended as much for the candidates themselves. These had to prove to the district conferences that they knew it inside out; otherwise they would be dropped immediately. It was on the manifesto and it alone that candidates could draw in campaign meetings; it was on their skill in adapting the manifesto's contents to local needs that voters would judge them. The vice-president of the electoral commission was very explicit on this point: 'It will be ridiculous – and in fact it won't be possible – for a candidate to talk about his election symbol. Nor will there be a chance for a candidate to attack his opponent.'[46] As candidates no longer had the right to promise special favours for their district, their role in the elections can be seen to have been considerably reduced. The manifesto specifies without qualification, 'The fact of voting implies simply choosing capable men with the spirit and skill necessary to uphold unfailingly the policy adopted by TANU and the Afro-Shirazi Party.'[47]

Through this strategy, the contradiction, often noted in past electoral studies of Tanzania, between the national character of elections as institutions and agents of political integration, and the essentially local emphasis of most of the campaigns is, to say the least, limited. The themes of unity and nation-building are reinforced. One paragraph (the eighth) in the manifesto is nominally devoted to nation-building, with its economic and developmental connotations, and the theme recurs throughout the manifesto. It is the same when the MP's role is examined. The MP (*mbunge*) as such is mentioned specifically only in the manifesto's third paragraph and, in passing, in paragraph seven ('Socialism and Self-Reliance'). Everywhere else, it is the parliament in general (*Bunge*), and the·party in particular, that is referred to. What is more, the third paragraph makes clear that in future the MP is only one of a team of three in his constituency:

> *Collective leadership* [the exact meaning of the Swahili title being 'Importance of collective leadership']: apart from the collective functions of Parliament which are described in the foregoing paragraph, there are other functions which must be performed by Members of Parliament in their individual capacities. The party is currently putting great emphasis on the need for collective leadership. It is for that reason that the State constitution was recently amended so as to make the electoral constituencies to be the same geographical areas as the party districts. According to established procedures, political functions are normally carried out at a meeting properly convened by the Party or by government. In his own district, a Member of Parliament is just one of a team of District party leaders, the others being the District Chairman and the District Secretary, and he will be expected always to collaborate with his team-mates and carry out his duties by utilising the party organs which have been constitutionally provided.[48]

Popular legitimacy and the supremacy of the party

The MP now finds himself, therefore, restrained within very narrow limits: his role has come increasingly to be defined as that of an animator elected at the local level, and less and less as that of a legislator. This could lead to the weakening of the parliamentarian's function and, in consequence, of parliament itself. One must await the end of the 1975–80 legislature to judge the performances of the new-style parliament. However, authorised commentators and the President himself have on several occasions insisted that the constitutional reform should not be interpreted as the relegation of parliament to an accessory role in government. In his last speech before the National Assembly elected in 1970, President Nyerere recalled the defining characteristic of the parliament. Even in a system where the party is without dispute the country's guiding power, parliament remains the only institution which has the power to make laws. 'The purpose of the change in the Constitution is to make law conform to what we believe and practise. But the changes do not reduce the work of Parliament or the respect due to the President. All that they do is to remind us that by belief, by practice and now by the laws we follow, our country is led by our party.'[49]

If parliament retains the power to enact laws, it is TANU's National Executive Committee that has the legal power to work out the political decisions of which the law is ultimately no more than the official formulation. Parliament could scarcely fail to ratify what had been adopted by the party leadership.

There has been some decline in the legitimising function of elections. For historical reasons, the party is unequivocally both the source and the embodiment of all legitimacy. It led the struggle for national liberation that brought independence and has governed the country since. It has also won every election: those of 1958–9 and 1962, when it was not the only party, and those of 1965 and 1970 (under a new Constitution). Equally, it possesses a kind of revolutionary legitimacy, manifested by its writing its socialist objective into the preamble of the Constitution adopted in June 1975. Parliament, then, is no longer the source of the regime's popular legitimacy: it is one of the instruments of popular control exercised, through the intermediary of elected representatives, over the government and the state apparatus, in order to insure that neither deviates from the party line. But since TANU has still not clearly decided between being a party encompassing the whole population, and being an *avant-garde* party with only committed socialists as members, parliament[50] remains the only institution that represents all citizens. The party declares,

> The division of responsibility among the party organs at the national level under the new setup of the constitutional Supremacy of the party is that the National Executive Committee sets out the objectives, and Parliament, using the procedures mentioned above, supervises the implementation of those objectives. Furthermore, the Government itself, that is the Cabinet, is appointed by the President of the Republic from among the members of Parliament. It is therefore evident that Parliament is a very important institution having special and specific responsibilities within the political system. This is why the party is most anxious to ensure that those who will be elected to Parliament will be people who fully understand the party policy and are fully committed to it, as a consequence of which they will be in a better position to supervise the implementation of that policy by the government and various para-state institutions.[51]

Universal suffrage still confers a special prestige on parliament, which transmits a little of its legitimating power to the government chosen from among its members by a president who is himself also elected by universal suffrage. In both cases, however, the impression remains that, whatever the importance attributed to elections, it is the party that carries the greatest weight.

> Even if we get rid of the attitude of regarding the National Assembly as a body 'representing' people because of the good reason that in our situation the party is the voice of the people, there is still the need to emphasize the importance of the National Assembly. It is obvious that the National Assembly is an organ of the party, for according to the party Constitution, the Assembly is a special committee of the party conference.[52]

Apolitical elections?

The central power, the party, has reinforced its control of elections and the parliament that is their outcome. But to describe the evolution of Tanzanian institutions in this way is to ignore some questions. Even if there is really control, to accept that the central power is not a homogeneous body, but is itself riddled with contradictions and run by politicians whose aims are not always the same, makes it more difficult to say in whose advantage the control is exercised.

The dominant conception of elections, as elaborated particularly in the manifesto, is that they are a unifying force in the building of a nation and in the promotion of development, conceived as the achievement of a certain number of concrete goals. In Tanzanian conditions, it would be absurd to expect from leaders a Gramscian lecture on the nature of state power or the political implications of state appropriation of the means of production. But it is striking, none the less, that the manifesto is ultimately an apolitical document in the sense that socialism, as it is defined in it, derives more from a list of tasks to be achieved than from a vision of the future organisation of the country for which the people are now being mobilised. The document has an astonishingly timeless character; for example, in the paragraphs devoted to agriculture and to socialism and self-reliance, neither the Ujamaa villages nor the villagisation campaigns are mentioned, even though these were questions that had been at the centre of the political debate in the three years preceding the elections.

The manifesto's tone is radically different from that of the press or of the President's speeches during the previous period. For more than a year, Tanzanians had been able to read or hear violent criticisms of bureaucrats and corrupted officials. They witnessed spectacular personnel changes in the officers of the police force, army and some administrative services. Referring to the popular designation of parliamentary representatives as those in charge of overseeing the implementation of party policies, the manifesto contents itself with outlining a moral portrait of the ideal MP, without dwelling any further on the problems which had been encountered at the leadership level up to that point. As a result, the number of MPs of working class or peasant origin will go on decreasing.

The nature of Tanzanian elections does not seem to have changed much. They can still be

> understood as a compromise (implicit in all probability) between two opposing factors in the leadership stratum, a compromise which allows them on the one hand to speed up the reconstruction of a society in which political tensions between the authorities and citizens would be attenuated to the maximum extent so that power, however it be defined, could not be dangerously threatened, and, on the other, to transfer political conflicts to settings where the orientation of the economy was at issue, but also where, through directly confronting the citizenry with concrete political and economic realities of daily life, the choice of mode of development could be made effectively and with fewer ideological detours in speeches that the majority of the population is not prepared to listen to.[53]

THE DEFORMING MIRROR

If the 1975 elections saw greater control exercised by the central power, with all its contradictions, and if they led to the designation of an Assembly whose legal powers came to be specified within a restraining framework, they appear none the less to have assumed a political importance that they did not have before. That was the final paradox in these elections.

Some signs of this increased importance can be singled out. The manifesto stayed silent on the political problems that dominated life in the country; on the other hand, the severest attacks on corruption and the bureaucracy were made by the President during a pre-election tour in Shinyanga and Mwanza regions, the very territories where the negative vote was to increase to a relatively large extent.

Large number of educated Tanzanians who had hitherto felt no pressing need to seek election to parliament sought to obtain nomination by the party. This does not signify that it is necessary to put them *en masse* in the same category as that ill-defined group called the bureaucracy, but the educated constitute nevertheless the stratum of society from which the latter draws its recruits. Leaders, or aspiring leaders, therefore, were more clearly in the public eye than in the past, finding themselves almost physically confronted with popular choice.

Finally, elections remain the privileged medium for the expression of multi-faceted popular discontent, as well as being the occasion for a dazzling show of widespread popular adherence to the regime, an adherence for which the motivations are also very complex.

In so far as the struggle for power cannot show itself openly, elections are still only an upbeat in the *andante* movement of Tanzanian political life. But they are beginning, very slightly, to reflect, albeit with distortions and delays, the contradictions at work in Tanzanian society in the 1970s, without yet being able to influence directly the course that they take.

7 Syria Returns to Democracy: the May 1973 Legislative Elections

ELIZABETH PICARD

THE RECTIFICATION MOVEMENT AND ITS ELECTORAL PROBLEM

A longstanding electoral tradition

Syria knew a long period of democracy between the collapse of the Ottoman Empire in 1918 and the creation of the United Arab Republic (UAR) when Syria joined Egypt in 1958. But under the French mandate and after independence (1946) individuals and groups consolidated themselves in coteries around a single personality (the ζaim) rather than in political parties. This led to a personalisation and regionalisation of power. Relations with the electorate, based upon tribalism in the country and clientelism in the towns, were characterised by a notable absence of popular base and a paucity of ideological content in election programmes. The consequent weakness of political coalitions was translated into governmental instability (nine assemblies between 1920 and 1958, and forty-one cabinets, not counting minor ministerial reshuffles) and the avoidance of fundamental problems such as Syrian nationalism and the social upheaval accompanying economic development. However, the majority of Syrian elections until 1962 may be considered pluralistic, competitive and relatively free. The pronounced taste of its citizens for debate and public controversy – in short, for the parliamentary game – shows that Syria served its apprenticeship of Western-style democracy all the more willingly.[1] The country sailed between two reefs: on the one hand, there was a complacent anarchy of a traditional elite wishing to conserve a socio-political order favourable to itself; on the other, there were authoritarian attempts at transferring the political power from this traditional elite to young intellectuals, army officers, and the growing middle class.

Elections without Choice

Syria began its independent life with a splintered parliament. After only three years, the country became profoundly disappointed in the government's failure to overcome personal and regional conflicts. In 1949 was staged the first of Syria's numerous coups and the new leader abolished political parties. A counter-coup followed. Syria knew its first period of dictatorship (1949–54) under Colonel Shishakli. When the army had restored the government, cabinet succeeded cabinet under various coalitions of conservatives, progressively threatened by left-wing radicals. General elections, party competition and political paralysis marked the last democratic periods in Syria – 1954–8 and 1961–2 – before and after an unsuccessful attempt to unify the country with Egypt in the United Arab Republic.

A Ba'athist army officer, General Amin al-Hafiz, put an end to a series of confusing events by seizing power in the name of the Ba'ath Arab Socialist Party (BASP). Frequent changes of government and widespread violence reflected the contest between the moderate and extremist wings of the Ba'ath party in power from 1963 to 1970.

General Hafez al-Assad initiated a policy of rectification (*tashihiyya*), in contrast to the hard line posture of his Neo-Ba'athist predecessors.

A return to democracy

General Assad's regime dates from November 1970, following the Ba'ath Party's Tenth Extraordinary Regional Congress. Placed in a minority position by the Neo-Ba'athist power-holders, the General removed the Regional Command from office and, with the support of a broad section of the army, of which he was the tutelary minister, set up a provisional Command. This was a 'white' *coup d'état* directed against the revolutionary BASP, made unpopular by its excesses and failures.[2] Founded in 1940, and increasingly strong after 1954, the BASP had seized power in 1963. Setting forth a pan-Arab, Marxist-influenced secular ideological rationale based on the motto 'unity, freedom, socialism', it had progressively infiltrated the armed forces, radicalised the regime, intensified socialist measures and driven the country into isolation within the Arab world.

General Assad intended to give back to his country the military and diplomatic strength to lead the struggle against Israel, by serious preparation for the October 1973 war, an increase in the USSR's logistic support, and co-ordination with its Egyptian ally. Domestically, he set himself to return politics to the routine, stimulating economic activity through a series of measures intended to rally opponents of the Neo-Ba'athists, particularly the bourgeoisie of the former regime. But on his accession to power General Assad had practically no popular support and still less the sympathy of intellectuals and students. He had friends in various circles, but these had little influence.

In the months that followed, rationalisation, the relaxation of rules restricting entry into the political arena, and international events brought the out-of-office Ba'athists the support of various political groups, particularly that of the Nasserists and the Communists. This limited return to multi-party politics went hand in hand with a process of re-establishing constitutional norms that had been abandoned by the Neo-Ba'athists in 1966. Starting on 16 February 1971, a People's Council of 173 members appointed by General Assad settled down to the task of formulating a permanent constitution. The General, who was then President of the Council, had renounced any precipitous rushing into elections, fearing that he might not be able to exercise effective control over voting and that liberalisation might degenerate into a sterile clash of political forces. With the support of the appointed Chamber he hoped to embark on a gradual return to constitutional democracy through electoral consultations, a necessary part of his plan for political stability and economic development.

The socio-economic context in 1973

Syria in the 1970s is undergoing profound change. It definitely remains a predominantly rural country in which tribal and clan structures are still healthy, despite accelerated settlement of the Bedouin population (7 per cent of the 6,300,000 inhabitants in 1970) and the exodus of rural peasants (58 per cent) followed by proletarianisation and rapid growth of the main towns. Another of its characteristics is the existence of religious communities functioning as separate quasi-ethnic entities with distinctive cultural patterns. Beside the Sunni Arab majority (60 per cent of the population) the country contains numbers of non-Arabic Sunnis (Kurds 8 per cent, Turks 3 per cent), and various groups of non-Sunni Arabs: Alawis in the Latakia region (12 per cent of the population), Druzes around Swaida (3 per cent), and Christian minorities (9 per cent). Linguistic, regional, religious and cultural differences thus cross-cut society, each community being marked by strong internal loyalty and solidarity. The Syrian's first level of allegiance is local, familial or even personal, and plays an essential role in his social life. More abstractly, Syrian aspirations operate at the level of the Arab nation, within a framework set by Nasserist, anti-Zionist and, more often, Ba'athist pan-Arab ideologies. These evade the issue of the Syrian state's intermediate position between communal and Arab loyalties.

The Rectification Movement, striving to induce moderate behaviour, gave priority to nation-building, backed up by a rapid economic development favouring the middle classes and a technocratic elite. In the economy, Assad's regime reaped the fruits of the agrarian reform implemented by the UAR and built upon by the Ba'athists, and the grandiose infrastructural and industrial projects (such as the Tabqa dam) started with the aid of Soviet and Arab capital. These transformations included a profound social change characterised by a growth in education, increasing urbanisation, developments induced by light industry and greater consumption, and enlargement of the working-class proletariat. Traditional ideologies and structures offered only a weak resistance to the identity crisis that permeated Syrian society, as it did the societies of other Arab countries. This crisis was aggravated by the acuteness of the Arab – Israeli conflict, and the situation brought about the rise of radical ideologies, which at this time of change became especially attractive. The Rectification Movement became doubly threatened by the conservative Moslem Brethren, on the one hand, and the revolutionary Marxists backed by Palestinian extremists, on the other.

Electoral operations (1971 – 3)

Invoking 'the return of sovereignty to the people', General Assad set about a succession of electoral operations meant to shore up his new authority and endow his regime with a legality that it possessed only doubtfully at its origin. The speed with which he acted seems to indicate that he had conceived this 'popular democracy' plan prior to his seizure of power. On 12 March 1971 General Assad, nominated by the BASP Supreme Command, was the only candidate for the presidency of the republic. Official sources showed him elected by 99·2 per cent of the votes cast.[3] On 1 September 1971 his offer to federate Syria with Egypt, Libya and perhaps the Sudan was approved by 96·4 per cent of the voters. These levels of acceptance indicate that a plebiscite was created by the chief of state, rather than real unanimity of popular opinion. The Reconstruction Movement's third plebiscite was the constitutional referendum of 12 March 1973 after political forces had had the chance to accommodate themselves to the new power. The text of the new Constitution,[4] which had been adopted in February by the People's Council, gave rise to some heated controversies, particularly the references to Islam as the principal source of Syrian law and the chief of state's religion. In addition came the problem of Article Eight, which related to the Ba'ath party's leading role within the National Progressive Front (NPF), an alliance established on 7 March 1972 between the BASP and the four progressive authorised parties: the Union of the Arab Socialist (UAS), Nasserist in outlook; the Socialist Unionist Organisation (SUO), which had been a dissident Ba'ath party group since 1967; the Arab Socialist Movement (ASM), which drew its authority from the Hama leader exiled in Beirut, Akram Hawrani; and the Syrian Communist Party (SCP), which had split in 1970–1 over the merits of collaborating with General Assad's Ba'athists. These issues were the major causes of the demonstrations that inflamed the large cities in February and April 1973. Moslem brethren, numerous Ulama and General al-Jarrash's pro-Libyan socialists in Aleppo called for a boycott of the referendum. The Nasserists openly showed their disapproval of Article

Eight. Finally the Neo-Ba'athists, supporters of the former rulers, added their protest to those of other opponents.

Officially the vote was a complete success[5] and government commentaries stressed the huge vote in some regions containing large minorities, notably Alawis and Christians. Observers agree in concluding that in the three plebiscites voting was controlled, limiting the freedom accorded to the 'sovereign people' by the new Ba'athist regime.

In one case, it seems, President Assad tried to let elections proceed freely: the election of representatives to the Mohafaza councils (regional councils) in 1972. The division of the fourteen regions into small electoral constituencies favoured candidates whose support was regional and even local, because it scattered the votes, and the relative freedom of the vote brought about the defeat of the central power. After two days of balloting (the number of voters was very small on the first day, 3 March), the Minister of Local Administration announced a turn-out of 50 to 55 per cent of eligible voters. The BASP obtained a majority in the Tartous, Deir-ez-Zor and Djezireh regions, as well as in Latakia (the capital of the Djebel Alawi), but it received only 25 to 30 per cent of the total votes for 6897 candidates. In Damascus, for example, only eight of the ninety members of the regional council were Ba'athists, and in the conservative Sunni quarter of Midan the whole list of candidates presented by the Ulama and sheikhs was elected. The same thing happened at Bab, in the Aleppo region, where the opposition won a majority of the seats. It was worse still at Homs, where, in spite of the power of the Communist Party, which contested the elections in alliance with the Ba'ath Party, the full list presented by the Moslem Brethren was elected, with a majority of 11,000 votes.

THE ELECTIONS OF 25 MAY 1973

Eager to confirm the new People's Council's democratic appearance by respecting the freedom of the vote, the Syrian authorities paid particular attention to the offering of candidates and nominations.

The limits of pluralism

The candidature rules set out in the Election Law (Presidential Decree no. 26, 14 April 1973) are at first sight flexible. Candidates were to be at least twenty-five years old, know how to read and write, and present to the election surveillance committee, presided over in each electoral constituency by the regional prefect, a written candidature request containing a brief statement of their election platform. The examination of these requests by representatives of the Ministers of the Interior and Justice and, in case of difficulty, by the Minister of the Interior himself, gave rise to hardly any disputes. According to this minister, only ten requests were subjected to an in-depth examination and of these only one was rejected. But the restrictions preceding nomination meant that party competition was limited. The parties that had dominated political life since 1920 and again in the 1954 and 1961 elections remained proscribed. Their traditional leaders, having been exiled or imprisoned, were not able to offer themselves as candidates. The same applied to the Neo-Ba'athist leaders of the 1963–70 period, who stood trial after General Assad's victory.

Only four political parties authorised since 1966 (the SCP) or re-authorised in 1971 (the UAS, SUO and ASP) were allowed to campaign together with the Ba'ath party. The National Progressive Front, constituted on 7 March 1972, consolidated these four authorised parties and the Ba'ath around a covenant which was simultaneously a governing programme and a platform for the legislative elections. The Communists campaigned in two separate groups, which had split in 1970–1 over the merits of collaborating with General Assad's Ba'athists; Khalid Bakdash, their traditional leader, had opted for participation in power, while Daniel Nehme and Riad al-Turk's group opposed collaboration in the name of national communism, free from Moscow's control. As for the Union of the Arab Socialist Party (UAS), most of its militants had followed the party leader, Jamal al-Atasi, in his refusal of the BASP leadership inside the Front and his decision to boycott both the constitutional referendum and the legislative election. A minority kept the name of the UAS and stayed within the NPF.

The election law apportioned seats between two electoral bodies: 50 per cent for the peasants and wage-earners (list A) and 50 per cent for the rest of the population (list B). But the peasant candidates ('those who work the land, alone or in a collectivity, whose harvest is their primary source of income and who have not been touched by agrarian reform') necessarily came under the control of the pro-government agriculturists' union. Likewise, 'wage-earners in the employ of the state or the socialist or private sectors' were organised by the Ba'athist union. Hence, the incumbent power was certain to control 50 per cent of the representatives to be elected, whoever they might be.

An important modification of the Election Law, as compared with its predecessor of 19 September 1949, was that non-Moslem communities were no longer granted a number of seats proportional to the size of their population. The deconfessionalisation of representation conforms to the Ba'ath's secularising spirit and took place at the expense of minority groups which were not able to win in the election as many seats as they had been granted traditionally.

The manipulation of candidacies

The number of candidacies was high at the beginning of the campaign (nearly ten per seat) but dropped as the campaign progressed, leaving only 699 (nearly three per seat) on the eve of the election.

Some individuals had sought to use the campaign for commercial or, more rarely, political publicity. They never seriously envisaged becoming members of the legislature. From the outset the different members of the Front tolerated numerous individual Ba'athist, Socialist, Communist and independent candidacies having identical political profiles but receiving the support of different power-holding groups. The distribution of nominations to a number of candidacies corresponding to the number of contested seats gave rise to bitter bargaining within the Front's central leadership, particularly between Ba'athist factions and between the two rivals groups forming the SCP.

In the days preceding the election, the BASP and its Front allies put strong and effective pressure on their militants to decide exactly who their candidates were. This pressure included promises concerning careers or benefits for the families of withdrawn candidates, appeals for discipline and even threats. The most resounding success in this campaign of intimidation occurred in the Latakia region, a Ba'athist fief of the Alawis. The Front's candidates alone remained after the withdrawal of dozens of independents.

Besides the candidates nominated by the Front, there were also hundreds of candidates campaigning as individuals or with the support of only a local interest group. As for the few dozen remaining opposition candidates, they were drawn from traditionalist Sunni circles, from business circles close to the proscribed conservative parties, or from extreme leftist groups opposed to the SCP's policy of collaboration.

There were fifteen constituencies, comprising the city of Damascus and fourteen regions. The number of seats per constituency was calculated as one for every 40,000 citizens. For example, electors in Damascus had to choose twenty-two deputies, eight representing the peasants and wage-earners, and fourteen representing the other categories. Those of Kuneitra elected four (two and two). The vote in one ballot was pluri-nominal, candidates being elected on a simple majority: the candidates with the best score won the seats of the constituency. Candidates joined in lists and coalitions. To campaign in areas as vast as the Djezireh, or in cities as populous as Damascus and Aleppo, candidates had to have at their disposal a huge electoral machine, financed well enough to overcome the prevailing system of local allegiances and support. The fact that they had such a machine at their disposal meant that the candidates of the Ba'ath party and its Front allies dominated isolated opponents with a narrow electoral base. This is why the 1973 Syrian legislative elections were effectively non-competitive, although voters were offered choices on the ballot paper.

The election campaign

On the whole the campaign was rather dull, for electoral statutes enacted
by the Minister of the Interior imposed a strict limit on political activity.
No candidate was allowed more than half a dozen meetings, and
attendance was reduced because the meetings had to take place in private
houses. The Ba'ath party and its affiliated trade unions and social groups
(women, peasants, cultural, and so on) mobilised their militants to
distribute literature, to canvass, and so on, on behalf of Front candidates
obliged to hold joint meetings. Without any notable exceptions, the debate
stayed at a superficial level, consisting of Ba'athist slogans on Arab unity,
socialism and economic development and appeals emphasising Islamic
unity or a 'Third Way', neither Marxist nor capitalist. More rarely,
discussion took a critical turn, when focusing upon regionalist arguments
or directed against the person of the chief of state.

Independent candidates, by virtue of their excessive number and
endorsement by well-known traditional notables, drew upon a variety of
propaganda techniques. These included posters on walls and cars, and
parades with streamers and music. Damascus in particular was besieged by
a kind of electoral fever, which contrasted with the calm throughout the
rest of the country. An indignant editorial in the newspaper *al-Ba'ath*
complained of poster anarchy, the abuse of the loudspeaker and the firing
of blank bullets. Some candidates, especially a rich merchant from the
Souk Hamidie, used methods that characterised the former regimes,
distributing presents to potential voters.

Another source of agitation was the dispute going on between the
different factions of the Ba'ath party, and inside the SCP. The rival
supporters of the Minister of National Defence and the President's brother,
each of whom represented a faction within the BASP, actually came to
blows, after the Minister of Defence tried to disturb one of his rival's
evening meetings in Damascus.

The exercise of the vote

The Syrian authorities made a real effort to ensure access to the polls for the
3,350,000 potential electors. The electoral lists had been revised in
February and were open to the public for two days at the end of April, for
correction or challenge.

With the exception of soldiers and representatives of the regime, Syrians
at least eighteen years old whose names were on the electoral register were
able to vote in their district of residence. During the campaign, official
communications emphasised the chance given to citizens to participate in
national choices.

Before proceeding to vote, each elector had to present his national
identity card, which, however, was not stamped to indicate that the holder

had voted. A directive dated 7 May from the Ministry of the Interior enjoined regional commissioners to speed up the procedures for granting identity cards. A second directive (on 23 May) reminded polling-station officials – of whom each station was to have at least three, chosen from the region's civil servants and the Ministry of Justice – of their obligation to use private booths for voting. These elections, in which the citizen suffered hardly any coercion, may therefore be called 'free'.

In spite of this, the exercise of voting rights presented some difficulty to the average citizen, because of the complexity of the system. Party lists, more than a dozen in many constituencies, were given to the voter. Some contained the names of as many candidates as seats, but most contained fewer candidates than seats, since some lines were left blank for the voter to write in the name of his choice. All combinations of vote-splitting between Front and independent candidates were possible. Moreover, the lists carried names that were confusing to the voter because of their similarity. In addition to the Front list in Damascus, there was also a National list, a list of National Unity, an Independents' list, a Third Way list, and so on. Often an independent candidate slipped his name in with those of the Front, to ensure the success. The Ba'ath party itself, in order to confirm its primacy in the ranks of the victors, offered the electorate a list made up of Ba'ath party candidates only, thereby breaking with Front policy. Supporters of the most well organised candidates waited at the doors of the polling stations, offering to fill in a list when the choices were confusing to voters.

The leadership of the different parties and candidates, and particularly of the BASP, adopted a wait-and-see strategy on the first day of the elections, because voting had to go on to a second day if less than 51 per cent of the electorate had participated on 25 May. Except in Hasakeh and Idlib constituencies, none was close to having received 51 per cent of the votes. The second day of voting brought bitter bargaining. Each local notable enjoined his supporters to cast their ballot for his allies in other localities, in exchange for similar support there. Alliances were formed without regard for established lists and ideological considerations.

One of the election's great problems was abstention. Groups urging a boycott included Atasi's UAS and conservative Sunnis. This policy, however, left the field open to Front candidates, who were elected with record majorities in constituencies deliberately not contested by the opposition: in Homs, for example, official candidates each won 130,000 to 140,000 votes. In Damascus, where there was greater competition, the successful candidates received from 19,500 to 46,000 votes; the losing candidates got up to 15,000. However, the 1973 Damascus electorate was estimated at about 440,000 people and turn-out was around 20 per cent of the eligible electorate. Constituency size discouraged the majority of citizens from voting, and this left non-Front candidates with hardly any chance.

The count took place on the afternoon of 26 May with municipal representatives and civil servants from the Ministry of Justice always present. The success of four conservative Sunni opponents in Aleppo was the object of a dispute, and voting was started again in three polling stations. The result turned out the same.

The results

The counting of votes from each polling station was centralised at the Ministry of the Interior. The Minister himself proclaimed the results by radio on the afternoon of 26 May. He read the list of candidates elected in each constituency in order of votes, excluding all other information concerning the votes obtained by the different candidates, or diverse parties, or turn-out. That explains the limited analysis possible in this chapter.

As Tables VII.1 and VII.2 show, General Assad achieved his goal of an elected assembly made up of a majority of his followers. The opposition appeared extremely weak and unable to attract independents. Such results were not accidental, as three examples will show.

The Latakia region consists of about 260,000 voters, more than half living on the Mediterranean coast, particularly in urban areas in the process of profound economic transformation. The highland hinterland is the fiefdom of the Alawis, a dissident Islamic minority that furnishes Syria with an exceptionally large proportion of its military officers and Ba'ath party leaders. The BASP, especially well rooted in the mountains and the region's port and industrial areas, had hardly any difficulty in effectively mobilising its militants and pressing opposition candidates from the commercial *bourgeoisie* and liberal professions to withdraw for the BASP's own profit. The result was that the thirteen BASP candidates had no challengers and were elected with more than 100,000 votes each.

It was just the same in the Swaida constituency. There the Front candidates won without difficulty, but the victorious list included the names of Druze notables and clan chiefs who certainly owed their election more to traditional allegiances than to activities inside the Ba'ath party. The BASP wove itself into local structures, especially strong because the region has not been touched by any profound agricultural reform. From the start of the elections, local notables or their representatives had been assured of their success, because they were backed by the party machine.

The third case concerns an instance in which the electorate did in fact make a real choice. In Aleppo four deputies from an opposition list were elected, the only successful candidates not appointed by the Front. These opponents, led by a doctor and a sheikh, were the first named on a conservative list that met with great sympathy among Sunni, anti-Damascene and anti-Ba'athist groups in Aleppo. They came first, third and fifth respectively on the B list; the fourth, by contrast, was the last man

TABLE VII. 1
Distribution of Seats by Party, Syrian People's Council

Party	Number of seats
Ba'ath Arab Socialist Party	104
Syrian Communist Party	6*
Union of the Arab Socialist Party	6
Socialist Unionist Organisation	4
Arab Socialist Movement	4
	124 (56%)
Independents	58
Opposition	4
	62 (44%)

* Three for the Bekdash group and three for the al-Turk one.

TABLE VII. 2
Distribution of Seats by Profession, Syrian People's Council

Profession	Number of seats
Peasants	52
Wage-earners	43
	95 (51%)
Engineers	6
Judges and lawyers	35
Doctors and pharmacists	9
Teachers	26
Others	15
	91 (49%)

to be elected on the peasants' and wage-earners' list. As everywhere in the country, turn-out was very low in Aleppo. Observers generally report it as being somewhere around 15 per cent, The opposition victory was not obtained at the expense of Front candidates but in a competition among independents. The leadership had let this competition run freely, sure as it was of the comfortable majority of its own supporters.

FUNCTIONS OF THE ELECTION

Three years after the legislative elections took place, few traces of them remain in Syrian memories and they rouse hardly any passions. May 1973 evokes, instead, the memory of the severe Palestinian – Lebanese conflicts

and Syrian efforts at mediation, and Syrian journalists, politicians and
citizens are astonished that a researcher should show interest in the
electoral side of their country's political life. They emphasise the
subordinate character of the People's Council, and of the process of its
election.

However, if the leaders of the Rectification Movement chose to run a
risk – to be sure, a calculated one – offering an election to the Syrian
population, it was not only to conform to an established tradition but also
because they considered the election to be a means of consolidating their
power. It is important, therefore, to compare the functions that they had
assigned to it with the effect achieved in the short and long run.

Legitimation

The primary function that General Assad wished to see filled by the May
1973 legislative elections was that of legitimating the regime. He felt the
need for this all the more keenly since he had come to power, on 16
November 1970, by forcibly suspending the Ba'ath Regional Command
and naming a provisional Command, which in return elevated him to the
presidency of the republic. As for the People's Council that sat from
February 1971 to February 1973, it was designed by him and officials were
appointed by the leaders, not elected. The illegality of President Assad's
seizure of power was particularly resented in the regime's early days, when
he had hardly any popular support, and when militant student and
intellectual groups were uncertain of and even unfavourable to him.

Thus the legitimation of the Rectification Movement seemed necessary
both because of the population's non-attachment to Ba'athism and
because of the persistence of the democratic tradition in the country for
more than fifty years. The principal reason for disaffection was that, from
the time of its accession to power in 1963, the Ba'ath regime had weakened
itself through its increasing recourse to autarky and authoritarianism, and
to dependence on the military and police forces, abandoning parliamentarianism. Since 1919 a genuine parliamentary system had functioned in
Syria. Until the period of union with Egypt (1958–61) and even beyond,
Syrians retained by right the institutions of public debate and governmental responsibility. On the whole, they accepted badly the dictatorial
character of Ba'athist rule after 1963.[6] By professing his desire to redeem
this tradition and install a 'popular democracy' (*sic*), General Assad was
responding to a genuine popular aspiration and he anticipated that in
return he would receive support and legitimation for his undertaking.

However, in the short term this function has not been fully realised.
Perhaps the manipulations regarding candidates and the proscription of
undesirable challengers were inevitable after the failure in the regional
councils elections of 1972, but the result was a very high level of abstention,
reflecting weariness on the part of citizens indifferent to an insignificant

event and disillusioned because its outcome was determined in advance. Such parties as Atasi's UAS, unable to obtain representation in proportion to their popular support, showed their discontent by recommending abstention in many constituencies.

In the medium term, the elections may have been a positive asset for the ruling power. After these manipulated elections, there was a People's Council representing the whole of the nation. The government receives unquestioning support from the Council – first, because the Constitution leaves it hardly any latitude to contradict the executive, and, second, because the majority of its members were chosen for their sympathy with the regime and acceptance of the Rectification Movement's plans as their own. The Syrian leaders' room for political manoeuvre was enlarged by the election of such an assembly.

In any case, the 1973 election effectively delegitimated opponents, keeping from the People's Council politicians to the left or right of General Assad's Ba'athists. The General's re-authorisation of political parties in 1971 had been discriminatory. It recognised groups considered progressive, and ignored parties from the former regime who were representative of the commercial bourgeoisie and large landowners (for example, the National Party, the People's Party and the Parti Populaire Syrien). On the other hand, this authorisation did not include political groups close to the SCP or small militant leftist groups. The candidates of the traditional and Marxist political groups, as well as the Neo-Ba'ath supporters removed from power in November 1970, did not have at their disposal a party machine allowing them to confront the governing power's candidates. Their only hope was nomination by the Front after signing individual agreements with the regime's leaders. This was done by all the elected independent candidates (save the four from Aleppo) and even by the three dissident communists from the Riad al-Turk group. These victorious candidates paid for their electoral success with unquestioning allegiance to the Front's management. As for the proscribed political groups, their position outside the parliamentary system encouraged extremism. The democratisation undertaken through elections was simply a broadening of the dominant bureaucratic and military group's power base.

On the international plane, it was clearly in the interest of the Rectification Movement team to hold the May 1973 election, since this helped efface the ten-year-old negative image of the Ba'ath Party as characterised by instability and authoritarianism. International observers, conferring a diploma for democracy on President Assad's regime and welcoming this return to the Syria of old, were willingly taken in.

The 1970 Ba'athists were more especially concerned with renewal of their ties with the Arab states from which their intransigence had estranged them when the conflict with Israel escalated. The Charter of the Federation of Arab States provided for twenty elected MPs from each of the three members – Syria, Egypt and Libya – to participate in a federal assembly in Cairo. At that time Syria was the only one not to have an elected parliament; but following the May 1973 election it was at last able to participate in federal activities on an equal footing with the other members.

Education

The themes developed in the Front's official campaign in the month preceding the elections were intended to 'educate' popular attention away from political realities and the issues at stake. Putting some responsibilities into the hands of deputies pre-selected by the ruling power and with only a limited political role was in itself a depoliticisation strategy. The regime's relentless invitations to the voter to participate were centred on a plan for economic growth based on the stabilisation of social structures, and equally on nationalist themes – that is, the struggle against external enemies. These appeals tended to mask ethnic and religious tensions on the one hand, and class inequalities on the other.

Education by anaesthetising issues was more effective in rural areas than in towns. For more than twenty years, the Syrian peasants had fought alongside the Ba'ath party and against the traditional elites for agrarian reform. Being reluctant to countenance new destabilising forces, they more readily accepted, therefore, the decisions of a ruling power placating them with development projects in their own interest. But inside the towns discontent and opposition remained – though underground, and analysable at present only in terms of disaffection with the regime, and, in particular, abstention. Education in elections could subsequently be turned against the conservative ruling power.

Communication

Communication between the governors and governed seems to have been particularly badly realised in the May 1973 elections. During the campaign the ruling power developed an ideology of participation and progress that was not only artificial, but also detached from the country's social and historical reality. The election slogan of 'development' crudely hid a programme that was almost exclusively of interest to the elites. Such deception, significantly accompanied by quarrels and sharply abusive polemics, undeniably aroused popular scepticism, and even scorn.

The election was rarely used by the grass-roots to convey criticisms or aspirations to governors. Genuine political debate was absent from the meetings organised by the unions and circles of Ba'athist obedience. These meetings hardly reflected either opinions or choices; at the very most they may have given to the leaders a snapshot of Syrian society in 1973, of its social networks, its inertia and its potentialities.

From the time of its election the People's Council was not a place for communication between governors and governed. It remained on the margin of political life. During the campaign, communication occurred through the traditional clientele networks, as is proved by the election deals between Damascus neighbourhood patrons, as well as by the support given by some Ba'athist leaders to independents whose ties were clear from their political past, or even by independents to Communist candidates. The parties knew very well how to use these traditional exchange networks. In the Druze region, for example, the BASP allied itself with the feudal clan structures spared by agrarian reform. Thus the party grafted a socialist and nationalist ideology onto traditional clientele relationships through the intermediary extent patrons. The state conducted itself like a grand patron. Through its unions, it kept voters in a dependency position and assured them of protection, thereby combining class consciousness and a sense of national integration.

The resolution of tensions

In Syria's current state of economic and political underdevelopment, elections are most significant as influences upon tensions between the different groups coming to power or seeking power.[7]

These groups first of all benefited from the political liberalisation and the sharing of responsibilities that the establishment of the NPF in March 1972 had initiated. The composition of the Front itself and the distribution of the seventeen seats on its Central Committee – nine to the BASP and eight to its four allies, the SCP, the UAS, the SUO and the ASM – give an idea of the power relationships within the alliance. The ascription of nominations to the various candidates in the legislative reflected the supremacy of the Ba'ath party, which won 104 seats to twenty for other members of the Front. Multi-partyism within limits was thus realised.

The Front's consecration by an electoral battle fought as a team was accompanied by the removal of political groups that refused to accept the comfortable but authoritarian protection of the Ba'ath party. By withdrawing from the Front a few days before the elections, Atasi's UAS in particular condemned itself to underground opposition of little effect in the short term.

The bitterest negotiations and rivalries occurred between factions in the BASP itself. As for the Communist Party divided into two rival groups, the fate of the six seats reserved was of no less importance. But even here the Ba'ath party solved the problem by giving three seats to each of the principal factions. It remains a moot point whether these confrontations between the various power groups reflected ideological divergences about economic and political liberalisation, or whether the arguments were only pretexts for a power struggle that grew bitter as economic projects expanded and personal interests came to be more mixed up with them each day. One would tend to adopt the latter interpretation. The same high-level officials who, as part of the Ba'ath Party's Regional Command, were involved in sponsoring candidates in the legislative elections acted as intermediaries in allocating important state contracts.

General Assad's plan was to enlarge his 'presidential majority', initially limited to the faction of the Ba'ath party that had supported him in his rebellion, to include other categories of the political elite, to whom he proposed to 'reform the system from within'. The composition of the February 1971 Constituent Assembly indicates groups which it was important for Assad to rally to his regime:[8] pre-existing oligarchies that had been outside political life during the seven years of Ba'athist rule between 1963 and 1970, and the middle strata that benefit from the country's economic evolution. The elected members of the 1973 People's Council had economic and tribal ties that associated them with the close-knit bureaucratic military group running the country and with the traditional class of upper bourgeois and 'feudal' leaders.

The outcome of the election was not exactly the 'liberalisation in favour of the country's various progressive forces' promised in the Front's Charter, nor was it the type of liberalisation anticipated by the Communists. Protesting against the dialogue with luminaries from the *ancien régime* and categorically refusing to allow them to enter government, the SCP formulated an illuminating critique of the strategy followed by the Rectification regime and of its decisions about economic liberalisation and overtures to the political right-wing. All these indications are valuable for understanding the evolution of Syria's foreign relations and the twists of its domestic policy after the elections.

The Syrians did not escape the democratic mythology that prevails throughout the world. The election was judged a success by the majority, since it made for the emergence of a popular assembly and also, many say, because it kept the country from extremist rule. But is this not precisely where the illusory character of these elections lies, in ignoring awkward problems and opposition so as to gain adhesion through fear and immobilism? Instead of working to integrate citizens into the leadership, promoting elite mobility, or translating the popular will, these elections were a failed encounter between Rectification Movement leaders and the aspirations of the nation.

8 The Impact and Meaning of 'Non-Competitive, Non-Free and Insignificant' Elections in Authoritarian Portugal, 1933–74[*]

PHILIPPE C. SCHMITTER

Any analysis of elections in authoritarian Portugal (1933–74) must appear either, at best, a harmless instance of scholastic trivia designed to show off the researcher's technical wizardry or, at worst, a dangerous example of insidious apologia intended to place that defunct regime in some more favourable light. It is hoped that the following essay is neither, but it does seem pertinent to raise *ab initio* such questions as: what could one possibly learn from a national voting experience of over forty years during which, through repression, manipulation, exclusion, distortion and outright fraud, a regime managed to win every single election for every single office contested? What conceivable meaning could elections have had in a situation where they were non-competitive, non-free and without consequences – to categorise them in the terms offered us in Chapter 1 by Guy Hermet? Why did that manifestly anti-liberal, anti-democratic regime bother to hold even a simulacre of elections at all? And why did the Portuguese citizenry bother to participate when no one had any doubt as to their issue?

Perhaps in answering such questions we shall gain some additional insight into the generic nature of this particular mode of political domination or regime type, and so be better able to understand the past and prevent a similar situation from occurring in the future. In addition, focusing on this apparently extreme case – with all its anachronisms and

* This research was made possible by a grant from the Social Science Research Council in 1971 and by subsequent support from the Social Science Divisional Research fund of the University of Chicago.

atavisms – may teach us something about the less visible and less *confessable* qualities of ostensibly competitive, free and significant elections held elsewhere, or, for that matter, in Portugal since its liberation from authoritarian rule in 1974.

THE OCCURRENCE OF ELECTIONS IN AUTHORITARIAN PORTUGAL

It seems that, since the establishment of the Estado Novo (New State) in 1933, no country in Europe has had as many national elections (excluding plebiscites and referenda) as Portugal. It had no less than seventeen, five more than Greece, six more than Ireland, eight more than France, and more than double the number in Italy. Of course, neutrality in the Second World War and the fact that presidential terms (seven years) and congressional terms (four years) did not coincide account for much of the exceptionally high frequency. Even more remarkable (if unnoticed) is the regularity with which these 'contests' occurred. Except when a president died in office (1951) and one term of the National Assembly was strategically cut short (1945), the Portuguese voters were called to the polls with a predictableness which rivals that of Switzerland or Sweden.[1]

This is not to say that they went with the same enthusiasm or assiduity. Table VIII.1, which covers only elections to the National Assembly, shows the historical pattern of enrolment and actual voting from 1934 to September 1973, only seven months before the revolution. The inscribed electorate, itself far smaller than the proportion of the population eligible to vote by age, sex and literacy qualification, grew rather gradually during the first decade of the regime (1934–45) reaching only 7 to 8 per cent of the total population. With this very small (and, we shall see, select) electorate, turn-out (actual voters as a percentage of enrolled voters) initially reached impressive proportions (83 to 86 per cent). After 1945 the absolute number of those enrolled and of those actually voting took a step-level increase and then again stagnated, barely keeping pace with the increase in population. Abstention increased. This level of electoral participation during the 1960s (11–15 per cent of the total population, 19–23 per cent of the age eligible population) placed Portugal eighty-eighth out of ninety-two countries in the world in terms of voter turn-out, followed only by Sierra Leone, South-West Africa, South Africa and Rhodesia.[2]

By no stretch of the imagination, therefore, could it be suggested that Salazar sought to use the electoral process as a mass-mobilisation device. Illiterates (31·3 per cent of the population in 1960) were barred from voting, as, until 1968, were women, unless they could prove that they were 'heads of families' and/or had paid a certain amount of real-estate taxes. But the key to the electoral base of both the Salazar and Caetano governments lay in the controlled *minutiae* of the voter-registration process. Basically there were two procedures: official enlistment, in which local

TABLE VIII. I
Electoral Support for Authoritarian Rule in Portugal:
Elections for the Legislative Assembly, 1934–73

	Actual votes	Inscribed electorate	Total population	Turn-out[a] (%)	Participation[b] (%)
1934	377,792	478,121	7,148,046	79·0	5·3
1938	649,028	777,033	7,505,554	83·5	8·6
1942	668,785	772,578	7,830,026	86·6	8·5
1945	569,257	992,723	8,045,774	57·3	7·1
1949	948,695	?	8,333,400	?	11·4
1953	991,261	1,351,192	8,621,102	73·4	11·5
1957	1,030,891	1,427,427	8,908,766	72·2	11·6
1961	1,112,577	1,440,148	8,932,000	77·3	12·0
1965	1,211,577	1,609,485	9,234,400	75·3	13·1
1969	1,115,248	1,784,314	9,582,600	62·5	11·6
1973	1,320,952	1,965,717	8,564,200[c]	67·2	15·4

Sources: Antonio Rangel Bandeira, *As Eleições em Portugal* (Toronto: Brazilian Studies, July 1975) p. 3; *Anuario Estatístico*, 1957, p. lvi; *O Século*, 11 Nov 1973; *Keesing's Weekly*, various numbers.

[a] Actual votes/inscribed electorate.
[b] Actual votes/total population.
[c] The 1965 and 1969 values for total population are interpolations. The 1970 census revealed an unanticipated net decline in population since the previous decennial census.

authorities compiled names and certified eligibility, and individual petitions for enrolment, which citizens could use if they 'discovered' that they had not been placed *ex officio* on the rolls. Apparently very few took advantage of the latter provision, because they did not know they were not enrolled, because the period provided by law to petition for enrolment was so short, or, most likely, because they were indifferent to disenfranchisement. From all accounts, the officially compiled lists were shamelessly manipulated. Clauses in the electoral code denied registration and voting rights to 'those not enjoying their civic and political rights', 'those who profess ideas contrary to the existence of Portugal as an independent state and to social discipline' and 'those who notoriously lack moral fitness'. There is little evidence that these formal exclusions were resorted to extensively.[3] Rather, local officials simply seemed to have 'cooked up' the list of voters best suited to fit their interests and those of the regime. In one case, we have some interesting evidence of the sort of electorate this tended to produce. Prior to the 1969 elections, Marcello Caetano, as part of his 'renovation in continuity' and as the result of extending the vote to women without restrictions for the first time, ordered a thorough overhaul of voter registration records and for the first time opposition candidates were given an opportunity to see and copy the rolls for the districts in which they were competing. Previously this was a privilege available to only the official party, the União Nacional. One enterprising CDE candidate in the district of Castello Branco used this newly acquired data in a speech. If his record was correct (see Table VIII.2), the four urban *frequesias* of Covilhã, a minor textiles town of about 23,000 inhabitants, had only 2671 inscribed voters (11·6 per cent – about the national average at the time). More

TABLE VIII. 2

Breakdown of the Electoral Polls of the City of Covilhã, c. 1969, by Profession

1. *Public employees*
   A. Civil servants, corporatist functionaries   962
   B. Armed forces, Civilian Police Force and
   National Republican Guard   357
   C. Retired civil servants   16
         1335 (50·0%)

2. *Property-owners*
   A. Industrialists   142
   B. Merchants   119
   C. Rural landowners   79
         340 (12·7%)

3. *Middle class*
   A. Priests and nuns   72
   B. Professionals   23
   C. Commercial agents   22
   D. Students   10
         127 (4·8%)

4. *Workers*
   A. Urban proletarians   144
   B. Rural workers   11
   C. Various services and without professions   4
         159 (5·9%)

5. *Housewives*   347 (13·0%)

    Total enrolled   2671 (100%)
    Total population (1970 census)   23091

Source: António Alçada Baptista. *Documentos Políticos* (Lisbon: Moraes Editores, 1970) pp. 70–1.

revealing was the fact that 1335 of those voters were employees of the state! Living in Chicago, I am not unaccustomed to paid public officials playing an important electoral role; however, the fact that one-half of those likely to vote were themselves employed by the power for which they were voting must constitute some sort of record for political incestuousness! Property-owners outnumbered workers by almost two to one. There were almost as many industrialists (142) as there were proletarians (144)!

The restricted and selective nature of the electorate constituted the stable ecological base upon which the authoritarian rulers of Portugal could rely with such frequency, regularity and predictability. However, given this controlled and unrepresentative context, what conceivably could have been the function of exercising it so often to produce such ritualistic and routinised results?

THE FUNCTIONS AND MOTIVES OF ELECTIONS IN AUTHORITARIAN PORTUGAL

Portuguese elections seem to fit securely in the most negative of Hermet's taxonomic profiles. Opposition candidates were a rare occurrence (1945, 1949, 1958 in presidential contests; 1953, 1969 for congressional elections) and never an effective threat. The registration of voters, the selection of candidates and the conduct of campaigns were subject to considerable (but variable) regime control. The consequence of the whole process was minimal, considering the prior control over candidacies, the 'domesticity' and organisational weakness of the government (but not governing) party, and the extensive powers of the executive. And yet the very existence of elections could and did create problems and costs to the regime. While they can hardly be credited with contributing much directly to the overturn of authoritarian rule in April 1974,[4] they were a factor in blocking Caetano's attempt at 'renovation in continuity', and they did lay some of the bases for the explosion in popular participation which immediately succeeded his demise.

Let us begin with Hermet's sensible proposition that 'the fact of organising elections in a certain form and at a certain time never constitutes a gratuitous act'. In short, elections, even those with foregone conclusions, involve costs as well as benefits. If they are held, they must have some reason or motive; they must contribute in some way to sustaining (or undermining) the mode of political domination. They must have some functions – positive or negative, manifest or latent, intended or unintended – or they would not exist.

This functionalist perspective would be valid only if elections were not merely a ritualistic habit inherited from the past and, hence, produced no effect upon either civil society or the state. In the specific case of Portugal it would be difficult to argue that the Estado Novo's decision to incorporate them into the new constitution was an act of instinctive 'electoral conscience' or civic fetishism. The previous electoral experience of the country was hardly exemplary.[5] Novelists such as Eça de Queiroz delighted in satirising the scandalous conduct associated with them. Under the monarchy from 1834 to 1910, there were forty-three general elections, and the ensuing republic produced no fewer than nine during the sixteen years of its existence. The general pattern was one of governmental rigging, *caciquismo* and widespread public apathy. The party in power almost invariably won; electoral laws and registration procedures were frequently changed for partisan advantage; violence and intimidation were commonplace; recourse to *coup d'état* and insurrection were a constant temptation for losers.

Salazar himself once ran for election during the republican period (1921). He was elected a deputy, but returned home in disgust after attending only a few sessions of parliament. He since repeated on numerous occasions his hostility to partisan struggle and electoral competition, and longed for an integrally corporatist order in which the representation of individual citizen interests would be replaced by the representation of organic family and social ties. In the mid-1920s, he confidently predicted that 'we are drawing near to that moment in political and social evolution in which a political party based on the individual, the citizen or the elector will no longer have sufficient reason for its existence'.[6] Yet, when he drafted 'his' Constitution in 1933, he placed in it both elections and territorial representation (albeit granting a very subordinate role to parliament) and relegated his ideologically preferred 'Corporative Chamber' to a purely advisory, honorific status.[7]

One possible motive-*cum*-function for tolerating elections was purely external to the regime – to legitimate it in the eyes of foreigners (*para inglês ver*, as the Portuguese would say). Given the mood of the time (the mid-1930s) and Salazar's repeatedly expressed dislike and disregard for liberal democratic regimes,[8] this is not a very plausible answer – at least not for the initial period. Later, especially after the defeat of Fascism and National Socialism, this function would become more salient. Under tremendous pressures in 1945, Salazar once went so far as to promise the Portuguese people (and the outside world), 'Free elections, as free as in England', but that, needless to say, never materialised.

Nor does internal legitimation seem quite as salient in the case of Portugal as in other, more 'plebiscitary' authoritarian regimes. One can find citations of both Salazar and Caetano invoking electoral legitimation. Foz example, after the 1958 presidential elections, the 'closest' ever held, Salazar could claim,

> In the next-to-last presidential elections [1958] it was verified that the opposition candidate received a little less than one-quarter of the votes. Thus we know how many Portuguese prefer other methods of governing, more conspicuous and unforeseen, over the present. . . . The same

comparison of numbers unequivocally demonstrates the legitimacy of a mandate that comes from more than three-quarters of the electorate and from the massive adherence of those consciences – in fact, the largest number – that did not have the means to express themselves at the polls.[9]

The last phrase gives it all way. By recognising the massive abstention that was prevalent and claiming it as evidence of support, Salazar revealed the weakness of his particular electoral strategy as a legitimating device. Had it been a serious 'functional' preoccupation (as it perhaps was to Caetano in 1969 and 1973), the regime would have had to alter the form, the volume and even the content of the civic act. By the time his successor made a timid effort to do so, it was too late. The entire farce had simply become too politically discredited and too closely linked to the class structure through heavily stratified participation.

A national sample survey taken shortly before the 1973 elections reveals this quite clearly (see Table VIII.3). If the function of elections generally is to legitimate power by accentuating the 'false universality' of those who govern, by socialising citizens to believe in their access to power, by

TABLE VIII. 3
National Survey Responses to Questions Concerning Elections, 1973

1. Percentage of those interviewed who say they follow electoral campaigns with

	much attention	little attention	no attention
Social status			
Upper and upper middle	57·6	33·7	8·7
Middle	35·1	47·8	17·1
Lower Middle	19·1	49·0	31·9
Lower	19·7	34·0	46·3

2. Percentage who could name a *deputado*:

	could	could not
Social status		
Upper and upper middle	45·5	54·5
Middle	25·3	74·7
Lower middle	10·1	89·9
Lower	3·6	96·4

3. Percentage who said they voted in the 1969 Legislative Assembly elections:

	voted	did not vote	no answer
Social status			
Upper and upper middle	33·1	62·8	4·1
Middle	27·0	71·3	1·7
Lower middle	14·5	84·1	1·4
Lower	9·1	85·2	5·7

Source: *Os Portugueses e a Política – 1973* (Lisbon: Moraes Editores, 1973).

mobilising voters to participate in political actions which rise above class, sectoral and regional cleavages, and/or by calling on individuals to take part in a collective *fête national*, there is no evidence that elections in authoritarian Portugal promoted any of these ends. Relative to a declining scale of social status, interest, information and participation all fell off dramatically and monotonically, until in the popular mass of the population they became virtually non-existent. When the entire sample was asked what national traits they most admired, 0·9 per cent gave 'the political system' as their first answer, no one mentioned 'deputies' and only 7·4 per cent said 'government and authorities'. Internal legitimation may have been a motive of growing importance for the maintenance of authoritarian rule in Portugal, but elections were decreasingly effective in performing that function. By 1973 they had probably become counter-productive. Each successive election under the old rules and actors was further delegitimising the existing mode of domination.

Guy Hermet suggests that there exists an 'anaesthetic' function of non-competitive elections – that, by granting to the populace occasions upon which it can cleanse itself publicly, even raucously, of accumulated resentments, the installed rulers can then expect greater acquiescence in the interim. Repeated doses, according to Hermet, serve to socialise the citizenry both to the futility of the existing opposition and to the legitimacy of the situation. Leaving aside for the moment the fact that the treatment sounds more closely analogous to an enema than to an anaesthesia, one could find traces of this function in the Portuguese body politic as a by-product of its seventeen elections.

Nevertheless, such a comforting functionalist diagnosis would be misleading. First, it is doubtful that this was an initial intended consequence or motive. Salazar does not seem to have envisaged that his 'form' of electoral scrutiny would eventually result in the formation of a party-like opposition. Rather, the Uniaỗ Nacional (UN) was established shortly before the first elections as a catch-all (or, better, catch-some) party from the numerous right-wing political formations that were squabbling for their share (and more) of the inheritance from the 1926 coup: monarchists, *integralistas*, clericalists, *sidonistas*, conservative republicans, nationalists and so forth. Its status and statutes as a civic organisation, rather than as a party or movement, implied that whatever competition or opposition was tolerated under the Estado Novo would be channelled into and occur within its ranks. This would have given Salazar, as its leader, the capability to manipulate all dissension from above without any need for the messy, unpredictable and potentially corruptible process, which he so strongly abhorred, of recourse to the public political market-place. The UN would simply have had to present every four years a unique list of candidates to the electorate for ritualistic approval.

To an extent this did indeed occur until 1945. The end of World War II, however, invalidated such a co-optive grand design, and after that the regime had to contend regularly with an extra-UN electoral opposition. While denied by law the right to structure itself as a permanent political party, 'formations' offering alternative candidates and programmes appeared shortly before elections and took as much advantage as possible of the relative relaxation of repression and censorship which was 'guaranteed' during the prescribed one-month campaign. Frequently the opposition withdrew from contention at the very last moment rather than face inevitable defeat. Occasionally it did not self-destruct and actually went before the electorate to compete for a share of votes. During this period (1945–65), elections may have served a newly acquired, if initially unintended, 'anaesthetic' function. Outbursts of enthusiastic opposition were interspersed with longer periods of despair and hopelessness. Even then, however, on at least one occasion (the assasination of General Humberto Delgado in early 1965) it was felt necessary to eliminate physically one of the attending physicians in order that the patient body politic might safely continue to be anaesthetised in the future.

After 1965 and especially after the accession to power of Marcello Caetano in 1968, the whole operation began to take on a different meaning, phenomenologically as well as functionally. Caetano needed elections for purposes of internal and external legitimacy in a way that Salazar had not.[10] So that they might perform that function, they had to be 'cleaned up' and the opposition had to be given somewhat more honest and fair treatment. The immediate effect was again anaesthetic, at least until the election was held. Mário Soares, leader of a Socialist faction (CEUD) in the 1969 elections refers to the 1968–9 period as 'a deceptive experience' and notes that, immediately after the elections had made it clear that the liberalisation was only cosmetic, 'a heavy silence again fell on Portuguese society'. 'Paradoxically, the electoral victory of Marcello Caetano diminished the possibilities for accelerating the political process in the sense that the new President of the Council found himself condemned to repeating the actions of Salazar, if not in form at least in substance.'[11] The repeated doses of anaesthesia, in other words, had not only begun to lose their potency, but had begun to have an effect upon the physician in charge. To the extent that Portugal teaches us anything about electoral anaesthesiology in authoritarian regimes, it is that partial applications are dangerous, that its effects in any case are of short duration, that it is difficult to administer unless coupled with major surgery on other parts, and, finally, that it may result in the loss of the physician rather than the patient.

Hermet's third macro-function for non-competitive elections is communication, by which he seems to mean their use as a device to transmit *mots d'ordre* to the population and/or to local elites. He also suggests that choosing – or, in the case of Portugal, ratifying choices already made for the voter – tends to open up a channel of knowledge and mutual relation between citizens and local notables which may subsequently be exploited for purposes of interest articulation or influence peddling. It is very difficult to find much evidence in Portugal to support this hypothesis. As we have seen, the electoral process barely touched the masses and was conducted in such a low key and ritualistic manner by the government party as to be incapable of passing any comprehensible *mots d'ordre*. As far as anyone can tell, most of the interest and influence linkages, downwards as well as upwards, passed through state and para-state (for example, corporatist) institutions, not through party or parliament.

What Hermet missed was the communicative process in the other direction. As one cynic put it,

> The periodic election of a President has merely provided the regime with an extremely good opportunity to bring its police records up to date. By means of allowing a rationed thirty days of freedom, during which censorship was relaxed, a number of otherwise quiet citizens would come into the open, either as members of Candidacy Committees, guest speakers or electoral campaign heads. . . . The Government's candidate having been duly renominated, conditions reverted to the usual pattern. For some time, under the cloak of silence provided by censorship, all those law-abiding citizens who had come forward in support of the opposition candidate were 'investigated' or became unknowing 'lighthouses' for the Police as they circulated amongst their friends.[12]

Admittedly, this sort of indirect functional appropriation of the electoral process for repressive purposes was not systematically exploited and probably produced little that the police files did not already contain. Nevertheless, it was a positive, latent and probably unintended factor contributing to regime persistence.

Very little is known about a second-type of upward information flow. Since voters could pick individual candidates on the UN list (whenever a list received the most votes, and the UN one always did, the entire list for that district was proclaimed the winner), the top *cadres* of the regime had a sort of internal popularity poll available to them which could have served to get rid of laggard, unpopular candidates and to promote more successful ones. This in turn might have affected factional strength where it counted the most – that is, in naming ministers and higher administrative personnel. Some of this might have occurred, since Cabinet shifts generally preceded or immediately succeeded elections, and the rate of turnover in individuals occupying Assembly seats was rather high; but it is not clear whether detailed scrutiny of the electoral returns (not available publicly, incidently) were used for this purpose.

Another possible communications function 'hidden' within non-competitive elections is the utilisation of information about specific changes in opposition strength to determine the nature and location of public policy outputs. Presumably the regime could either have chosen to reward those *frequesias, conselhos* or *districtos* which expressed increased dissatisfaction, in the hope of dampening further opposition, or it could have punished them for their obstreperous behaviour. Some research in this vein has been conducted on central-government allocations to states in Mexico,[13] but no comparable data or analyses yet exist for Portugal. To the extent, as we shall see, that regime-supportive voting is heavily concentrated in the classes and regions that least benefited from the recent development of the Portuguese economy, the presumption is in favour of a 'reward' rather than a 'punishment' model, although one could argue, counterfactually, that Portuguese development might have been even more unevenly distributed had the regime not intervened to protect and subsidise its supporters in the economic and geographic periphery of the society.

Reviewing our discussion so far of the functions of Portuguese non-competitive, non-free and insignificant elections, our conclusion might well be that, even added to each other, they are insufficient to explain why and with what effect, on seventeen different occasions from 1933 to 1974, Portuguese voters were called to the polls. So far, it simply does not seem that either the regime would have been willing to bear the costs, especially the indirect ones, or that the individual citizens would have bothered to go through the motions – even taking into consideration their selective number and massive abstention. Of course, to a degree, voting is an habitual, ritualistic civic act (although, as we have seen above, there are reasons to doubt this at least with respect to Portugal, prior to the establishment of the Estado Novo) and, as such, is not subject to the sort of cost – benefit ('What is in it for me?') or functionalist ('What good or harm will it do the system?') calculation that we have assumed so far. Elections exist because elections have existed; elections happen and nothing else will happen.

But this arational and afunctional answer is itself theoretically un-satisfactory, as well as empirically non-demonstrable. Elections in authoritarian Portugal had costs and an impact, as they were perceived to have. *Ergo*, they must have responded to the motives, interests or imperative needs of political actors, especially and perhaps exclusively dominant ones. But what were these, and how did they affect the electoral process?

The most compelling but still speculative answers come from the fourth and last set of functions sketched out by Hermet, although not always for the reasons nor by the means he advances. Non-competitive elections, he suggests, 'reflect and influence the distribution of power among the groups that control the government'. They are 'often motivated by the need to give public sanction to the rivalries of the different factions of the elite, by the wish to capture new elements whose support is sought by the rulers, or, in some circumstances, by the will of those who govern to weaken traditional forces'. Perceptive as this is, this functional observation remains too limited both in terms of the nature of actors potentially involved and the range of 'managerial' tasks possibly served. The experience of Portugal suggests that it should be replaced with the following hypothesis: *the principal function of non-competitive, non-free and insignificant elections*[14] *is contrapuntal: to articulate a dominant coalition between segments of a divided political elite and conflicting fractions of the superordinate economic class; and to disarticulate any potential rival coalition between elements of a dispersed political counterelite and components of subordinate economic classes.* In sum, such elections obey the dualistic but complementary formula of *une et impera* and *divide et impera*.

On the one hand, they serve to bring together and reward with minor patronage, minimal policy responsiveness and anointed status a heterogeneous set of supporters, dispersed geographically, divergent in interests, diverse in resources and divided in ideological affinities. While the corporatist complex of state-controlled interest associations (*grémios*) and functionally specific government agencies processed and placated many of the economic and class interests quite independently of partisan or electoral channels in Portugal,[15] this still left a considerable variety of specifically localistic and narrowly social interests unattended. The União Nacional and periodic electoral 'consultations' filled this vacuum in political space with minimal and barely sufficient effectiveness (and in the process prevented other types of political organisation from occupying the same space).

This loose, 'catch-some' aspect of the structure of the UN, later Acção Nacional Popular (ANP), was well described by someone who ought to know, having been its leader and having discovered its limitations when he tried to transform it as part of his abortive reformist strategy – Marcello Caetano:

The government was based on a civic organisation created in 1932 under the name União Nacional with the intention of bringing together around the programme of the Movement of 28 May 1926 [which overthrew the parliamentary republic], as reformed by Salazar, all Portuguese of whatever party or political colouration who agreed to join, without giving up their own ideological particularism, in order to collaborate in a common effort at national salvation.

By 1968 the União Nacional was, therefore, a simple organisation of *cadres* grouping local notables in each district or *conselho* for action during electoral periods. Since it was constantly stressed that it did not constitute a party, one was careful not to concede it any sort of political monopoly and, hence, it was not exclusively from its ranks that men were recruited to occupy governing positions, nor was it permitted that there should be any attempt to give it special influence in the activities of the public administration so that it could obtain favours for its members or their friends or collect prestige that could be used to acquire improvements or other local successes. In this way the União Nacional was weakened and, worse yet, divided, because by taking away tasks it was frequent that men leaving and men entering it become rivals.[16]

Behind this minimal organisational façade and through its perfunctory electoral activity, a number of 'managerial', alliance-consolidating tasks were accomplished. During the 1930s, it served to neutralise a group of fascistic ultras, the National Syndicalists,[17] as well as placate extreme clericalists and monarchists. It co-opted a substantial number of conservative and nationalist republicans who had been active under the previous parliamentary regime, in effect withdrawing them from potential opposition to Salazar's emergent authoritarian state. Later elections served as a pretext or cover for the periodic reshuffling of Cabinet and higher administrative officials engaged for other motives. Not only could impending or recently completed elections be used to justify such intra-elite changes, but, in addition, positions in the National Assembly (along with seats in the Corporative Chamber and on boards of directors of state-dominated firms) could be used to 'park' notables who had outlived their usefulness or become somehow embarrassing. Finally, elections and the compilation of party lists were a convenient device for recruiting new talent, rejuvenating a political elite which was becoming increasingly gerontocratic. As I have shown elsewhere,[18] there was a considerable turn-over in the ranks of the UN deputies to the National Assembly. The high point was reached in 1969, when Marcello Caetano concocted a UN slate in which ninety-six of the Assembly's 120 members were neophytes. Some of these were deliberately selected in an attempt to incorporate a new group of moderates or liberals into the ranks of the government party. Whatever its functional intent, the effort failed and several of the co-opted liberals subsequently resigned their positions.[19] Again, the generic mode of domination of which non-competitive elections are but a subordinate component intervened to distort and, in this case, dialectically to transform their effect.

Equally important and more effective, however, was the impact that holding such controlled elections had upon the actual and potential opposition. Without these public contests, they might have been forced to weld a clandestine unity in adversity; with them, they periodically rose to the surface of political life and, in so doing, provided a convenient target for the ridicule of those in power and an inconvenient mechanism whereby the latter could discover the diversity of their reactions to, and their programmes for opposing, authoritarian rule and the economic order.

Elections under the Portuguese formula, by allowing a one-month 'conditional probation' under which the usual censorship and repression of political formations denied all other visible existence were eased, tended to make the opposition look even more impotent, isolated and in the minority than they really were. The government reinforced that impression by emphasising the Manichaean aspects of the choice. On the one side was a *situação*: powerful, orderly guarantor of actual social peace; paternalistic provider of welfare and security; enlightened embodiment of wisdom and concern. On the other was an *oposição*: impotent, disorganised purveyor of potential social chaos; vague promiser of illusory equality and class violence; abstract representative of intellectual dogmatism and totalitarian intervention. Witness the following testimony by a frustrated opposition politician:

> We ourselves have to put aside the idea that, just as there are 'specialists' in government, there are 'specialists' in opposition. We have to put aside the idea that, before the animosity of Power, there are in every city of the country a half-dozen professionals with some civic courage who get together for four years at the same café table and then, at the moment of the elections . . . take the initiative to remind people that there are things like justice and freedom. . . . Those half-dozen people have created, in the view of some, their own statutes and have organised their life more or less safe from the reprisals of Power. . . .
>
> Despite what is established by law, the activity of the opposition is treated as if it were illegal. . . . *We are transgressors.* These thirty days, every four years, are conceded to us and we don't even know why. . . . We are treated as transgressors; and, naturally, we are regarded as transgressors. The populace regards us with surprise, admiration and the distance from which one usually regards the transgressor of an unjust law, with whom, out of fear of reprisals, one hasn't the courage to deal. But, in the last analysis, we *are* transgressors. If only because it is in the transgression of an unjust law that man effectively realises his freedom.[20]

Two factors, one sociological, the other ideological, tended to reinforce this impression of transgression, this effort at stigmatising the opposition as a group isolated from the 'real' civil society of Portugal. About the only segment of the population who could 'organise [their] life more or less safe from the reprisals of Power' were the liberal professionals – themselves a socially and economically privileged elite. While the government's list of candidates could show a relatively balanced representation of local notables, prominent bourgeois, eminent professors and 'ordinary folk', the opposition's ticket was much more 'skewed' socially. Of its 139 candidates in the 1969 parliamentary elections, fifty-three were lawyers, twelve writers, ten students, nine physicians, nine university and high-school professors and five journalists. The remaining 30 per cent consisted of a smattering of other liberal professionals, with only three workers and eight who could be considered 'owners of the means of production'.[21] The UN's victorious candidates were hardly a socially representative sample of the entire population and certainly no less privileged in the aggregate, but they were a great deal less concentrated in the service –

distributive – intermediate sector and, hence, less visibly 'parasitic' and removed from productive forces and social authority than was the opposition.

The opposition's high level of educational attainment and professional status also contributed to a marked tendency to articulate their campaign in rather abstract, ideological terms. Precisely because of the hopelessness of their position with respect to obtaining even a share of power, they were not compelled by the process of electoral stuggle to forge 'realistic' alliances, aggregated around compromises over prospective policies. That element of 'competition for the middle ground' which plays such a central role in all game-theoretic models of the democratic electoral process was conspicuously absent. As Alçada Baptista, our repeatedly exploited 'witness' to the dilemma of opposition in authoritarian Portugal, put it, proudly but a bit apologetically,

> This 'conditionalism' and hopeless state of mind has meant . . . that the expression of our thought was not submitted to any type of strategic consideration, even if legitimate, that the probability of victory would have obliged us to take into account. In all the documents, in all the statements that I have made, I am conscious of not having made any kind of concession, of not having used any form of subtlety [*astucia*], and I sought to have them contain that which, within the 'conditionalism' of the campaign of October 1969, I could best know and say.[22]

In addition to not being a formula for winning or even for augmenting one's ranks to include others, the purist, intellectualism to which the Portuguese *electoral* opposition were confined (and confined themselves) was highly propitious for generating yet further schisms and divisions, which in turn contributed even more to their image as an isolated, unrealistic and ineffectual minority. Looking over the accounts of the 1969 election, it is instructive (and depressing) to observe how much of the energy and attention of the opposition were devoted to an internecine dispute between the CDE and the CEUD, representing (but not clearly or distinctively) communist and leftist Catholic, and socialist and social-democratic factions, respectively.

One is, therefore, forced to agree with Mário Soares, that 'after forty-five years of struggle and sacrifice, no sector of the opposition, even the best organised, ha[d] sufficient power to impose, alone, a change of regime'.[23] This pessimistic, but realistic, conclusion (written presumably in 1971–2) was, of course, in large part the direct result of regime policies of systematic intimidation, repression, and violence. But it was also a product of the peculiar form under which what may be termed 'asymmetrically com-petitive, episodically free and contrapuntally significant elections' were held in Portugal. Had the rulers not permitted elections to exist at all, had they not so restrictively regulated access to the voting rolls, had they

Elections without Choice

not tolerated a modicum of carefully encapsulated 'free' articulation of opinion, had they not attracted such a specific and narrow social – professional sector to man the ranks of the opposition, had they not so cleverly reinforced the image of the opposition as a troublesome minority, they would have found it a good deal more difficult to sustain their authoritarian mode of domination for so long. Only once the regime itself began to depend on elections for more positive functions, such as legitimation, co-optation and rejuvenation, did these negative functions of disaggregation and segregation of the actual and potential opposition begin to take on a new significance, if not yet to acquire a new polarity.

THE STRUCTURE AND PERFORMANCE OF ELECTIONS IN AUTHORITARIAN PORTUGAL

Having speculatively identified the possible functions and motives for holding 'asymmetrically competitive, episodically free and contrapuntally significant elections' in authoritarian Portugal, we can now briefly turn to some empirical questions about the actual structure and performance of the electorate. It should be clear by now that, unless certain constraints on its collective behaviour were effectively obeyed and/or enforced, the Portuguese citizenry might have been able to use the electoral process with systematically disturbing effects. The positive consequences of the elections – from the point of view of the established authoritarian regime – depended upon a certain longitudinally stable pattern of performance, itself firmly rooted in social-structural inequalities. If the supportive electorate had proven to be temporally fickle, if the opposition had succeeded in creating a socially and geographically concentrated nucleus of supporters, if the class barriers to enrolment had been widely breached, if the level of extensive abstention had changed significantly, elections might, even in the Portugal of Salazar and Caetano, have taken on a different meaning.[24]

At the least, Portuguese elections should have obeyed the following empirical patterns to fulfil reliably and predictably their positive and negative functions for the authoritarian regime that established and controlled them:

(1) they should produce, from those actually voting, large majorities for the government party list;
(2) the territorial basis of this support should be stable over time;
(3) the social-structural basis of this support should be anchored in distinctive, reliable and economically dominant social classes, and should also be stable over time;
(4) enrolment to vote should be controlled in such a way as to exclude distinctive, unreliable, economically subordinate social classes and

such disenfranchisement should be stable over time or expand only gradually and predictably;

(5) high level of abstention on the part of the enfranchised portion of the population could be tolerated (even encouraged), but it must correspond to individualistic factors, not to class or territorially distinctive properties (i.e. it should not become a means of hidden collective protest); and

(6) opposition voting may be tolerated (within predictably narrow limits) but must correspond to individualistic factors and/or be socially and territorially dispersed. At best, it should be random with respect to social or collective attributes.

In a sense, this set of propositions about electoral manipulation suggests that Portugal had a latent four-party system: (1) the regime-supporting party (measured as the percentage of the population eligible by age to vote who actually voted for the UN or ANP); (2) the abstention party (measured as the percentage of registered voters not voting in a given election); (3) the disenfranchised party (measured as the percentage of the eligible population not registered to vote); and (4) the opposition party or parties (measured as the percentage of the eligible population voting for any non-UN or non-ANP party). Each of these parties, or strategies of electoral choice,[25] should have had a distinctive ecological basis, according to our set of derived propositions. In some cases this basis would have been firmly and significantly grounded in class structure and territorial units; in others it would have been dispersed or uncorrelated with respect to such collective attributes, and have been predictable (if at all) only in terms of individual-level characteristics such as age, sex, literacy and religion.

Restrictions in the availability of voting data[26] confine our analysis to the two last legislative elections under authoritarian rule, those of 1969 and 1973. Both were held under the 'new management' of Marcello Caetano and their district-level results were made public. To these dependent variables we have juxtaposed data gleaned from the (incompletely published) national census of 1970, various editions of the *Anuario Estatístico* and other sources on class or occupational structure. These data include class variables [percentage of the economically active population in each of the following categories: (1) landowners employing others, and independent cultivators; (2) agricultural workers; (3) industrial workers; and (4) owners and self-employed in urban occupations, and those employed in service, managerial and liberal professional tasks] and social variables [(1) percentage of couples who chose a Catholic marriage ceremony; (2) percentage of the total population who emigrated (1957–67); (3) percentage of illiterates in the population (1960); and (4) a vitality index based on the ratio of births and deaths to the respective age categories of the population].[27] Associations among these variables were analysed at the level of the electoral districts, of which there were twenty-two, including three in the Azores and one for Madeira.

Returning to our list of derived propositions-*cum*-formulae for electoral manipulation, there is little to be gained by discussing at any length the first one. If the official party had not regularly obtained large majorities in its favour from *those actually voting*, no elections would have been held at all. However, Table VIII.4 shows that regime-supporting party, while beating the opposition party by more than seven to one in 1969, was in both elections considerably smaller than the disenfranchised party.[28] The abstention party held a very steady 14 percent of the potential vote in both 1969 and 1973.

The second point of interest is the stability of the government party's vote over time. While it is politically useful to have opponents and abstainers vary greatly in number and identity from one election to another, authoritarian regimes need a steady predictable core of sup-

TABLE VIII. 4

The Four 'Parties' of the Portuguese Electoral System and their Performance in 1969 and 1973.

	1970	
Total population eligible by age to vote (male and female population over twenty years of age)[a]	4,828,375[b] (100·0%)	

	1969	*1973*
'Regime-supporting party' (votes for the UN – ANP)	980,800 (20·3%)	1,391,999 (28·8%)
'Abstention party' (registered voters who did not vote)	694,934 (14·4%)	702,726 (14·6%)
'Disenfranchised party' (voters eligible by age who were not registered)	3,018,595 (62·5%)	2,733,659 (56·6%)
'Opposition party' (votes for the CDE and CEUD)	134,046 (2·8%)	withdrew (0·0%)

[a] As this represents the male and female population twenty years of age and older, and in 1969 and 1973 voters had to be at least twenty-one, the relative size of the 'disenfranchised party' is slightly exaggerated.

[b] The 1970 census revealed that the total population had decreased slightly since the 1960 census. It is therefore not unreasonable to assume that the age-eligible constituency remained roughly constant over the period covered by this table.

porters within each territorial unit. Even if its party were to obtain ample margins of victory over the opposition(s) in every election, if this were to be composed of radically different actors and social groups each time, that would introduce a serious element of instability and even potential regime vulnerability. Naturally, aggregate data analysis does not reliably prove that, when there exists a high correlation in the voting percentages for successive elections, the same individuals have performed in the same way; but it does constitute a presumption in that direction. Scatterplotting the results of the 1969 and 1973 Portuguese elections against each other across all voting districts yields the extremely high correlation coefficient 0·894, which not only shows very convincingly that where the UN did well in 1969 it also tended to do well in 1973, but strongly suggests that the same persons and social groups were involved in both supporting actions. A glance at the residuals from that regression equation shows that the UN – ANP tended to gain in the northern and coastal areas (for instance, Aveiro, Coimbra, Viana do Castelo, Vila Real, Braga and Leiria); stayed about the same in the centre and south (Beja, Evora, Faró, Lisbon, Santarem, Setúbal – but also Porto, Bragança, Guarda and Viseu); and declined proportionately in the islands (Horta,[29] Funchal, Angra) and the interior (Portalegre and Castelo Branco).

Table VIII.5, however, provides us with the most significant clues to the longitudinal pattern of Portuguese voting. The regime-supporting party vote, as we have just seen, was very stable across the two elections (0·894), but it was almost matched in this respect by the disenfranchised party (0·891). As one might expect, the correlation between support in 1973 and disenfranchisement in 1969 in the twenty-two electoral districts was a very high, negative 0·864. Abstention as an electoral option in the two 'contests' was more weakly but still highly correlated (0·815), and, of course, owing to its withdrawal in 1973, there is no direct way of measuring the

TABLE VIII. 5

Zero-Order Bivariate Correlation Matrix of Voting Patterns, 1969 and 1973

	Regime-supporting party 1973	Abstention party 1973	Disenfranchised party 1973
Regime supporting party 1969	0·894	0·356	−0·806
Abstention party 1969	0·222	0·815	−0·513
Disenfranchised party 1969	−0·864	−0·601	0·891
Opposition party 1969	0·109	0·076	−0·126

'Parties' as defined in text and Table VIII. 4

longitudinal – geographical stability of the opposition. Nevertheless, it is important to note the low correlation between its proportional share in 1969 and the subsequent pattern of support, abstention or disenfranchisement in 1973.

We are now ready to consider the class and social-structural conditions that underlay Portugal's pseudo four-party system and served to perpetuate authoritarian rule through 'asymmetrically competitive, episodically free and contrapuntally significant' elections. Table VIII.6 broadly differentiates between those structural features linked to ownership and occupation (class) and those representing certain potentially significant social conditions: Catholicism, emigration, age distribution and illiteracy. Our general hypotheses that regime-supportive voting and disenfranchisement should be class-related in opposite directions and that both abstention and opposition voting should be individualistically or randomly associated are strikingly confirmed.

Voting for the UN – ANP in 1969 is quite well (and positively) predicted by one class variable: the percentage of the economically active population who are landowners employing others or are independent agricultural cultivators (0·822). Another class variable is a relatively good negative indicator of the size of the supporting vote: the percentage of industrial workers. On the social side of the table, the high positive correlation with emigration (0·505) suggests that, the greater the number of Portuguese who left a given district to seek work abroad, the more likely it was that the remaining ones would vote for the 'party of the situation'. Catholicism also seems to have been significantly linked to a pro-regime voting pattern.

The pattern of 'support' for the disenfranchised party is almost the exact inverse. Again, class variables are specifically more significant than social ones. Landownership and peasant cultivation decrease disenfranchisement; working in the industrial labour force increases it. Predictably, illiteracy is positively associated with disenfranchisement at the aggregate level (individual illiterates not being formally entitled to vote – although accusations of fraud and abuse in rural areas were common). Unpredictably, the more emigration, the less likely was it that those who remained would not be registered to vote.

Abstention was much less clearly linked to the class structure – with the possible exception of a hint (0·260) that urban bourgeois and *mesoi* groups who were registered might have refused or neglected to actually go to the polls in 1969. The level of illiteracy in a given district was associated negatively, and aging and moribund population positively, with abstention. As predicted, abstaining once one had become a registered voter seems to have been an individualistic choice – which about one-sixth of the age-eligible population regularly chose.

Finally, in 1969, nothing in the class structure or social composition of the districts predicted the proportional size of the opposition vote. Scattered ineffectually across all units – although proportionately and

TABLE VIII.6

Zero-Order Bivariate Correlation Matrix of Voting in 1969 and 1973 by Class and Social Variables

| | Class indicators | | | | | Social indicators | | |
| | Percentage of economically active population who are: | | | | Percentage of all marriages which are Catholic | Rate of emigration | Index of age and vitality | Illiterates as percentage of total population |
	landowners and peasants	agricultural workers	industrial workers	urban bourgeois and mesoi				
1969 elections								
Regime-supporting party	0·822	−0·082	−0·482	−0·247	0·373	0·505	−0·098	−0·207
Abstention party	−0·011	−0·145	0·002	0·260	−0·068	−0·204	0·234	−0·357
Disenfranchised party	−0·706	0·156	0·392	0·103	−0·300	−0·366	−0·008	0·343
Opposition party	0·175	−0·002	−0·158	0·008	0·135	−0·088	−0·015	−0·068
1973 elections								
Regime-supporting party	0·827	−0·145	−0·428	−0·235	0·544	0·425	0·056	−0·259
Abstention party	0·066	−0·245	0·062	0·225	−0·142	−0·049	0·353	−0·369
Disenfranchised party	−0·667	0·282	0·272	0·025	−0·308	−0·314	−0·253	0·361

'Parties' as defined in text and Table VIII. 4.

absolutely highest in Setúbal and Lisbon, the most urban, industrial and modern of Portugal's electoral districts – the CDE plus CEUD vote was exactly what the manipulative formula sought to make it: socially isolated, territorially dispersed, individually almost random.

The pattern of the 1973 election is hardly worth discussing in any further detail, since it so nearly replicated the 1969 pattern, despite the absence of any opposition party or parties. The class-linked nature of support and disenfranchisement was again demonstrated, the individualistic nature (age and illiteracy) of abstention reaffirmed.

When one passes from bivariate to multivariate regression, the successful manipulative formula becomes even more evident. Whereas the class categories predict UN voting and disenfranchisement with impressive efficiency (0·823 and 0·836 for the former in 1969 and 1973; 0·723 and 0·717 for the latter), they are insignificant estimators of either abstention (0·279 and 0·284) or opposition voting (0·205). The set of social variables does slightly better for abstention (0·458 in 1969 and 0·554 in 1973), but nothing, even in combination, 'explains' the voting proportions obtained by the CDE and CEUD in 1969.

CONCLUSION

At first view, elections in authoritarian Portugal seemed to fit snugly and securely into that most negative of typological syndromes: 'non-competitive, non-free and insignificant'. Upon closer inspection, we characterised them somewhat differently: 'asymmetrically competitive, episodically free and contrapuntally significant'. Opposition elements could and did present alternative candidates and programmes, although never with any prospect of winning. Controls on freedom of speech and assembly were relaxed during the brief, one-month campaign preceding the election, but opposition parties were otherwise prevented from leading a legal and continuous existence. Elections did play a major role in drawing together and rewarding elements of a fragmented and dispersed ruling elite, and in putting aside and punishing an even more fragmented and dispersed counterelite – even if they did not perform significantly the classic electoral functions of leadership selection, policy influence, regime legitimation, political communication and citizen socialisation. Furthermore, we have shown empirically that the viability of this formula for using frequent and regular 'public consultations' in support of an authoritarian, i.e. a non-publicly accountable, regime depended upon systematic patterns of class inclusion (with respect to regime-supportive voting) and class exclusion (with respect to disenfranchisement), and on dispersed or random patterns of individualistic effort (with respect to opposition voting) and individualistic non-effort (with respect to abstention). At least for the limited period we were able to scrutinise in any detail (1969–73), these complex patterns were quite stable over time and showed no marked tendency to degenerate or disintegrate.

This speculative conclusion about the function of elections in authoritarian Portugal reinforces (if not merely reiterates) an interpretative perspective I adopted earlier in discussing that country's corporatist system of interest representation. The role and consequences of that system, I suggested, 'must be assessed not primarily in terms of what it openly and positively accomplishe[d] but in terms of what it surreptitiously and negatively prevent[ed] from happening'.[30] The electoral process fits the same mould. It did accomplish some positive and acknowledged functions – most saliently that of locating, articulating and coalescing a territorially dispersed and potentially conflicting set of dominant class interests – but its most important ones were negative and not openly admitted: to identify, isolate and disaggregate elements of potential opposition, forcing them to participate in a structurally rigged political arena. As with state corporatism, state electoralism in authoritarian Portugal operated *pre-emptively* within categories set out and controlled from above; *preventively*, by occupying a certain physical, temporal and ideational space foreclosing alternative uses of that space; *defensively*, by encouraging the opposition to act primarily in the defence of its precarious rights, rather than in the aggressive promotion of new projects, interests or alliances; and *compartmentally*, by confining conflicts to a narrow spatial and temporal context and orienting them inward rather than toward wider publics and longer time periods.

Of course, elections did have their costs and dysfunctions for the regime. Had there not been some hope of eventually affecting policy, personnel or the nature of the regime itself, there would have been little chance of the opposition's participating in them, even as sporadically and dispiritedly as it did. Occasionally elections did produce unanticipated and unwelcome results for those in power, who then responded with intimidation, harassment, fraud, forced exile, repression, violence and, on at least one occasion, assassination. Nevertheless, owing to their constitutional status and their frequent and regular occurrence, elections in Portugal became a part, if a subordinate one, of the ritual of governing. Even when their functions and consequences began to shift – as they clearly did following the accession to power of Marcello Caetano – the regime could hardly have abrogated them. To have done so would have removed the carefully cultivated patina of institutionalisation so crucial to regime continuity and peaceful executive succession, encouraging the opposition to even greater efforts, since they would certainly have interpreted such a move as a sign of weakness.

Despite the evolving change in significance and some changes in form under the successor to Salazar, there is no sign that elections or the electoral process contributed directly or indirectly to the liberation of

Portugal from authoritarian rule. Elsewhere I have analysed this un-expected revolution in terms of exogeneous factors related to the conduct of colonial war and indigenous contradictions within the apparatus of the state, without reference to electoral decay or civilian opposition.[31]

Once liberation had occurred under other auspices and inspiration, the latent consequences of having tolerated 'asymmetrically competitive, episodically free and contrapuntally significant' elections were consider-able. The new regime inherited some *cadres* and even a few popular political figures ennobled by their honest, tenacious and self-sacrificing efforts in the previous opposition. It also inherited most of the organi-sational cleavages and personal animosities of that Quixotic experience. To the astonishment of many, the Portuguese people went massively and enthusiastically to the polls within a year of their liberation and articulated their preferences in an orderly and rational way despite what initially appeared to be a fantastic and confusing plethora of party and programme choices. For a people supposedly lacking in civic spirit and definitely lacking in experience with meaningful electoral choice it was a magisterial performance.

Perhaps the greatest significance of elections under Salazar and Caetano will ultimately prove to be ironic. From 1933 to 1973 a subject population was taught how the mere formal existence of repeated, regular and ritualistic 'popular consultations' could be rigged and distorted to support unpopular rule. Since that population recovered its citizenship status and rights in 1974, it may insist with even greater conviction that elections must be both procedurally equitable and substantively meaningful and that the only way to ensure this is to make them competitive, free and significant.

9 Elections in Communist Party States

ALEX PRAVDA

Elections in Communist Party states have traditionally been seen in the West as grotesque parodies of liberal democratic originals. As such, they have been described so as to reveal the bogus nature of their democratic pretensions.[1] With the decline of the 'totalitarian school' and the advent of a less doctrinaire approach to the study of Communist Party systems, elections have been given more attention and more complex analysis. For the Soviet Union we now have detailed, largely descriptive accounts of the mechanics of Soviet elections and some analysis of their functions. A considerable body of material deals with the composition of elected representative bodies, and some attempts have been made to use voting as an indicator of political dissent.[2] In Eastern Europe, where elections offer a potentially more fruitful field for research, treatment has been piecemeal: only Poland has received anything like detailed coverage.[3]

Since no attempt has been made to compare elections in Communist Party states or systematically to analyse their development, this analysis has the following objectives: first, briefly to survey the background and development of elections to national parliamentary and local government bodies in Communist Party states; second, to detail a typology of elections in these states; and, third, to examine the main functions performed by these elections and assess the variations in functions between types.

The study focuses upon the degree and kind of the choice or non-choice provided by elections in Communist Party states. Any attempt to evaluate the democratic or non-democratic nature of these elections is deliberately eschewed. The very different meanings assigned to the concept of democracy in liberal thought and in Marxism – Leninism make use of the term a hindrance rather than an aid to clear analysis. Although the study covers elections in all the Communist Party states of the Soviet Union and Eastern Europe, constraints of length rule out detailed treatment of elections in all nine states. Evidence is therefore drawn largely from Soviet,

Czechoslovak, Polish, Hungarian and Yugoslav elections; between them, they provide good examples of the whole range of elections in Communist states.[4]

The view of elections in Marxist – Leninist ideology is ambivalent. On the one hand they appear to be in a weak and subordinate position. As part of the state superstructure, elections are seen as deriving their real nature from their socio-economic content. Because elections are supposed to reflect the infrastructure, they have constantly to be adjusted in order to keep pace with developments; hence the frequent and often confusing changes in Communist electoral laws and regulations. Another factor contributing to the ideological weakness of elections is their notionally temporary nature. As part of a system of representative democracy, elections in their present form are scheduled to be superseded by more advanced direct democratic processes in the course of evolution towards full Communism. On the other hand, for the foreseeable future, ideology endows elections with considerable legitimacy. By contrast with the treatment accorded to elections by fascist and Nazi regimes, in Communist Party states they are lauded as essential channels for expressing popular sovereignty and socialist democracy. As the eschatological elements of the ideology continue to give way to those legitimating the political status quo, so the position of elections becomes more firmly entrenched.[5]

General political traditions, however, undermine the position of elections. It is extremely important that none of these countries, except for Czechoslovakia and East Germany, has a historical tradition which endowed elections with a strong authority prior to Communist rule. The weakness and deficiencies of the Russian electoral tradition are particularly important. The only elections which took place under the Tsarist regime were to the Duma between the 1905 and 1917 revolutions. Designed to ensure the dominance of the propertied groups, the system divided electors into five *curiae* and heavily favoured the landowning class. Furthermore, the Imperial Duma was indirectly elected through a multistage system of assemblies which effectively eliminated all vestiges of lower-class influence. Just as traditional Russian authoritarianism largely shaped the nature of the Soviet regime, so the Tsarist electoral system formed the basis for post-revolutionary elections till the mid-1930s.[6] The tradition of controlled elections, functioning as instruments to be used by the ruling minority to enhance its power, imbues Soviet elections to this day.

Electoral traditions in Eastern Europe prior to the establishment of Communist Party states were also weak by Western standards. No country, except Czechoslovakia, enjoyed an unbroken period of free elections affording voters real political choice. Nevertheless, the political tradition of many of these countries was less authoritarian than that of Russia, and the citizens of Poland, Czechoslovakia and what was to become East Germany had some experience of competitive multi-party elections in the inter-war period.[7]

The influence of these pre-Communist traditions was twofold. First, some of the old structural features were retained in the constitutions of the new People's Democracies, including non-Communist parties and pro-portional representation. Second, the experience, short as it was, of participation in competitive elections affected popular attitudes and expectations and thereby coloured the subsequent development of elections.[8]

The influence of such elements was more than offset by the political structure and style of the Communist Party states, which built upon and greatly reinforced the authoritarianism characteristic of many of these countries' historical traditions. The concept of the Communist Party's leading role in society and the operation of democratic centralism have made non-party representative bodies, and elections to them, instruments for the implementation of Communist Party policy.[9] Any changes in elections are dependent upon changes in the exercise of the party's leading role, and this in turn hinges on developments in the general political situation. One way to approach the whole problem of election develop-ment, and its relationship to systematic change, is to outline the main stages through which elections in these states have passed, and identify their salient features.

(1) In the 1920s in the Soviet Union and in the late 1940s in Eastern Europe, elections took place in conditions of political stuggle; they can be designated 'semi-civil-war elections'. Their nature was shaped by two sets of circumstances. First, in most cases the Communist Party had taken part in competitive elections before assuming power, but in none had it succeeded in obtaining a clear majority. Second, the Communist parties thus found themselves in power in a hostile political climate, without a basis of popular support or popular legitimacy. From these circumstances stemmed a general anxiety to hold elections which would endow the new regime with the popular legitimacy it lacked. In order to ensure a favourable result in what were at best unsure political conditions, various precautions were taken: those groups most likely to oppose the new regime were disenfranchised, voting was by show of hands, and an element of indirect election was introduced. Opposition parties were so emasculated that the Bloc or Front led by the Communists appeared the only viable choice.[10]

(2) The establishment of firm political control and the execution of fundamental 'socialist' transformations in the social and economic spheres brought about the second stage: Stalinist plebiscitary elections. The defeat

of 'class enemies' made safe the introduction of universal suffrage, direct
elections at all levels, the secret ballot and all the other trappings associated
with free elections in the West. In the Soviet Union, where the new
electoral system formed part of the 1936 constitution, these changes were
explained as reflecting the new socialist stage of development. Whereas in
the period of outright proletarian dictatorship it had been necessary to use
elections as an instrument of class power to forge unity, in a basically
harmonious socialist society the role of elections was to give unimpeded
expression to existing unity. Similar arguments were employed in Eastern
Europe, where parallel electoral reforms were accompanied by new
constitutions in the early 1950s.[11]

On paper, Stalinist plebiscitary elections were the very model of
electoral rectitude. However, their coincidence in time with the highest
levels of monolithic Stalinism and hyper-centralisation of the power
structure meant that these rules and regulations had little practical
impact, and many were customarily violated. Held in a climate of coerced
unanimity, these elections approximated very closely to an ideal-type
plebiscite, in which all parts of the process, from the selection of candidates
to the counting of votes, were bureaucratically manipulated and co-
ordinated to produce the desired result.[12]

(3) The process of de-Stalinisation can be seen as the most important
factor operating in the third stage of election development, from the
mid-1950s to the mid-1960s. A relaxation of centralisation and a decline in
police powers gave somewhat greater control over elections to state, as
against party, authorities. More importantly, the new emphasis on
socialist legality and constitutionalism reduced the violation of electoral
rules and enhanced the standing and role of representative bodies. The
decompression of the general political climate and the new stress on active
and voluntary popular participation in public life combined with the
above to encourage voters to take advantage of their formal electoral
rights.[13]

The minimal effect of de-Stalinisation was thus to reduce a little the
chasm which had existed between formal electoral rules and election
practice. Where, as in Yugoslavia and Poland, de-Stalinisation was
transformed into far-reaching reform of systemic proportions, the plebiscitary nature of elections was itself changed qualitatively by the introduction of elements of real choice. It is a token of the political
significance of elections that elections offering choices between political
parties were seen as one of the most important guarantees against the
return of Stalinism.[14]

(4) The current stage of election development, since the mid-1960s, has
been characterised by a steady leavening of the plebiscitary lump and a
general spread of limited-choice elections. Two sets of changes in the
outlook of Communist Party leaderships have fuelled this process: first, the
growing realisation that the achievement of increasingly secularised goals

in a highly complex modern society requires considerable decentralisation of decision-making powers and administrative responsibility to non-Communist Party bodies (this has led, *inter alia*, to the elevation of the role and powers of parliamentary and local government bodies and to a greater emphasis on the need for deputies and councillors of high ability[15]); and, second, the recognition that the most effective way to underpin political stability and maintain economic progress is to provide more institutional opportunities for the expression of different interests within the community, and closer links between the electorate and their representatives.[16]

These changes in thinking have moved election development further away from bureaucratic control and toward greater voter choice, but their impact has varied with political conditions. Where strong concern with the maintenance of very close control over all political processes persists, as in the Soviet Union, Czechoslovakia or Bulgaria, proposals advocating the introduction of elements of choice and competition have remained on paper.[17]

In other Communist Party states, such as East Germany, Hungary and Romania, varying elements of electoral choice have been offered to voters. Even in Poland and Yugoslavia, where a degree of choice has long been an established part of elections, measures have been taken to enhance its scope and encourage its utilisation. It is difficult to generalise about regime motivations, but election changes have often been part of a larger package of reforms making the political system more responsive. The introduction of electoral choice has invariably been officially depicted as proof of advances in 'socialist democracy'. This underlines the ever-increasing importance accorded by the regime to representative bodies and to public opinion.[18]

In all instances where choice has been introduced, the Communist Party's leading role has continued to be beyond electoral challenge. There is no question, even in Yugoslavia, of voters being given a choice between the Communist Party and an organised opposition. Only in one case, that of the abortive Czechoslovak reform movement of 1968, has a Communist Party put forward proposals to allow electoral contests involving several parties with differing platforms. And even these proposals stipulated the maintenance of the leading role of the Communist Party for some considerable time to come.[19]

A TYPOLOGY OF ELECTIONS IN COMMUNIST PARTY STATES

As a result of the developments outlined above, elections in Communist Party states vary significantly, even if they do so within the limits imposed by one-party rule. In order to clarify the situation, elections to representative state bodies at all levels have been categorised according to three sets of criteria: (1) the degree of contest permitted, the main factors here being the number of candidates standing for every seat and the scope of programmatic differences in election campaigns; (2) the scope made available for the expression of voters' preferences both at the polls and in the selection process; and (3) the consequences of election results, in terms of the tenure of political power and in terms of policy.

As can be seen from Table IX.1, elections in Communist Party states at present fall into two main types: plebiscitary elections and limited-choice elections. Because the latter has evolved from the former, and both are set within similarly structured political systems, the two types share many characteristics and in some respects are separated by only slight differences. The number of candidates per seat has been selected as the key distinguishing factor, because of its salience to this study. This is not to imply the existence of a direct correspondence between the number of candidates standing and the degree of electoral choice. Without qualitative differences between candidates, their numbers can be almost meaningless. Furthermore, electoral choice is not restricted to polling day, but can occur at the selection stage. Lastly, any assessment of the degree of choice in these elections must take account of the size and composition of the body of choosers, and of the extent to which they take advantage of the opportunities proffered them. It is not so much the availability of choice as its actual use which ultimately determines political reality.

Plebiscitary elections

In terms of political forms, there seems to be no necessary connection between plebiscitary elections and the existence of the Communist Party as the only political organisation. In the Soviet Union, which provides the prime example of this type of election, the Communist Party is in a monopolistic position – i.e. there are no other political parties, and the electoral Bloc, uniting the Communist Party with all social organisations, functions only during elections. On the other hand, Czechoslovakia and Bulgaria combine plebiscitary elections with a political structure incorporating non-Communist parties organised in a permanently operating Front in which the Communist Party has a dominant position. While the presence of such satellite non-Communist parties can contribute to the introduction of electoral choice, the way in which the Communist Party exercises its power is far more important. Plebiscitary elections are most firmly grounded where the Communist Party behaves in a monopolistic fashion even if structurally it is in a position of hegemony.[20]

Nothing in electoral law prohibits more than one candidate standing for any seat; indeed, provision is often specifically made for such a contingency. The defining characteristic of plebiscitary elections is that this legal possibility is not translated into electoral practice.[21] The standard official justification of the absence of electoral choice has been that there is no political conflict in socialist societies; to insist upon several candidates

TABLE IX. 1

A Typology of Elections in Communist Party States

Type	No. candidates/no. seats	Election platform and campaign	Voting	Selection procedure	Consequences	Current examples
Plebiscitary elections	One candidate per seat	One election platform. High levels of pressure, to ensure unanimity	Direct voting for single-member constituencies. Facilities for secret ballot, but demonstrative voting encouraged; unmarked ballot counted as a positive vote	Usually determined by executive decision; voter choice largely formal except occasionally at lowest levels	None for tenure of power. None on national policy; possible minimal consequence for local policy	USSR 1937 – Czechoslovakia 1954 – Bulgaria 1953 – Albania 1954 –
Limited-chance elections	More candidates than seats, particularly in local elections	One national election platform; some variation in individual candidates' interpretation	Multi-member constituencies, in-built bias in favour of official candidates; *or*	Greater voter choice and say, especially at local level	None for tenure of power. Minimal for national policy; some for local policy	Poland 1957 – East Germany 1967 –
			single-member constituencies. Greater secret voting; unmarked ballot invalid. Mixture of direct and indirect voting	Considerable legal rights possessed and more influence exerted by voters' meetings, especially at local level		Yugoslavia 1953 – Hungary 1967 – Romania 1975 –

would be to create disunity where none exists. Moreover, it is claimed that, because the selection process allows the widest possible say to all those who wish to participate, the lack of alternatives on polling day in no way infringes voters' freedom of choice.[22] The anxiety to justify the situation belies a certain defensiveness, which has recently given way to some expression of unease and doubt. Several Soviet academics have pointed out that the established political custom of allowing only one candidate per seat might be doing more harm than good, and that the introduction of an element of electoral choice would probably stimulate popular interest and improve the quality of candidates. To this end, proposals have been put forward advocating the introduction of electoral contest at local levels for a trial period, but there is no evidence that they have been acted upon.[23]

The presumption of consensus embodied by the custom of one candidate per seat is reinforced by the election campaign. All candidates stand on the 'unbreakable' platform of the Bloc or Front, which unites all social and political organisations under the leadership of the Communist Party.[24] Great stress is laid on the fact that all candidates have equal access to campaign facilities, but the legitimate use of such facilities is restricted to those canvassing in favour of those standing; no mention is made of the right to campaign against candidates.[25] Indeed, all campaigning is co-ordinated and steered by the Communist Party's agitation and pro-paganda departments to project the best possible image of party and government achievements and plans. Throughout the three weeks or so of the campaign national policies are lauded and not discussed. At nomination and campaign meetings, criticism is sometimes voiced of the performance of local government bodies and demands are raised about matters such as housing and transport, but national political issues are studiously avoided. Some additional opportunity for discussing local issues is provided by door-to-door canvassing, but the main thrust of these visits is to convey the achievements of the Communist Party and the govern-ment.[26]

Considerable criticism has been voiced in the Soviet Union and Czechoslovakia about the monotony and lack of imagination evident in campaigning, and the call raised for a more varied and sensitive approach. Yet, given the unchanged nature of the ruling purpose of the campaign – to ensure that the entire electorate demonstrates its un-animous support for the Front or Bloc – it is not surprising that blanket mobilisation remains dominant.[27]

The citizen has very little real choice about whether he votes in plebiscitary elections. There is no legal compulsion, but the overwhelming social and organisational pressures to turn out make the difficulties of absenteeism far outweigh the inconvenience of voting. As a result, electoral turn-out since the 1960s has ranged from a 'low' of 99·4 per cent in Czechoslovakia to a 'high' of 100 per cent in Albania. The missing percentile fractions are being steadily eroded and should be ascribed mainly to organisational shortcomings rather than to determined absenteeism.[28]

Voting procedures facilitate the expression of support and discourage dissent. To register a vote in favour of the candidate the elector has merely to place an unmarked ballot paper in the box; those who wish to vote against the candidate have to delete his or her name. As secrecy of the ballot is constitutionally guaranteed, voting booths are provided for this purpose. In the circumstances, however, their use can be interpreted as indicating dissidence. These conditions, in addition to the strong campaign pressures to vote 'demonstratively', result, at least in the Soviet Union, in an estimated 1 – 5 per cent of the electorate using the booths to cast a 'secret' ballot. Several academic commentators have criticised existing voting procedures for their failure either to assure secrecy or to afford electors the opportunity to express their opinions. It has been suggested that positive marking of the card should be required, encouraging all voters to use the booths.[29]

Given existing arrangements, which so strongly militate against the negative vote, it is not surprising that the number of such votes rarely exceeds 0·5 per cent of the total votes cast. These votes appear to be largely protest directed against local policies and performance and against unpopular local candidates; only at village level are they sufficient to bring about the defeat of any candidates – in Soviet elections, approximately one in every 10,000 fails in this way.[30]

Electors' rights do not end with a ballot on polling day. The right of recall has long been highlighted as exemplifying the high level of popular control and choice made available in all socialist elections. In the Soviet Union since the late 1950s, increasing stress has been placed on the voters' right to recall any deputy who has failed in his duties or betrayed his constituents' trust. The organisations nominating a deputy have the right to raise the question, which is then examined by the executive of the representative body of which he is an elected member. If this body decides there is a case, it organises a vote on the matter. Interestingly enough, in the campaign leading up to this vote, canvassing is permitted against as well as for the incumbent. The actual question of recall is usually decided by a show of hands at a local electors' meeting and, if it proves necessary, a by-election is then held. Inbuilt executive filters make it a highly controlled process which restricts actual incidence of recalls to a very small number of cases, involving misdemeanours; recalls do not occur where policy questions are involved.[31]

One of the standard official explanations offered for the absence of choice at the polls is that voters have already exercised their choice in the course of the selection process. Formal selection procedures appear to grant considerable powers of choice to work-place meetings of voters: all nomination proposals have to be submitted to them for approval; and, even after the registration of nominations, further voters' meetings have the right to alter the lists. The entire process is purportedly designed to give the voter the decisive say in determining who stands for elections.[32]

In practice, selection is a far more closed process offering only a limited degree of choice to small groups. As one would expect, the Communist Party, whose role is glossed over in the formal procedures, exercises a decisive influence over the outcome of selection. It is evident from written accounts, and from the remarkable consistency of the composition of deputies, that central party directives are issued for every election which lay down definite guidelines according to which candidates are to be selected. These guidelines stipulate the overall proportion of candidates in terms of social – occupational status, political and organisational affiliation, age, sex and so forth. Party committees, particularly at the district level, then break down the overall proportions for their own areas and issue appropriate recommendations to other organisations involved in selection, including Front committees. These proportions vary in specificity, and leave the Communist Party and, in Bulgaria and Czechoslovakia, other organisations, at district and at the lowest levels, with a good deal of discretion in selecting names to fit the bill.[33]

It is within circles of local officials that most of the real selection takes place, accompanied by a good deal of consultation and bargaining. The resulting lists of proposed candidates are then presented to nomination meetings of voters at their places of work. Usually there is little discussion of or challenge to any of the nominees.[34] Nominees are then registered as candidates and duly presented to voters' meetings. These are generally rather tame affairs, at which a few questions are addressed to candidates and electors' instructions are issued. Such instructions or mandates, which are supposed to guide and not totally bind candidates when elected, are often drawn up by local campaign officials and merely formally ratified by the meeting. At the lowest levels in local elections, where issues and individuals are better known, both nomination meetings and those between voters and candidates tend to be more lively and occasionally result in the replacement of official candidates.[35]

The reality of candidate selection thus departs from the avowed principles of broad voter involvement, choice and influence. Several aspects of the process have prompted critical comments and proposals from academic and official platforms.

First, some Soviet academics have underlined the need to strengthen links between nomination and representation, between those who select candidates and those whom the candidate is elected to represent. Under the existing system of nomination at work-places, and elections for territorially based constituencies, such links are often tenuous and, for some voters, non-existent. To solve this problem, some have advocated nomination rights for territorially based voters' meetings and the election of deputies on a mixed territorial – production basis; others favour a return to the pre-1936 Soviet production-based constituencies. On a different tack, but with the same end in view, one writer has proposed that candidates standing for re-election should as a rule do so in their old constituency, rather than be moved elsewhere as at present; they should certainly not, as often happens, be foisted on new voters without the latter's being given some idea of their previous record.[36] The contention of all these critics is that, were such proposals enacted, those participating in nomination meetings would have a greater interest in choosing the right candidate, and the capacity to do so.

The second concern is the gap between the voters' formal prerogatives in selection and their use of these rights. Soviet academics and party spokesmen and some Czech local councillors have deplored the general hastiness and superficiality of nomination meetings and the lack of real discussion and questioning of candidates at voters' meetings. The official answer to this is a call for greater activism on the part of the rank and file. Academics, on the other hand, have suggested procedural changes to strengthen the influence of nomination and voters' meetings over selection.[37]

Predictably, none of the Soviet critics sees the passivity of the voters in selection as the direct function of the bureaucratic domination of the process. No attempt had been made to suggest a change in the principle of party 'supervision' over selection. This is deemed to be necessary in order to prevent any 'spontaneity', i.e. uncontrolled grass-roots activity, which is regarded in all Communist Party states, but particularly in those with plebiscitary elections, as a heinous offence. What is suggested instead is that all nominating organisations consult local activists and voters more fully and take greater care to put forward candidates of the highest calibre who command genuine popular respect and support.[38]

While there is no evidence of any of the specific proposals for structural and procedural change being put into effect, there are signs that steps have been taken in the direction of fuller consultation. In a few cases, official candidates have been withdrawn in favour of those chosen by votes at work-place nomination meetings. Developments along such lines would extend the exercise of selection choice from 'roomfuls of officials' to assembly halls at places of work. Such an extension would not necessarily diminish greatly the level of bureaucratic control, but it would bring the selection process closer to fulfilling its supposed 'primary election' function.[39]

Limited-choice elections

As with plebiscitary elections, there is no uniformity of political structure among the states whose elections are of this type. The existence of non-Communist parties is not prerequisite of limited-choice elections: the Communist Party retains a monopoly of organised political activity in Yugoslavia and Hungary, but these countries offer a greater amount of electoral choice than do other Communist states. What distinguishes them from their plebiscitary counterparts is higher levels of political pluralism, stemming in part from a greater social heterogeneity, and in part from a more flexible party attitude toward political expression.[40]

The distinguishing characteristic of this type is the extension of voter choice from the selection stage to the polls. In all these elections it is established practice for there to be more candidates than seats. The degree of electoral contest and choice does, however, vary considerably from country to country.

In East Germany the element of competition and choice is kept to a minimum. The list of candidates for the multi-seat constituencies comprises two groups: the 'seat' candidates (listed first), equal in number to the seats to be filled; and the so-called 'surplus' candidates. The electoral chances of the two groups are very different. In order to become deputies the 'seat' candidates merely have to get a simple majority of the votes cast. On the other hand, the 'surplus' candidates, even if they poll 99 per cent of the vote, have no chance of becoming deputies, unless one or more of the 'seat' group fails to get a majority. In the event of there being no such failure, 'surplus' candidates who get 51 per cent or more of the vote become what are called 'substitute' deputies, and can be brought in to fill any vacancies which may arise between elections.[41]

The Polish system provides for a far more equal and meaningful contest. As in East Germany, the list is divided into 'seat' candidates and 'surplus' candidates, but in this case the number of votes received is decisive. Those candidates who poll the largest number of votes, over and above a simple majority, become deputies regardless of their status. The success of the 'surplus' candidates is thus not conditional upon the failure of one of their 'seat' counterparts. The latter, however, have one considerable advantage – namely, that an unmarked ballot paper is counted as a vote for the 'seat' candidates alone.[42]

No such bias is present in the Romanian, Hungarian or Yugoslav systems. In none of these is there any limit to the number of 'surplus' candidates allowed; nor do they suffer under any formal voting handicaps. It is interesting to note that the Hungarian and, especially, the Yugoslav electoral systems also incorporate an important element of indirect election; this might be seen as an inbuilt safeguard against excessive voter influence.[43]

Just as the formal regulations vary, so do the quantitative levels of choice. Yugoslav elections have produced the highest ratio of candidates to seats. In 1967 this ranged from approximately 1·5 to 1 at national level to 2·5 to 1 in local contests. In Poland the legal surplus of 50 per cent has rarely been fully achieved, though levels have usually not fallen far below a 40 per cent excess of candidates over seats. The only Romanian election to have offered any real choice, that of 1975, had slightly higher levels, while the Hungarian record makes it numerically less competitive than East

Germany. The general pattern is that, the lower the level of election, the greater the quantitative choice available. Several factors can be held to account for this. At the local level there is greater involvement and therefore a greater tendency on the part of organisations and groups to insist that their candidates stand for office. Because the political importance of such elections is small, central authorities are more likely to allow most nominations to go through. At higher levels central controls are more stringent; many seats are held *ex officio* and fewer candidates are willing to risk defeat by standing in contested constituencies.[44]

Although the excess of candidates over seats is an essential precondition for electoral choice, it is the existence of qualitative differences between the contestants which determines the reality of that choice. The first overall factor limiting the differences between candidates is that they all stand on the same electoral platform, that of the Front or its equivalent, which is based on the programme of the Communist Party. Repeatedly it is officially emphasised that the choice with which voters are presented is one between personalities and not between policies. Individual candidates may interpret certain aspects of their common programme in slightly different ways, but they all, regardless of political or organisational affiliation, stand for one party line. In practice, such consensus is generally maintained; only in some Yugoslav election contests have candidates ever questioned the policies embodied in the official election programme.[45] Despite such programmatic unity, it is only in East Germany and Poland, where the electoral system almost guarantees who will be elected, that the electors are given a choice among individuals who hold important political or administrative office. In Hungary, Romania and Yugoslavia, where electoral contests are more equal, officials from the higher or even middle echelons of the party and other organisations almost invariably stand unopposed. Officials of lower ranks are sometimes put up in contested seats, but usually only against officials of similar standing. Were Communist Party officials to stand against rank-and-file candidates and be defeated, this would reflect on the party's image, despite official insistence that all differences are merely personal.[46] A similar tendency emerges when one examines the electoral position of the larger 'core' of deputies who seem to enjoy almost permanent elected office. These sitting deputies are generally placed in safe seats, the contested ones being reserved in large part for their 'one-term' colleagues.[47]

As far as Communist Party members as a whole are concerned, it is difficult to discern any definite patterns. They seem to form as large a proportion of competing or 'surplus' candidates as they do of the other categories. This is the result of deliberate party policy. In order to assert its presence and maintain certain set levels of saturation in all representative bodies, the party makes sure that its members stand in what can be identified as unsafe as well as safe situations. Lastly, there is usually very little difference between competing candidates as regards their social – occupational status; at the most, workers stand against foremen or the latter against works engineers.[48] Distinctions between candidates, and thus choice, are narrowed down to differences in individual experience, popularity and ability to carry out what remains a common programme.

The entire election campaign is directed towards underlining the unity of outlook and interest of all candidates, and obscuring the differences separating them. As in plebiscitary elections, campaign effort popularises the positive aspects of past national achievements and future plans. Appeals are made, if in somewhat less strident tones, for the electorate's wholehearted support and unanimous endorsement of the Front platform. The attention given to publicising individual candidates and their views still tends to be very secondary by comparison.[49] Polish surveys show that the majority of voters do not have sufficient knowledge to assess candidates' relative merits.[50]

The rules and conventions governing the campaign still explicitly prohibit canvassing against candidates, and even efforts by individuals to win votes for themselves are frowned upon. All candidates are meant to act the same. All have to get exactly the same amount of publicity and press coverage. Even in Yugoslavia, where campaigns have been freer than in other limited-choice elections, attempts to attract support by making promises to promote local interests are condemned as 'demagogy'. Despite such restrictions, competitive electioneering has occasionally occurred. In the Polish elections of 1957 and in Yugoslavia in 1967 and 1969, some contests assumed a combative nature, with candidates playing on local grievances and even running their own campaigns in opposition to the official machine.[51]

Official endeavours to minimise differences between candidates notwithstanding, these elections present voters with some opportunity to express their preferences. In addition to the black-and-white options available in plebiscitary elections – of voting or not voting and of casting a positive or a negative vote – there are further possibilities for choice. In Hungary, Romania and Yugoslavia, many electors have a straight choice from two or more candidates; in East Germany and Poland they can either vote for the 'seat' candidates or for those in the 'surplus' positions on the list, or opt to vote for a mixture of individuals. Voting procedures facilitate the use of these options. Passive voting is still encouraged by the Polish and East German systems, where unmarked ballot papers are counted as votes for the 'seat' candidates. In Hungary and Yugoslavia, however, unmarked ballot papers are considered invalid; this makes it easier to vote secretly without incriminating oneself as an opponent of the regime. Finally, procedures governing the recall of deputies give Hungarian and Yugoslav constituents a greater say than they would enjoy in plebiscitary elections. Grounds for recall are somewhat broader and the control exercised by executive bodies over the whole process is less prohibitive. Yet there is still widespread feeling that recall is under-utilised because it is not sufficiently open to voter influence.[52]

What use does the electorate make of the opportunities offered by limited-choice elections and what preferences do voting figures reveal? Election turn-out tends to be lower and a good deal more volatile than in plebiscitary elections ranging from a low of 90 per cent in Yugoslavia to 96–98 per cent in Poland, Hungary and Romania.[53] The figures reveal the usual pattern of lower turn-out in local elections and in rural areas; consistent regional and nationality group variations; and fluctuations corresponding to changes in policy. The less highly charged election atmosphere and less intensive mobilisation efforts allow for the greater use of absenteeism as a means of registering indifference to or even disagreement with regime policy.[54]

A more direct indicator of such disagreement is the number of protest votes, i.e. votes cast against all the candidates standing. The availability of choice does not seem to reduce the number of such votes, though many of those who supported the introduction of an element of choice probably hoped it would. On the contrary, it appears to result in a significant increase. Negative votes constitute 1–2 per cent, and in Yugoslavia up to 7 per cent, of all votes cast. Once again, the slightly more tolerant election climate must be held to account in large part for this phenomenon. Organisational factors, however, are of less importance than in turn-out, and voter apathy does not cloud the political meaning of this act. It is clear from the Polish and Yugoslav data that negative votes reflect both underlying political antipathies and short-term reactions to changes in political course.[55]

It is difficult for voters to express their political preferences when presented with a straight choice from two or more candidates of equal status standing on the same platform. Even where one of the candidates is known to be officially sponsored, the evidence indicates that voters tend to decide on the basis of candidates' individual qualifications and past record, and not on the basis of their official standing. Although being the unofficial candidate is no handicap, it is not necessarily an advantage either. Those candidates who have successfully stood as independents in Yugoslav elections have achieved their success not because of their contradiction of the Communist Party line, but because of their promises to promote local interests.[56]

Polish elections, which demarcate clearly between official ('seat') and unofficial ('surplus') candidates, shed more light on this point. Given the rarity in these states of the opportunity to choose between official and unofficial standpoints, one might expect the 'surplus' candidates to do very well. Yet very few of them are elected and then only at lower levels in local elections. Several factors might be held to account for this. First, the voting system: to get elected, the 'surplus' candidate needs to combine a large personal vote with concentrated voting against one of the 'seat' candidates.

Second, careful selection: this not only excludes most potentially un-popular candidates but also often ensures that popular and able in-dividuals are placed in the 'seat' positions. The voters are therefore not presented with a choice between unsuitable official candidates and able unofficial ones. As a result, only a very small minority of electors, usually in tightly-knit communities, have the knowledge and motivation to vote against a particular 'seat' candidate, let alone for a particular 'surplus' candidate.[57]

While the vast majority of voters do not, therefore, attempt to defeat the official slate, enough vote against the 'seat' candidates to alter substantially from the original listing the order in which they are elected.[58] In this way voters in Poland can make their preferences felt without implying any wholesale rejection of the official election platform. At first sight, these changes in order seem to operate against Communists and in favour of candidates from other parties and the unaffiliated. On closer inspection, however, it emerges that the apparent anti-Communist Party vote is secondary to one directed against office-holders. The functionaries who are usually placed first in the list of 'seat' candidates are often well known and sufficiently unpopular with the electorate to attract a number of negative votes, which result in their demotion to the bottom of the 'seat' group. This seems to be the case whether or not they are members of the Communist Party. Because the majority of Communist candidates hold some kind of office, they poll a lower percentage of votes cast. Although it can be argued that electors do not use their vote against Communists *qua* members of the Communist Party, it is mistaken to claim, as does Wiatr, that these consistent changes in the order of seat candidates are essentially non-political. By deleting the names of party and government apparatchiks, a small yet significant number of voters do make effective use of the system to voice their political opinions.[59]

The formal stages of selection in many ways parallel those in plebiscitary elections. The right of proposal is universally possessed by social and political organisations, meetings of working people and of electors. In some instances it extends to groups of citizens and even to individuals. By a process of consultation, organisation representatives draw up lists of nominees, and these are submitted to voters' meetings or to conferences of elected voters' delegates. Such meetings or conferences are generally empowered to reject names on the lists and put forward nominees of their own. A vote decides the composition of the list of proposed candidates, which goes to the election or Front committees and is then forwarded to official bodies for registration. Even after this stage, meetings of voters with prospective candidates can alter the final election line-up.[60]

The formal rights of voters' meetings vary considerably. In Poland and East Germany their powers are as nebulous as in plebiscitary systems. While the meetings can change the lists of nominees submitted to them, the election or Front committees are obliged merely to take these views into account. The meetings are seen as no more than sounding-boards to facilitate the consultation of voter opinion. In Yugoslavia and Hungary, these meetings or their equivalents have far more extensive and more closely defined powers. Yugoslav regulations lay down that the decisions of meetings comprising set minimum proportions of voters must be confirmed by the electoral commissions, unless there are strictly legal grounds for their rejection. Hungarian electoral law stipulates that all nominees who receive a third of the votes at electors' meetings must be put forward for registration by the Front committees. In both cases, therefore, the decisions taken at voters' meetings are legally binding and not merely views to be taken into account.[61]

In practice, by far the most important stages of the selection process still take place within the Communist Party and the main social and political organisations. Although the scope for choice afforded by party guidelines is similar to that in plebiscitary selection, influence is brought to bear by a wider range of opinion. First, the selection procedures within organisations are more open. While the majority of nominations for national level bodies continue to be issued from central executives, all other nominations are decided by conferences of delegates. In Poland, for instance, not only have Communist Party nomination conferences taken on the character of primaries, but they have also been opened to non-Communist activists, who thereby have an opportunity to influence the composition of party nominees. Yugoslavia offers the best instances of nomination lists being drawn up by a process of hard bargaining and trading between delegations from the main social organisations. The Communist Party still exercises a guiding role but does not always seek to get its own way.[62]

Any attempt to assess the impact of voters' meetings on the lists of nominations produced by the organisation 'primaries' must take into account the differences between selection of candidates for national representative assemblies and selection of candidates for lower-level bodies. In the first category, voters' meetings and conferences seem to leave little impact. In Yugoslavia in 1965 and 1967, for example, voters' meetings put forward a large number of nominees for election to federal office, but many were disallowed on what were often spurious grounds. In Hungary, the reluctance of voters to propose nominations from the floor has combined with the authorities' determination to secure the adoption of their candidates to prevent anything more than occasional changes being made in the lists. When candidates are rejected by these meetings all that usually happens is that a substitute candidate is put forward by the Front – the umbrella body which co-ordinates the main organisations' election activity – and is endorsed by the same or by a second meeting. Only very rarely is a candidate 'spontaneously' proposed from the floor added to the final list.[63]

At local level, voters' meetings and conferences have greater influence. Because controls are less tight and because participants know a good deal about the merits and demerits of each nominee, searching questioning often takes place. As a result, a small yet significant proportion of the names submitted is rejected; in the Polish local elections of 1965, for instance, 4 per cent of village-level candidates were changed in this way. The most common objection raised against these candidates was that they were not locals and would therefore be unlikely to understand and represent constituency interests. The nominations put forward by such meetings show a bias towards locals or towards those who can convince voters of their determination to promote local interests. This criterion appears to far more important than political affiliation, though, in Poland at least, there is some prejudice in favour of candidates who are not members of any party. The alterations made by voters' meetings to the lists of nominations fare differently from country to country. In Yugoslavia, for instance, most of the changes proposed get through to the final lists, while in Poland election committees use their discretionary powers to neutralise much of the meetings' impact.[64]

FUNCTIONS

As all elections in Communist Party states exclude the possibility of choice between competing national programmes, it is often assumed that their functions are confined to mobilisation and legitimation of a crude and uniform kind. In point of fact, they perform a range of functions which in many respects resemble those associated with classic Western elections.[65]

Mobilisation

Organised mass activity is a salient feature of public life in all Communist Party states, involving up to half the adult population. Elections are an important occasion for the mobilisation of the normally passive members of the community. In plebiscitary elections, overwhelming emphasis is placed on achieving extremely high levels of turn-out. Electoral participation is almost exclusively 'stalactite', i.e. the result of organisational pressure from above, including occasional voting by election officials on behalf of absentees. In limited-choice elections, high turn-out is still worked for, but greater priority is accorded to encouraging participation of a more 'stalagmite' nature. These differences in approach largely account for the differences in turn-out between, to take the two extremes, Albania and Yugoslavia.[66]

Getting out voters is not the only dimension of election mobilisation. Improving disappointing attendance at meetings throughout the election period is also important. Low attendances can present a serious problem where voters' meetings play an important part in selection; in Yugoslavia many nominations have fallen through because of the lack of a quorum at meetings. Yet it is contradictory for elections stressing voter choice to employ plebiscitary pressures to ensure that choices are made.[67]

Elections provide a unique opportunity for all political and social organisations to collaborate on a national political mobilisation which is in many ways the political equivalent of the launching of a Five Year Plan. Economic issues pervade all campaigns; in Czechoslovakia and Hungary the parliamentary term of office has recently been extended to bring it into line with the period of the economic plan. In Eastern Europe elections are the only occasion at which otherwise semi-moribund Fronts come into effective operation to co-ordinate the activity of the Communist Party and its partners. More generally, elections test the organisational and propaganda abilities of the various apparatuses and offer an excellent opportunity to activate the mass memberships. Officials carefully monitor all aspects of electoral mobilisation for signs of organisational strength and weaknesses.[68] In both types of election, mobilisation is a demonstration on the largest scale of the regime's political control and organisational effectiveness. While differences between the types are largely ones of degree and emphasis, mobilisation in limited-choice elections is somewhat less dragooned and inflexible.

Political education and socialisation

All these elections are occasions for the intensification of political education and socialisation. Their sheer duration and frequency give them weight. In the Soviet Union, for instance, elections occupy up to two months in three out of every four years.[69] Elections open up a greater variety of channels for political communication. Political information is given even greater media prominence than usual and direct contact with the electorate is made possible, if not always utilised, by meetings at places of work and residence. In addition, agitation points and centres are established and used for political discussion and the distribution of election literature. Finally, canvassing operations are mounted on a massive scale, particularly in plebiscitary elections. Most families are visited at least once in the course of the campaign and given a political-education talk and some opportunity to discuss local problems.[70] It is difficult to assess the impact made by such methods. Very wide coverage is achieved, but much of the campaigning remains perfunctory and usually too much is crammed into the final weeks of the campaign period. Because the flow of political propaganda is continuous, the majority of the population has considerable resistance to indoctrination. In these conditions the concerted use of communications channels during elections probably reduces the credibility of the messages conveyed.[71]

In both types of election, campaign themes are invariably taken from the last Party Congress or Central Committee session. The election programme of the Bloc or Front and election addresses tend to highlight the work of parliamentary and local government bodies.[72] In local elections considerable effort is made to weave matters of local concern into campaign material. This is particularly the case in some limited-choice elections. In Poland since 1965, election programmes have been formulated for local councils. The introduction of electoral contests has led, in Hungary, Poland and, especially, Yugoslavia, to candidates' expounding their own views of election issues. On rare occasions even national-level elections, as in Yugoslavia in 1967 and 1969, have witnessed public argument and conflict. What has happened more often, however, is that contest has enlivened discussions and helped to make elections into more of a two-way exchange of information and opinion.[73]

Participation in such discussions forms part of the socialisation effect of elections. Attendance at election meetings usually involves between a third and a half of the electorate, if only to a minimal extent, in the campaign and thereby in the whole political process. The act of voting is more significant in socialisation terms, because it constitutes the culmination of elections as civic rituals of participation and commitment. In some plebiscitary elections, Czechoslovakia in 1971 being a case in point, electors are strongly encouraged to vote with their fellow workers, to strengthen the collective ethos which figures so prominently in the ideal political culture.[74] All this underlines the importance of elections as May Day demonstrations writ large.

Very large numbers also participate in elections through working in election commissions and committees, in canvassing groups and at polling stations: one in sixteen did so in the Soviet local elections of 1967.[75] Such active involvement is likely to create some feeling of co-responsibility, even if only as a result of its being ascribed to this group by the non-involved. By far the most far-reaching involvement and socialisation is undergone by those elected to office. The very high rates of turn-over associated in particular with plebiscitary elections – 50 per cent plus is common – exist partly for reasons of socialisation. In the USSR, the Soviets are seen as 'schools of ideological and political upbringing', though greater concern with representatives' performance and their links with constituents has prompted calls for a reduction of turn-over. Such concern may account for the lower turn-over – of one-third – in recent Hungarian elections, and for the falling rate in Poland.[76]

The effectiveness of elections as agents of political education and socialisation must be assessed in the context of regime objectives. In the Stalinist stage, the overriding objective was to convey a few simple messages and socialise all into compliant behaviour; convictions were of secondary importance. Plebiscitary elections are still geared to and largely succeed in achieving these objectives. Since the late 1950s, however, the socialisation goals of those states which retain plebiscitary elections have become more complex. They now incorporate some desire to produce participation based on a conviction that elections truly express popular sovereignty. Measured against such aims, plebiscitary elections fail dismally. Levels of information and interest seem to be low; one Soviet survey found that under 10 per cent of electors knew the names of the candidates they had elected. Czech surveys in 1968 revealed enormous discrepancies between the officially propagated image of elections and popular attitudes; in one national poll only 1 per cent of respondents shared the official view that the existing election system was the best system for the 'democratic' expression of the people's will.[77]

Limited-choice elections are better suited to newer socialisation objectives and seem to do marginally better in achieving them. Research conducted during the Polish elections of 1958 and 1961 showed increasing levels of information and high levels of interest, even though some of the latter should be discounted as the result of conscious effort to give the 'right' answer. Yet what is worrying from the standpoint of newer socialisation objectives is that the polls revealed that under 10 per cent of voters believed in the 'socialist democratic' nature of elections. Even in Hungary and Yugoslavia, where electoral contest is more equal, 'tolerant cynicism' is widespread and it is unlikely that this will be transformed into enthusiastic participation without the introduction of some choice of programmes.[78]

Integration

Even in Communist Party states, which have a whole array of integrating mechanisms at their disposal, elections still perform a useful role.[79] Both types of election enable party leaders to appear as national figures and to appeal to all citizens on a national rather than party-political platform. Election declarations are notable for the care they take to give weight to the achievements and contributions of all groups and for the emphasis they place on their interdependence. Not only are the politically unaffiliated made to feel equal to their Communist fellows, but, in addition, attention is paid to those groups distanced from the centre by their geographical, social, ethnic or spiritual location. In Poland and Hungary, for example, party leaders stress the alliance with the Catholic Church.[80] Elections are fought on a platform uniting organisations representing a wide spectrum of interests and identities, and not by the Communist Party alone.

Integration by way of a public image of unity and equality is accompanied by integration through representation. The main rationale behind the party's guidelines on the composition of candidates is to achieve a balanced and proportional 'mix' of occupational, ethnic and minority groups. The assumption is that the presence of group representatives will assure the identification of all the groups concerned with the election process and the political system as a whole. As the elective offices involved have little political influence, proportional group representation seems a convenient way of furthering integration without jeopardising control.[81]

The flaw in this reasoning is that, for such representation to operate effectively, the groups concerned must feel that they are being given a meaningful say in public affairs. Yet, the more meaningful that say becomes, the greater the risk of its undermining a system of integration based on the principles of democratic centralism.

Integration in states with plebiscitary elections is conceived as a top-down process. The role of an elected representative is primarily to ensure local compliance with central directives and not to press local interests. Accordingly, the ideal representative is a respected and exemplary member of his group, and not a local politician. Indeed, while it is stressed that he should do his best to fulfil constituents' mandates, it is made clear that in any conflict precedence must be given to national interests.[82]

This concept of integration through representation has several weaknesses. First, it produces many deputies and councillors unable to cope with the tasks involved; this in turn contributes to constituents' dissatisfaction with representatives.[83] Second, unless candidates enjoy genuine popular support, their ability to perform linkage and integrating functions is weak. Shared social-group membership is not sufficient for popular support. Czechoslovak, Polish and Yugoslav evidence shows that voters tend to put experience and capacity to represent local interests first.[84]

The logic of the situation leads to a different concept of integration in many limited-choice elections. By giving voters a greater say in selection and a choice of candidates, these elections move from the principle of group membership ordained from above to a more flexible combination of group membership and popular choice. While the deputy or councillor is still urged to place national interests above local ones, there is greater emphasis on his discretion and on the need to harmonise the two, rather than subordinate one to the other. This approach has the potential to produce integration founded on local identity and involvement, but it carries with it the danger that candidates will campaign on a platform of promoting local interests over and above all others. Though controls remain tight, Yugoslav elections show that greater voter choice can produce representatives who foment rather than stem parochialism, thus weakening integration.[85]

Legitimation

Legitimation is by far the most important function performed by elections in these states. In a strict sense, the leading role of the Communist Party is beyond questioning by elections. Nevertheless, they legitimate it in at least two ways. First, as a large proportion of candidates are Communists – 60 to 70 per cent at national level and 40 to 50 per cent at local level – elections constitute a vote of confidence in the Party.[86] Second, elections confer legitimacy on the whole political system, of which the Communist Party is the core. By voting in favour of candidates standing on a single platform, the electorate is said to be voicing its approval of the performance and plans of the party and government. Electoral success is taken to signify not only agreement with plans but also a firm commitment to work for their implementation. Votes are interpreted as the political equivalent of the pledges given by work-forces to fulfil production targets ahead of schedule. Furthermore, the very high votes received by party and government leaders, all of whom stand in parliamentary elections, are interpreted as popular votes of confidence; they can be seen as fulfilling the leaders' psychological need for mass public support.[87]

By conferring legitimacy, elections also make illegitimate any political alternatives. This is particularly important when a regime's overall legitimacy is in doubt. The Hungarian election of 1958 and the Czechoslovak election of 1971 were held with the express purpose of showing that opposition elements had no popular support and that their attacks upon the regime had no substance. In both cases the 99 per cent plus majorities were heralded as conclusive demonstrations of legitimacy, and arguably this had some impact on the domestic and international front.[88]

Plebiscitary elections provide legitimation by a guaranteed and unanimous demonstration of mass support. Insistence on one candidate per seat is a logical part of a concept of elections as primarily acts of affirmation, and only secondarily procedures whereby individuals are selected for office.[89] The legitimacy provided by plebiscitary elections has several weaknesses. First, it may not stand up under pressure. Events in Poland and Hungary in 1956 and in Czechoslovakia in 1968 revealed the lack of legitimacy of regimes with excellent election records. Second, insistence on extremely high levels of electoral support means that any falling below those norms might be dysfunctional. Lastly, it follows from the principle of one candidate per seat that all votes cast against candidates can be seen as votes against the regime.[90]

The legitimation sought in limited-choice elections is of a somewhat different kind; greater importance is attached to the quality of electoral support. Appeals for unanimous support are frequently but not invariably made, but are couched in different terms; rather than reminding voters of their obligation to register support, they ask for approval of the election programme.[91] The introduction of choice between candidates breaks the direct connection between votes against officials and system rejection. But there are also disadvantages. Although all electoral defeats are depicted as reflecting upon only the personal qualities of the candidates concerned, they can negatively affect regime legitimacy, because of official insistence on the indivisibility of the election platform. As has been noted, the introduction of choice between candidates increases rather than siphons off the totally negative votes. Finally, the higher status of popularly elected bodies might weaken the legitimacy of those not formed on that basis, namely party bodies.

The contribution made by elections of both types to regime legitimacy is very minor when compared with other factors, particularly economic performance. Yet the official emphasis on popular sovereignty and the long tradition of holding elections has made them necessary rituals the removal of which, to put their importance in minimal terms, would weaken legitimacy. In situations of economic and political flux their legitimating role increases considerably. The postponement of elections in Hungary in 1956 and in Czechoslovakia in 1968, when it was feared that they would have a negative effect on stability, and their advancement in Poland in 1972, when it was thought they would legitimate a new leadership and a new programme, testify to this.[92]

Influence on public policy

The policy process in all these states is highly bureaucratic and decisions are largely confined to the upper echelons of the party and government. Nevertheless, the last twenty years have seen a certain opening up of policy-making, creating some scope for the expression of popular attitudes toward policies through electoral barometers.[93]

Nomination meetings and meetings between candidates and constituents provide forums for the expression of voters' opinions on matters of local concern. Even in plebiscitary elections, views are aired at such meetings and in canvassing, – on housing, transport and local government performance. The introduction of greater choice stimulates discussion and produces a greater polarisation of opinion, though this still revolves overwhelmingly around local issues.[94] Careful note is taken not only of views expressed at these meetings, but also of complaints and suggestions made to canvassers.[95]

Greater differences between the types of elections emerge from the way in which they communicate public opinion by means of the ballot. In plebiscitary elections the minute levels of absenteeism and votes against are probably of very limited significance to policy-makers. In limited-choice elections, voting reveals a good deal more. In Poland, for instance, patterns of turn-out and negative and selective voting are sufficiently marked to make possible the grouping of regions and cities according to levels of political acceptance.[96] From the policy-makers' standpoint, such data provide some indication or confirmation of the location of conformity and non-conformity. The selection of certain types of candidate reveals something of the attitudes of local voters, and particularly of local activists.

The information derived from campaigns and from voting probably has a very limited effect on local policy; it forms only a small part of a large fund of information which is systematically gathered in all these states by means of sociological surveys as well as by nationwide discussions and organisation reports. Only when election information is corroborated by other sources is it likely to have any policy influence.[97] The most direct impact made by elections has been on electoral policy. The tightening of election regulations in Poland in 1957 and 1960 and their easing in Hungary in 1970 can be attributed in part to the results of preceding elections, as well as to changes in political climate. In terms of general policy, however, only in conditions of political flux have elections made any impression. And even in such situations – Poland in 1954, 1957 and 1972, and Czechoslovakia in 1971 – their influence has been indirect. Elections have been treated as showing certain policy tendencies, and have been used by the party leadership to justify their extension. There is no hard evidence to substantiate Wiatr's contention that Polish elections influence the way in which the country is ruled.[98]

The potential policy influence of elections is restricted by the small extent to which they affect the composition of representative bodies and by the marginal influence exercised over policy by those bodies. This circumscribed scope for influence has been enlarged, however, by several related developments. First, in both types of election, fulfilment of electors' mandates has improved.[99] Second, as a result of limited-choice elections, the presence of greater numbers of constituency-centred and politically-oriented deputies and councillors increases the likelihood of efforts being made to influence policy. Lastly, the chances of such efforts being successful improve with the growth in policy activity of parliamentary and local government bodies.[100]

CONCLUSIONS

All the evidence indicates a general movement towards greater choice. Twenty years ago only two Communist Party states, Yugoslavia and Poland, had limited-choice elections; now five have. Within plebiscitary elections, the scope for voter influence on selection, and for closer links between constituents is growing. Proposals have emerged, at least in the Soviet Union, advocating a transition to limited-choice elections. The likelihood of such a transition depends in part upon the balance of advantages and disadvantages of limited-choice elections. On the plus side, limited choice appears to endow elections with a marginally greater popular interest and credibility. Greater voter say in selection and election tends to produce representatives closer to and better able to serve their constituency. All this can increase the value of the legitimacy conferred by such elections. The list is longer on the minus side. Greater voter and local activist choice means a commensurate loss of central and local executive control and even a certain weakening of party control over the composition of state representative bodies. More importantly, the very existence of electoral choice and contest breaks with the tradition of an indivisible party line.[101] The reality of Hungarian, Polish and especially Yugoslav elections has not always conformed to the official picture of no policy differences or contests. Competition for voters' support has questioned government policy and brought a greater emphasis on local interests. Representatives may be more able, but by the same token they are also more capable of weakening executive control.

At first sight, the minuses seem to outweigh the pluses, yet many of the drawbacks appear formidable only if one assumes a static political system. Over the past twenty years Communist Party states have evolved in the direction of less rigid central control and greater provision for the regularised expression of interests. Yet such provisions have been insufficient to relieve the mounting pressure under which these regimes have to operate. Partly because of the lack of opportunity to exercise any political choice, there has been an overwhelming concentration on economic choice. The extractive attitude of the mass of the population towards party and government stems in part from its feeling of political powerlessness. As material expectations of voters rise faster than the capacity to satisfy them, so these regimes are likely to seek new ways in which to divert these pressures.[102]

Real electoral choice might create some feeling of political efficacy and thus reduce pressure on the centre. Limited-choice elections have failed to do this because they do not go far enough. By attempting to combine electoral choice with a monolithic policy platform, these elections have brought many of the disadvantages of competition without the considerable benefits accruing from the institutional expression of popular choice.[103]

It was this line of reasoning that lay behind the Czechoslovak Communist Party's proposals of 1968, outlining a system which would maintain the leading role of the party but also offer voters a choice of policies. This choice was limited by the stipulation that all candidates had to stand on a National Front platform, ruling out all those advocating non-socialist policies or questioning the party's leading role. Within these bounds, all parties and organisations were to campaign on their own behalf. All were entitled to put up as many candidates as there were seats in the multi-member constituencies; most of these seats were to be allocated by proportional representation to candidates standing on organisation and party platforms, and the rest were to go to those candidates standing as individuals who polled the highest number of votes.[104]

The Czechoslovak scheme is important because it constitutes the only really coherent proposal for Communist electoral reform which goes beyond limited choice. Even though the scheme is a logical projection of limited-choice elections, it cannot be put forward as the only possible next stage of development. The scheme emerged in specific political conditions and was meant to serve only for a period of political transition, after which it was hoped that insistence on the leading role of the party would be unnecessary. Subsequent electoral development was to depend on the evolution of the political situation and the political system.[105] This scenario underlines a point of cardinal importance: elections in all Communist Party states reflect political realities there: evolution is therefore totally dependent on the direction of developments within the political system as a whole.

10 Is Choice Enough? Elections and Political Authority

RICHARD ROSE

Electoral choice is not the only political institution of value, nor is choice an unambiguous good to be pursued at all times and by all means. Just as subjects of a one-party state can complain of too little choice when they troop to the polls, so citizens of Denmark or the Netherlands may complain of too much choice, when they learn that their collective ballots have returned ten to fourteen parties to their national parliaments. Multi-party competition carried to this extreme is alleged to produce weak government through a coalition of parties so numerous that they can have few positive policies or goals in common. Yet there are also times when a two-party system can be criticised for offering the 'wrong' choice, as in the First Austrian Republic between the wars. Its two-party system offered the alternatives of a clerical and authoritarian Christian Social Party or an embattled Austro-Marxist Social Democrat Party – with Pan-German Nationalists a small and even more extreme third party. Sometimes, both faults – 'too much choice' and the 'wrong' choices – can be combined, as in the Fourth French Republic, where half a dozen or more parties could claim seats in the National Assembly, and at times the anti-regime Gaullists and Communists were the two largest parties.

In a study devoted to elections without choice, it is important to emphasise the conditions and limit of electoral choice. These are usually taken for granted in Western countries, where classical elections and fully legitimate governments are found together. This is not the case in most parts of the world today. The alternative to the governing party is often a 'disloyal' opposition. Electoral defeat does not mean a change of office-holders within established institutions, but rather, the overthrow of the existing regime. Instead of looking forward to the swing of the pendulum returning them to office, defeated office-holders may anticipate the knock on the door that heralds imprisonment for 'crimes against the state', or the flight in the night, when exile is a better choice than imprisonment or even death.

The central concern of every political system, however its leaders are chosen, is the exercise of political authority. The authority of government reflects two complementary characteristics: compliance with the basic political laws of the state, and voluntary consent for the institutions of government – that is, the constitutional regime.[1] If the government enjoys popular consent, and citizen compliance, it is a *fully legitimate* authority. From Finland and Austria to New Zealand and Australia, this is normally the case where classical elections prevail. If governors find themselves without full consent and unable to get their subjects to comply with their decrees, then their authority is *repudiated*, and their regime is consigned to the wastebin of history. The Western as well as the non-Western world has seen many regimes repudiated in the twentieth century. Their successors too face problems of how to win consent and compliance. In the politically uncertain circumstances of a newly installed regime, most politicians will seek compliance first. If they can get their subjects to do what they are told, they will establish *coercive* authority. If they win support without compliance, then at best the regime will be *isolated* from its subjects, a position hard to sustain anywhere in the world today, even in African and Middle Eastern societies where loyalty to nominal rulers was once given, as long as rulers remained remote, making few demands upon those they claimed to govern.

The prime choice facing governors in most parts of the world today is not how to conduct elections but how to maintain such authority as they have or aspire to. If orderly compliance with their wishes comes first, then they will turn to the civilian bureaucracy, the police and the army, to make sure that subjects do what is expected of them. To supplement these forces, governors may use the mass media and a mobilising party to disseminate a traditional or imported ideology justifying their rule. Control of economic resources can be used to bribe people to do what government commands. By comparison with these techniques, elections appear of secondary importance in making people do what they are told. But the problem is not so simple, for the most economical way to make people obey government is to have them comply of their own volition. If government has popular consent, citizens will not need to be coerced or bribed to do what government wishes. Even though elections are not necessary to change or confirm the governors of a country, they are nonetheless employed almost everywhere, as a part of the complex efforts of governors in search of that popular consent needed to advance their aspirations to fully legitimate authority. The more consent authority has, the better its rulers can economise on the use of their limited resources for compelling compliance.

The prime choice facing citizens is not how or whether to vote, but, rather, whether to obey the government of the day. In a fully legitimate

Western political system citizens will do so, marking time until they can use their vote to 'throw the rascals out'. Citizens obey a government they vote against, because, when their party wins, they expect those who are on the losing side to accept majority rule too. However, in a country where elections do not determine who governs, a citizen dissatisfied with government can at best hope to remain in isolation, subject only to personal and extra-governmental authorities. If the state is well enough organised to penetrate his town or village, or if local chiefs and landlords are as unattractive as remote authorities, then an individual has but two choices: to rebel, or to be coerced into doing what government wants, while nonetheless refusing his moral consent.

The history of Western nations is replete with examples of groups of people who refused to give their full consent to the demands of established authorities. The American Revolution of 1776, the French Revolution of 1789 and the English Reform Bill of 1832 are landmarks in the development of fully legitimate governments resting on the consent as well as the compliance of the populace. The development of fully legitimate regimes has been marked by the assertion of many claims besides that of 'one man, one vote, one value'. Some grievances of clerical or anti-clerical groups or linguistic or national minorities were not resolved by electoral competition, but by *force majeure*, or the massive migration of peoples in the aftermath of total war. The success of socialist and bourgeois electoral parties has substituted for these non-bargainable value conflicts competition involving 'bargainable' demands that can be resolved by elected governments distributing the fiscal dividend of economic growth.[2] Thus, the politics of post-1945 Western Europe has witnessed the co-incidence of free elections and fully legitimate authority.

Every generalisation about politics requires exceptions, and much can be learned from deviant cases. This chapter examines the role of elections in two atypical parts of countries commonly regarded as paradigm examples of free elections and fully legitimate authority: the United Kingdom and United States. Like it or not, their national governors cannot deny that they have been responsible through the years for the government of Northern Ireland, and of the states of the American Deep South. The resolution of the Irish troubles after the First World War made Northern Ireland a technically subordinate though intermittently insubordinate subject of the Westminster Parliament. Similarly, the Northern victory in the American Civil War and the frustrations of Reconstruction left Washington nominally responsible for actions that it could not control *de facto* in the Deep South. In both places, free elections have been entrenched as firmly as anywhere else in the Anglo-American world. Yet the governments produced by majority rule could not claim fully legitimate authority. Each system has been challenged by a large minority – blacks in the Deep South and Catholics in Northern Ireland – to recognise rights that could not be secured by free elections.

The very different outcome in the Deep South and in Northern Ireland is a cautionary tale of the limits of electoral choice.

A PARADOX OF RIGHTS[3]

The political institutions protecting and advancing the rights of man are multiple, not singular. Citizens of Anglo-American lands rarely discriminate between civil, political and social rights. Yet these rights were not secured all at once, nor is any one necessarily dependent upon the other. The rule of law – the essence of civil rights – was secured centuries before the right to vote was granted to the masses in England. Today, the courts are meant to protect such rights as *habeas corpus* and free speech from the encroachment of executive agencies of elected governments. Political rights are advanced through representative government; elections not only make governments accountable to the governed, but also allow individuals (or, at least, those in the majority) to choose who governs. Social and economic rights, today the primary concern of the governments of mixed economy welfare states, do not depend upon free elections, but, rather, upon economic resources. Even a government elected by a massive electoral majority cannot enable its citizens indefinitely to continue consuming more than they produce. The fact that citizens of Western nations today take all these rights for granted does not mean that they are inevitably in harmony. Of fundamental importance here is the potential conflict between the civil rights guaranteed through the courts, and political rights guaranteed by electoral choice.[4]

Civil rights advanced through the courts and political rights advanced through elections together constitute a fundamental paradox. The decisions of the courts, like the outcome of an election, create losers as well as winners. In an election, the result is meant to be determined by counting heads. The majority wins, and the minority loses. In the courts, by contrast, judges are meant to weigh arguments. The losers in court cases are meant to be identified not by their relative fewness, but by the weakness of their arguments and evidence. The losers in each arena are meant to accept the decision as subjects of a political authority maintaining both electoral and judicial processes. They cannot refuse to recognise election results or the courts without defying political authority.

The right to vote in a free election is regarded as central to democratic government. Denying franchise rights to a substantial proportion of citizens is regarded as morally and politically wrong, something that might have been done by governments before the liberal era dawned, but can no longer be justified. But the grant of universal suffrage does not create 'self' – government, whatever that term could mean in a country of 5, 50 or 200 million people. It secures an individual the right to be governed by politicians chosen by an electoral majority. Universal suffrage does not guarantee the universal distribution of power and influence throughout society; it guarantees no more and no less than *majority* rights.

By contrast, when the law grants justiciable rights to citizens, these are inalienable rights of each individual citizen. These rights cannot be denied an individual by a popular majority. They are prior to or independent of the rights conferred by statute laws passed by elected legislatures. While philosophers, ordinary citizens and governors can differ about specific details, there is agreement in principle that some rights are integral to citizenship. To deny an individual these 'inalienable' rights is to make him a subject inferior to citizens retaining such rights. The doctrine of inalienable rights is given fullest legal expression by the Supreme Court's interpretation of the Bill of Rights of the American Constitution, which accepts that justiciable rights can be *minority* rights. Time and again the court has upheld claims of individuals, as against the collective weight of a government elected by a majority.

So long as majority and minority views are in harmony about actions of government, no problems arise in practice from the logically possible conflict between the franchise rights of the majority and the justiciable rights that may be claimed by individuals in a minority. If these claims are in conflict, then the theoretical paradox becomes an urgent political problem. Means to resolve conflicts between majority and minority claims are needed, short of that implied in the Second Amendment of the United States Constitution: the right of the people to keep and bear arms.

The government produced by free elections need not represent the choice of a majority. The lower the turn-out, the less likely any one party is to win the support of a majority of eligible voters. For example, in 1976 Jimmy Carter was elected President with the support of 27 per cent of Americans eligible to vote. The mechanisms for converting votes into parliamentary seats in the first-past-the-post electoral system of the Anglo-American world can award a majority of seats to a party with less than half the votes. No party has won as many as half the votes at any general election since 1945 in Britain or Canada, and Harry Truman, John F. Kennedy and Richard Nixon each won a Presidential election with less than half the vote. In the extreme case of the October 1974 British general election, Labour won an absolute majority of seats in the House of Commons with only 39·2 per cent of the popular vote, and in February 1974 it won office even though it had fewer votes than its Conservative opponents. In most countries of the Western world, proportional representation gives parties parliamentary seats approximately in proportion to their electoral strength, but the multiplicity of parties prevents any single party from winning half the popular vote. At only fifteen of 201 elections in twenty-two Western nations in the period 1945–75 did one party win as much as half the vote. Majority-rule government results from the mechanics of electoral systems converting one party's claim to less than half the vote into more than half the parliamentary seats, or from negotiations between parties in parliament leading to a majority coalition.[5]

If voting is to constitute government by a majority, at least four conditions must be met: (1) the ballot must concern membership in bodies that take politically important decisions; (2) a choice of candidates must be offered; (3) citizens must be able to vote without intimidation; and (4) the ballots must be honestly counted and converted into representative mandates in a 'not too disproportional' manner.

Voters who find themselves in a minority at a given election are not, *ipso facto*, deprived of influence.

(1) Power may alternate between the two largest parties seeking votes. If this condition is fulfilled, then a given majority will enjoy 100 per cent of the power, but not for 100 per cent of the time. By the law of anticipated reactions, the government of the day may be sensitive to an electoral minority's wishes, for fear that it may soon find itself in a minority.

(2) A social group that is too small by itself to constitute an electoral majority may join a coalition with others, bargaining support for its own wishes in exchange for endorsing interests of other members of the coalition, as agrarian parties have done in coalition governments in Scandinavia.

(3) Constitutional provisions can require more than a simple majority to approve constitutional amendments; or a bicameral legislature with an upper house representing a constituency different from that of a popularly elected lower house may be required to concur in legislation.

(4) The dispersion of power among popularly elected central, regional and local authorities can give groups that are a minority nationwide a majority in a number of local jurisdictions.

(5) A constitution may stipulate communal electoral roles, so that the votes of some social groups, typically minorities, are counted separately, thus allowing the direct election of their own representatives.

(6) Groups of voters in an electoral minority may find that cultural norms such as proportionalism[6] encourage the government to provide something for everybody, including groups too small to enjoy electoral influence.

The bulk of the mechanisms by which minorities may gain influence through elections are contingent, rather than certain. They operate only if political conditions are appropriate; they cannot be enjoined by court order. The swing of the electoral pendulum is at the discretion of voters, and the construction of winning coalitions is determined by party leaders and indirectly by voters. The power of minorities in local jurisdictions of unitary or federal states depends upon their geographical dispersion and numbers. Positive cultural attitudes favouring power-sharing with minorities may not be held to the extent that minorities might wish. Communal electoral roles ensure small groups some representation, but they may be used to manufacture a legislative majority for a minority, as in Rhodesia, or leave a minority politically weak because numerically weak, as with the Maoris in New Zealand. Requiring a more-than-majority vote gives a veto power to a minority, but, the higher the threshold, the greater the discrimination against the majority. In the extreme case of the old Polish Sejm, the principle of *liberum veto* allowed one member to determine the outcome by voting against the wishes of every other member of the Assembly.

Most nations in the world today provide a catalogue of rights in their constitutions,[7] but constitutional dicta do not *ipso facto* ensure citizen rights. Much else must happen if the will and whim of a government is to be regulated on behalf of minorities or individual citizens. In the first place, enumerated rights must be justiciable rights, that is, individuals can secure them through the courts. To have a right without a remedy is to have something of little value. This is particularly the case where civil rights are concerned, because the denial of the right to vote or freedom of speech cannot be justified by economic scarcity. Second, individuals must have access to the courts. In part, this is a matter of procedure; individuals must be allowed to bring suits to defend or advance rights and not be solely dependent upon the discretionary decisions of the government's own law officers. It is also a matter of resources: it costs money to bring law suits, and aggrieved citizens need competent legal assistance to press claims through the courts. Third, judges must follow rules of law when deciding cases, and not simply echo the views of the government of the day. There is little value in an aggrieved party marshalling overwhelming evidence and precedents, only to find the judge pronouncing the opposite. To stipulate that judges should follow the law is not to assert a discredited yardstick theory of a written constitution. It is to treat laws, legal procedures, previous decisions and dissents as rules of a game. If legislators can be expected to temper short-term partisan advantage by respect for unwritten legislative norms, one can equally expect judges, men much more creatures of custom, convention and rules, to attend to the rules of their game.

The decisions rendered in courts of law are not taken in ignorance of majority views, but it is going too far to say, as Mr Dooley alleged, that the Supreme Court follows the election returns. It would be fairer to say that justices are not ignorant of the political climate of the day, including the views of articulate opinion-leaders, whose voices carry political weight well beyond their number. Judges are often drawn from the ranks of former elected office-holders or are appointed by elected office-holders. The fact that judges are usually not elected does not make them non-political.

The procedures of the courts, and the adversary trial of cases emphasise disagreements about what rights an individual may have in a particular case. In multi-member courts, disputes between judges result in split decisions and controversial dissents or concurring opinions. Inconsistency of decisions at one or different levels of a judicial system emphasises that the law, at a given place and moment, is only what a majority of judges say it is. In balancing influences external to the legal system and those internal to it, a judge has many incentives to follow the practice of other self-governing professions and be most sensitive to professional influences, including decisions of superior courts. Because his peers apply legal criteria, the pressures that most immediately affect a judge will be pressures to think in terms of rules of law rather than majority rule.

When all the qualifications are stated, the central paradox remains: whereas minorities must always lose in an elected assembly, in a court of law the claims of members of a minority are equal to those of a popular majority. In a representative assembly, minorities must normally expect to suffer from vote reversal; the law is the opposite of that for which the minority votes. A minority, whether 1 per cent, 10 per cent or 49 per cent, has 0 per cent influence. The decision rules of the courts assume, in the Anglo-American system at least, a formal equality of plaintiff and defendant, or even a bias in favour of the individual defendant in criminal cases where the state is the plaintiff. The case – and not the numerical size of the parties to it – is meant to determine the outcome.

In a conflict between electoral preferences and rules of law, a vote-maximising politician has a well-defined role: he is expected to articulate majority opinion. A judge likewise has a clear role: he is expected to articulate rules of law. From this it follows that minority groups concerned with defending their rights should place justiciable rights before electoral rights. 'One man, one vote, one value' threatens electoral defeat to minorities. But 'Equal justice under law' can lead to victory in another political arena.

JUSTICIABLE RIGHTS BEFORE MAJORITY RIGHTS

For generations up to the Second World War, black Americans in the Deep South had effectively been denied both justiciable rights and franchise rights, notwithstanding their nominal status as citizens. The reasons for this can be traced directly back to slavery, the military victory of the North in the Civil War of 1861–5, and the political failure of Reconstruction afterwards. This left the Deep South a part of the United States in international law, but domestically exercising 'peculiar' or 'irregular' customs to maintain white supremacy. The autonomy of American states, in electoral legislation and in criminal law enforcement and non-enforcement, as well as in electoral legislation, gave great scope for the states of the Deep South – Alabama, Georgia, Louisiana, Mississippi and South Carolina – to develop electoral institutions specially suited to maintain white supremacy, albeit often discriminating against poor whites as well as blacks.[8]

Southerners maintained free elections in which one party, the 'lilywhite' Democratic Party, was always assured of victory. The mechanisms were multiple. First, of all, by legal or extralegal means, blacks were usually excluded from registering to vote. Second, blacks were not allowed to vote in the primary election of the Democratic Party, which was regarded as a 'club' activity, not an election in which any citizen could vote. The use of a 'run off' second primary, reducing the field to two contestants, like the second *tour* in France, was a further barrier against an intense minority winning because of fragmentation of the rest of the vote. Whites coalesced around a single candidate for each office at the general election. Their majority status guaranteed them victory so long as they remained united.

The crucial steps on the road to black citizenship in the Deep South were taken through the courts, rather than the ballot box. With financial and legal support from the North, blacks entered United States federal courts asking the courts to grant them their rights as federal citizens, and declare null and void practices endorsed time and again by a majority of voters in the home state. In so doing, the blacks were not defying authority, but rather the reverse: they were asking the federal government in Washington to come out of its splendid isolation, and enforce the equal-rights clauses of the United States Constitution in the hardest parts of the Deep South. Beginning in 1938 with *Missouri ex rel Gaines*, the Supreme Court consistently found in favour of black claims to justiciable rights.[9] The doctrine of segregation was finally declared unconstitutional in 1954.

At no point did blacks claim that they wished the court to do 'what the people wanted'. Survey evidence indicates that a majority of Americans did not want blacks to have the rights that the courts were prepared to grant. In its 1954 decision promoting integration, the court was going against, rather than following, the views of the white majority.[10] Black lawsuits declared that the courts should not allow representatives of an electoral majority to pass laws violating inalienable rights guaranteed to each citizen. While lawyers and judges disagreed about the definition of claimed rights in particular cases, they shared a belief that such rights had priority over the views of the elected government of the day.

Among the many rights that blacks sought through the courts was the right to vote. In 1957 Martin Luther King Jr proclaimed, 'Give us the ballot and we will no longer have to worry the federal government about our basic rights.'[11] To gain the vote blacks had to turn to the courts, first winning the right to vote in the white primaries, and then compelling voting officials to allow blacks to register and cast their votes, free from intimidation and gerrymandering. Congress was lobbied to pass laws giving blacks easier and stronger grounds on which to appeal to federal courts against discrimination by local election officials in the Deep South. Major demonstrations in the Deep South concentrated nationwide attention upon the denial of the ballot; the brutal means sometimes used to break up these demonstrations won blacks wide sympathy outside the South. They were not perceived as radicals seeking to overturn the political order, but rather as loyal citizens, demanding what white citizens already enjoyed – namely, the right to vote. The cycle of judicial litigation and pressure-group action was repeated in other fields: most notably, school desegregation.

Black success in winning voting rights in the Deep South has confirmed a basic proposition of majority rule: that minorities lose. From 1960 to 1971, the number of blacks registered to vote in each of the states of the Deep South rose greatly, reaching a level only 12 per cent below that of the whites. At the same time, however, the number of whites registered to vote also increased. In four out of five states, more whites than blacks were added to the electoral register. Overall, an extra 1,181,000 blacks were registered – and an additional 1,958,000 whites. Even if blacks registered in as high a proportion as whites, nowhere in the Deep South would blacks constitute as much as one-third of a state's electorate – yet over half the vote is needed for victory.

In consequence of the minority status of blacks, whites have continued to win all state-wide races for the governorship and Senate seats in the Deep South. The basic principle of franchise rights – 'One man, one vote, one value' – is the cause. In the words of a civil-rights document: 'This is usually a matter of demography: there are more whites than blacks.'[12] Blacks can and do win elections where a constituency is small enough to enable a group that is a minority in the state as a whole to be a local majority. This happens most often in small towns or rural counties, but only occasionally in Congressional districts with half a million residents.

When whites are divided, blacks can effectively exert electoral influences. For example, in 1976 the almost even division of the white vote between President Ford and Jimmy Carter made it possible for blacks (or, for that matter, Catholics or Jews) to claim that their support represented the winner's margin of victory. But in 1972 blacks could not elect George McGovern President, even though 86 per cent of blacks voted for the Democratic candidate. With 66 per cent of the white vote, Richard Nixon won a landslide victory.[13]

Court actions upholding the rights of the black minority have been of crucial importance in changing the behaviour of elected white politicians in the Deep South. To win election to major or minor offices, white candidates had to fall in line with white-supremacy doctrines. To do otherwise was to risk being 'out-segged' by an opponent and defeated (that is, made to appear weak in segregation before a pro-segregation electorate). Judicial decisions favouring blacks challenged the readiness of white Southerners (and such Presidents as Dwight D. Eisenhower and John F. Kennedy) to support the law of the land. Southern politicians, as much as Presidents, were sworn to uphold the law of the land. Particularly where election returns and state laws as well as *mores* favoured segregation, it was not easy to change the habits of a lifetime. But the courts gave elected politicians a spur to act, and a rationale for doing what the majority of their voters did *not* want done. Desegregation was gradually accepted in the Deep South, because, however unpopular it was with the majority, it was the law of the land.

'YOU HAVE NO RIGHTS'[14]: NORTHERN IRELAND

Ulster Catholics have not had the choice of strategies available to Southern blacks, for the unwritten Constitution of the United Kingdom does not grant individuals justiciable civil or political rights. The rights that an Englishman claims to enjoy are simply cultural standards generalised from customary behaviour. As long as nothing is done contrary to his expectations, no problem arises. But, if the government acts contrary to what he regards as his rights, an Englishman cannot expect the courts to defend them, so long as the government of the day is acting in accord with an ordinary Act of Parliament. The central doctrine of the British Constitution is that Parliament is sovereign; neither the courts nor a previous Act of Parliament can set aside any executive action authorised by the government of the day. Since the government of the day has the power to pass retrospective legislation (even after a court has ruled that it has done something without statutory authorisation), there is no effective limitation upon what a government can do and then claim authorisation for. In the view of Sir Leslie Scarman, a prominent English jurist,

> When times are normal and fear is not stalking the land, English law sturdily protects the freedom of the individual and respects human personality. But when times are abnormally alive with fear and prejudice, the common law is at a disadvantage: it cannot resist the will, however frightened and prejudiced it may be, of Parliament. . . . It is the helplessness of the law in face of the legislative sovereignty of Parliament which makes it difficult for the legal system to accommodate the concept of fundamental and inviolable human rights.[15]

In Northern Ireland, Protestants have rested their political power upon free elections, for Protestants constitute two-thirds of the population, and Catholics only one-third. The Unionist Party was the organisation maintaining majority rule. It won a sweeping majority of seats at every election held for the Stormont Parliament during its fifty-one years of life (1921–72). It did so by campaigning to defend the union of Northern Ireland with Great Britain, attacking its Catholic opponents for wanting Northern Ireland to become a part of a united Ireland governed from Dublin. Instead of a 'white primary', the Unionists relied upon the all-

Protestant Orange Order to scrutinise the political orthodoxy of its candidates. In its half-century of existence, the Unionist Party never nominated or elected a Catholic to Parliament, and normally all Cabinet ministers were Orangemen. The Catholic complaints of archaic local election laws and the gerrymandering of local electoral boundaries in such places as the City of Londonderry were *prima facie* reasonable. But Catholics could be in a majority in Derry only because the city constituted less than four per cent of the total population of Northern Ireland. So predictable were election results, because of the correlation of religion and party loyalties, that anything from 38 to 63 per cent of the seats at Stormont were uncontested. In the words of one Northern Ireland scholar, this was to be expected, for 'there is no floating vote on the Constitutional issue'.[16]

The application of the winner-take-all Westminster election formula to Northern Ireland meant that the government of the province was always in the hands of an exclusively Unionist (and Protestant) cabinet, as long as it was based upon majority rule. As in Westminster, there was no provision for the judicial review of the government's actions. And, as at Westminster, party patronage was exercised by the government to reward its own supporters, and give only token representation to its opponents.

Debarred from winning a majority of votes or winning minority rights through the courts, Catholics in Northern Ireland had a range of unpalatable alternatives. They could emigrate to a secular society, where Ireland's age-old divisions were of little consequence; over the years hundreds of thousands went to England, America and Australia. They could seek non-political substitutes, whether in a religious life or in careers freely open to the minority outside government – for instance, medicine, teaching in Catholic schools, bookmaking or keeping a pub. In theory, Catholics could reject the Irish identity that customarily went with their religion – but few wished to do so, and those that did won no influence with Unionist governments and had difficulty maintaining a political position within the Catholic community. Voting could promise victory only if the six counties of Northern Ireland were merged with the twenty-six counties of the Republic of Ireland, thus placing Catholic Irishmen in a three-to-one majority against Protestant Britons. But Irish unity could not come about through the ballot box so long as votes were counted on a six-county basis only. Moreover, Protestants in Northern Ireland were prepared to fight to maintain independence of Dublin, as Southern Irish Catholics had fought from 1916 to 1921 to win independence from a United Kingdom Parliament in which the majority did not wish to recognise a separate Irish state.

In 1968, in emulation of Southern blacks, Ulster Catholics turned to street protests to demand civil rights, including 'one man, one vote, one value'. No reference was made by the Northern Ireland Civil Rights Association to a putative right to Irish unity. Catholic protesters regarded their actions as technically illegal, but not as immoral. In Britain many, including members of the British Labour government, sympathised with this view. But the elected government of Northern Ireland at Stormont met illegal demonstrations with police action reinforced by Protestant vigilantes defending a government elected by a majority of the voters. The resulting intercommunal clashes led to the introduction of British troops in August 1969, to impose a 'peace line' between the majority and the minority.

The British government's policy was to neutralise the conflict by removing power from the elected Protestant government, without giving power to Catholics. But the Labour government could not claim to be acting 'above' party politics, as judges do. If a justiciable Bill of Rights had existed in Northern Ireland, as it did in the Deep South, then Westminster and elected Unionist government at Stormont, like white-supremacist governors in Alabama and Mississippi, might have managed to maintain the confidence of their voters, while making concessions to Catholics, by explaining that 'the law' meant that majorities could not have everything their own way. But Protestant or Catholic politicians elected by Ulstermen to Stormont did not feel themselves bound by the wishes or recommendations of politicians elected from British constituencies to the British House of Commons.

In default of constitutional channels of action (including 'slightly constitutional' street demonstrations), the gun once again came out in Ulster politics. In February 1971 the Irish Republican Army, pledged to the unification of Ireland 'by all means necessary', started a guerilla war by shooting British soldiers. In August 1971 Stormont government, backed by British Army manpower, introduced internment, arresting more than 300 Catholics on suspicion of anti-state activities, holding them indefinitely without charge or *habeas corpus*. Catholics who wished to protest such measures through the courts could do little. A few went to Strasbourg, to lodge complaints about torture under the European Convention of Human Rights. The plaintiffs at the European court, supported by the Irish government, won their case, but by the time they did so, in 1976, victory was empty. Republicans refused to recognise British courts; they preferred to make their protest known by force of arms. Bombings and shootings escalated greatly after internment, as many Catholics turned from passive compliance to active opposition to authority, violently or through such devices as a rent and rates strike.

In March 1972 the British government revoked the Constitution of the Northern Ireland government, abolishing Stormont and substituting direct rule by the British Cabinet in its place. This brought about the arming and drilling of tens of thousands of Protestant Loyalists to protect majority views that could no longer be advanced by a popularly elected Stormont government. The internal war became three-sided, with British, Irish Republican and Loyalist forces all in action. The death toll from shootings and bombings reached 467 in 1972 in land of 1·5 million people, the equivalent of 16,000 deaths in Britain, or 64,000 in a country the size of the United States. By the end of 1976, it stood at nearly 1700 dead.

British politicians thrust in to govern Northern Ireland without any claim to local electoral support quickly sought to reconstitute a directly elected government in Northern Ireland with Catholic as well as Protestant support. To encourage a biconfessional majority, it mandated upon Northern Ireland proportional representation by the single transferable vote. Proportional representation does not guarantee minorities more rights than the customary first-past-the-post British ballot. What it does is to make it much more difficult for any one party to win a majority of seats in an elected assembly. The British government gambled that proportional representation would split Protestant representation so that there would be a substantial bloc in favour of power-sharing and needing Catholic support in order to form a ruling coalition. As a further assurance of a power-sharing government of Protestants and Catholics, the decision about the formation of a new executive was placed in the hands of a British Cabinet minister, directed to transfer power back to Northern Ireland only if a biconfessional executive was formed. In effect, a Westminster majority was prepared to veto the formation of a Northern Ireland government backed by a clear electoral majority in the province but not wishing to share power with a Catholic minority.

The British attempt to make a government failed, for power-sharing parties could not win a majority of votes. About nine-tenths of Protestant electors voted for Loyalist parties opposed to sharing power with the Catholic minority, thus ensuring, even under proportional representation, an absolute majority at Stormont against Westminster's wishes. In the five elections held in the period 1970–5 for Stormont and Westminster representation, the Unionist–Loyalist bloc won between 61 and 64 per cent of the total vote; Catholic candidates, primarily standing for the Social Democratic Labour Party (SDLP) won 24 to 30 per cent of the vote; and biconfessional parties accounted for the few remaining votes.[17]

Twice the British government has sought to impose its wishes upon a majority of elected Ulster representatives. In 1974 it temporarily succeeded in establishing a power-sharing executive under Brian Faulkner, who had blurred the Unionist Party's stand when fighting the 1973 Assembly election. As soon as he made evident his willingness to share power with the SDLP, Faulkner was deposed as party leader. The Executive fell in May 1974, in the face of a successful general strike by Loyalist workers. The 'revolutionary' demand of the political strikers was for an immediate general election. The British government refused to test the popularity of the power-sharing Executive that it had made; and it also refused to use British troops in defence of its authority.[18]

To fill the vacuum created by the fall of the Executive, Westminster authorised a Northern Ireland Constitutional Convention. The Convention was to be freely elected by proportional representation, but its members were not to be free to recommend what the majority wished. Instead, the Convention was enjoined to produce a power-sharing Constitution. The 1975 Convention election gave Loyalists opposed to power-sharing an unambiguous majority of forty-seven out of seventy-eight seats. The majority promptly proceeded to recommend a Constitution based upon familiar Westminster practices, especially the doctrine that the party winning a majority of seats in Parliament deserves 100 per cent of the seats in Cabinet. The Convention report was rejected by Westminster; it was prepared to use its majority in Great Britain to veto the recurrence of any indigenous representative government in the province. It could not claim to represent Northern Ireland as well as Great Britain, for the Conservative and Labour parties are now unwilling to contest parliamentary seats there.

The inability of the British government to recognise *any* kind of rights in Northern Ireland explains its inconsistencies and successive failures. In 1968–9, while sympathising with Catholic protesters, a Labour government was unwilling to admit that the Catholic minority had 'inalienable' rights enforceable at law, or to suggest alternatives to extra-legal protest by which the minority could advance its claims.[19] In 1973–5, successive Conservative and Labour governments were unwilling to recognise majority rights. Elections demonstrated the majority wish for a Loyalist government without power-sharing, but the British government insisted that no government could be formed that did not incorporate SDLP members (representing one-quarter of the vote). As violence has continued, the British government has even lost interest in maintaining its right to exercise coercive political authority, negotiating a political truce with the Provisional IRA in 1975. The truce was followed by the intensification of civil war in which Ulsterman killed Ulsterman, while the nominal sovereign power could secure neither a fully legitimate nor an effectively coercive regime.

CHOICE WITHOUT CONSENT

The problems of governing Northern Ireland highlight the difficulty of exercising political authority far better than do the problems of governing England, or a United States where blacks now enjoy the rights of citizens. The issues about which Ulstermen fight today are those that traditionally divided and disrupted political authority: religion, national identity, language and race. These issues challenge authority, because the claims of differing races, religions, linguistic and ethnic groups are 'zero-sum'. What one side wins, the other loses, and no party to the dispute is prepared to accept defeat, whether in an election or in a court of law.

Full legitimacy, resting upon the freely given consent and compliance of citizens, is a distant ideal in most countries discussed in this book. In such lands, to hold free elections along classical lines would not increase authority, but destroy it, in so far as elections would only reveal the intensity of divisions within society. Free elections *follow*, rather than precede, the establishment of legitimate authority. When full legitimacy is lacking, a ballot can only measure the extent and intensity of divisions within the society.

The governors of non-Western nations do not have the choice of advancing majority rights through elections, or minority rights through judicial action, for both electoral institutions and justiciable rights are usually alien, recent and weak within their territory. Ethnocentric Westerners should not be surprised by this if they reflect upon how recent is the establishment of representative institutions and civil rights within European states.

The maintenance of some authority is the immediate problem facing politicians in countries where the regime itself is as uncertain as those established in the wave of decolonisation in the 1960s. To say that governors have a choice between survival and repudiation may be optimistic, because it implies that a new regime is not necessarily doomed to prompt repudiation. Where authority is uncertain, governors will look for compliance before consent. In this search, they will look first to institutions of order – the bureaucracy, the police and the military – rather than to representative institutions.

The chapters of this volume illustrate that these concerns need not be mutually exclusive. The very fact that an election is held, even without choice, is a tribute, however hypocritical, to the idea of government by consent. If Western politicians sometimes risk estrangement from voters who have effective power to dismiss them from office, the risk run by governors in one-party states is even greater. The need to mobilise voters is a test of the efficiency of the local political apparatus of the party. In so far as blank or void ballots are cast, even a 6 per cent show of opposition can be a warning signal to governors who have few reliable means of assessing popular evaluation of their government, short of revolt. The weaker the party and the stronger the clientelistic networks of a society, the more important an election is as an effective constraint upon central authority. The territorial nature of contests call attention to the importance of local leaders 'outside' the institutions of the regime.

Even within the confines of a one-party state, an election can stimulate a modicum of competition, if incumbent candidates for elective office can be rejected at the nomination stage. If the ballot is for membership in a body like the Soviet Parliament, with little or no real political power, competition for nomination is of no consequence. But Tanzania illustrates how intra-party competition for office can be used by a national leader of a one-party state to encourage responsiveness of members of parliament.

The study of elections without choice is much more than a collection of curious and pathological political information. It is one of the few readily available methods that we have for observing a classic problem of political authority – the relationship between governors and governed – in regimes where authority cannot be taken for granted, and the mechanisms for coercing subjects or insulating governors from potential rebels are often opaque.

While only a limited number of countries in the world today are fully legitimate, even fewer maintain order solely by coercion, or are in a state of civil war, like Northern Ireland. The majority of the world's governments do not depend primarily upon elections for registering consent; nor can they claim full legitimacy. Instead, they wish to claim some authority. By holding elections without choice, they recognise both the need for a positive response from subjects – whether freely given or coerced – as a condition of continuance of their authority. By refusing to admit competition, they also emphasise that the choice is not one of changing governors within an established political regime, but, rather, one of maintaining or repudiating established authority.

Notes

PREFACE

1. See Charles L. Taylor and Michael C. Hudson, *The World Handbook of Political and Social Indicators*, 2nd edition (New Haven: Yale University Press, 1972) Table 2.9.
2. For a comparative worldwide analysis distinguishing functions of elections for voters and whole systems, see Richard Rose and Harvé H. Mossawir Jr, 'Voting and Elections: A Functional Analysis' *Political Studies*, xv, no. 2 (1967).
3. Cynical democratic politicians can still be heard privately echoing the judgement that the musician Carl Maria von Weber gave of the public: 'Each individual is an ass, but the whole is the voice of God.' See Norman Del Mar, *Richard Strauss: A Critical Commentary on his Life and Works*, vol. III (London: Barrie and Jenkins, 1972) p. 188.
4. For a sweeping view of the evolution of these institutions and their political consequences, see Stein Rokkan, *Citizens, Elections, Parties* (Oslo: Universitetsforlaget, 1970).
5. F. W. S. Craig, *British Parliamentary Election Results, 1885-1918* (London: Macmillan, 1974) pp. 584-5.

CHAPTER I

1. For Samuel P. Huntington, 'democracy exists where the principal leaders of a political system are selected by competitive elections in which the bulk of the population have the opportunity to participate' – *Authoritarian Politics in Modern Society*, ed. S. P. Huntington and C. R. Moore (New York: Basic Books, 1970) p. 509. For Robert A. Dahl, 'polyarchy also requires that the principal limit on entrance into a position of political leadership, must be inability to win elections' – R. A. Dahl and C. E. Lindblom, *Politics, Economics and Welfare* (New York; Harper and Row, 1957) p. 315. Marx himself seemed to anticipate this point of view when he affirmed, 'Universal suffrage is the equivalent of political power for the working class of England' – 'The Chartists', *New York Daily Tribune*, 25 Aug 1852, cited in T. B. Bottomore, *Elites and Society* (London, C. A. Watts, 1964) p. 39.
2. The only thing which can make up for the handicap of those who are less gifted, and of those who are poor in economic, intellectual or political terms.
3. See above, note 1.

4. Marx, *La Guerre civile en France*, 1871 (Paris: Editions Sociales, 1968) p. 214; see also pp. 260 – 1 and 301, introduction by Engels to the German edition of 1891.

5. Antonio Gramsci, *Passato e Presente* (Turn: Einaudi, 1952) pp. 158–9.

6. Quoted in Bottomore, *Elites and Society*, p. 5.

7. Joseph A Schumpeter, *Capitalism, Socialism and Democracy*, 2nd edition, (New York: Harper and Brothers, 1947) p. 282.

8. A. Downs, *An Economic Theory of Democracy* (New York: Harper and Brothers, 1967) p. 295. Schumpeter (*Capitalism, Socialism and Democracy*, p. 38, note 7) quotes the witticism of a politician who says that 'what businessmen don't understand is that, just as they run on oil, I run on votes'.

9. For fuller documentation than can be given here, see Richard Rose, 'On the Priorities of Citizenship in the Deep South and Northern Ireland', *Journal of Politics*, XXXVIII (1976) 247–91.

10. The criteria of delimitation used here are simplified to the utmost. They leave open the degree of control exercised by the state and the differences which exist between the processes of direction and those of coercion. Neither do they take into account what one might call the positive criteria of non-classical elections, which would refer to the intrinsic characteristics of these elections, rather than to their definition *a contrario* by comparing them with free and competitive ballots. Positive criteria should be related to the ideological content of the different categories of non-classical elections, to the machinery of domination, social exclusion or mobilisation, to the historical stages to which they correspond, to the cultural substrata which condition them, and so on.

11. The clientelist dimension of non-classical elections is not considered in this chapter.

12. See *Authoritarian Politics*, ed. Huntington and Moore, p. 15; K. F. Johnson, *Mexican Democracy* (Boston: Allyn and Bacon, 1971) p. 20.

13. The pre-1974 Portuguese regime used both literacy qualifications for the electorate and temporary tolerance of some form of opposition in the elections.

14. J. Wiatr, 'Elections and Voting Behavior in Poland', in *Essays on the Behavioral Study of Politics*, ed. A. Ranney (Urbana, Ill.: University of Illinois Press, 1962) p. 251.

15. This remark does not mean that the more qualitative Nuffield-style analysis of elections is less valuable than American and French electoral sociology for the study of fully competitive ballots.

16. See the suggestive facts on the predominance of 'non-classical' elections collected in R. Rose and H. Mossawir, 'Voting and Elections: A Functional Analysis', *Political Studies*, XV, no. 2 (1967) 180–2.

17. John S. Saul, 'The Nature of Tanzania's Political System: Issues Raised by the 1965 and 1970 Elections', *Journal of Commonwealth Political Studies*, X, no. 2 (July 1972) 113–29; Goran Hyden and Colin Leys, 'Elections and Politics in Single-Party Systems: The Case of Kenya and Tanzania', *British Journal of Political Science*, II, no. 4 (Oct 1972), 389–420; J. D. Barkan and J. J. Okumu, 'Political Linkage in Kenya: Citizens, Local Elites and Legislators', report presented to the 70th Annual Assembly of the American Political Science Association, 1974; Denis Martin, 'La Houe, la maison, l'urne et le maître d'école: Les élections en Tanzanie, 1965–1970', *Revue française de science politique*, XXV, no. 4 (1975) 677–716.

18. We refer to the Franco regime in Spain, where the democratic process ended in

1936; to the Colonels' regime in Greece; and, to the post-1964 military regime in Brazil.

19. Guy Hermet, 'Electoral Trends in Spain: An Appraisal of the Polls Conducted under the Franco Regime', *Iberian Studies*, III (1974).

20. G. A. Fiechter, *Le Régime modernisateur du Brasil 1964–1972* (Leyden: A. W. Sijthoff, 1972) pp. 220 ff.

21. Hyden and Leys, in *British Journal of Political Science*, II, 401.

22. Quoted in Françoise Cayrac-Blanchard, 'Les Forces politiques indonésiennes et les élections générales de 1971', *Archipel*, IV (1972) 92.

23. Quoted by Martin, in *Revue française de science politique*, XXV, 680. Anti-liberal extreme right theorists like Donoso Cortes or Charles Maurras would accept Nyerere's idea.

24. Always in proportion as the population really believes in election results and its own unanimity. Incidently, non-rigged elections may be more alienating than outrageously fraudulent elections.

25. Saul, in *Journal of Commonwealth Political Studies*, X, no. 2, . One might conclude from these remarks that the anaesthetising effect of elections works best in little-differentiated societies where they bring effective, even if short-lived mobilisation, while it does not have the same capacity in authoritarian regimes established in more industrialised and socially more differentiated societies, where the population keeps aloof from the electoral manipulations of the rulers.

26. Thus the Franco government organised eleven political ballots in twenty-six years, from 1947 to 1973, their frequency increasing to six elections in the period 1966–73. The pre-1974 Portuguese regime held eleven elections in twenty-eight years, from 1945 to 1973, the frequency increasing to four elections in the fifteen-year period 1958–73.

27. See H. Alavi, 'The State in Post-Colonial Societies: Pakistan and Bangladesh', *New Left Review*, 1972, 59–81.

28. These authoritarian situations are not far from the 'capitalist reactionary way' described by Barrington Moore in *Social Origins of Dictatorship and Democracy* (Boston, Mass.: Beacon Press, 1966) p. 599. See in this respect Guy Hermet, 'Dictature bourgeoise et modernisation conservatrice', *Revue française de science politique*, XXV (1975) 1029–61.

CHAPTER 2

1. See Alain Rouquié, 'L'hypothèse Bonapartiste et l'émergence des systèmes politiques semi-compétitifs', *Revue française de science politique*, XXV (Dec 1975) 1077–1111.

2. Antonio Gramsci, *Nota sul Machiavelli, sulla Politica e sullo Stato Moderno* (Turin: Einaudi, 1949) p. 81, and *Passato e Presente* (Turin: Einaudi, 1952) pp. 158–9.

3. Hugues Portelli, 'Gramsci et les élections', *Les Temps modernes*, Feb 1975, 1013.

4. Joseph A. Schumpeter, *Capitalism, Socialism and Democracy* (New York: Harper and Brothers, 1947) p. 285.

5. Ibid., p. 270.

6. See V. O. Key Jr, *Southern Politics in State and Nations* (New York: Knopf, 1949) pp. 525–632; and Marie-France Toinet, 'La Concurrence electorale impar-

faite aux États-Unis', *Revue française de science politique*, XXVI (Oct 1976) 898–929.

7. See especially the comparison between elections in the American Deep South and elections in Northern Ireland made by Richard Rose in 'On the Priorities of Citizenship in the Deep South and Northern Ireland', *Journal of Politics*, XXXVIII (May 1976) 749–914.

8. See Pierre Gilhodes, *Politique et violence: la question agraire en Colombie* (Paris: Colin, 1974) pp. 72–4.

9. See J. P. Mackintosh, 'Electoral Trends and the Tendency to a One-Party System in Nigeria', *Journal of Commonwealth Studies*, I (Nov 1962) 207. See equally Tatiana Yanopoulos, 'Lutte de classe et guerre nationale au Nigeria', *Revue française de science politique*, XVIII (June 1968) 515–19.

10. Lucy P. Mair, 'Clientship in East Africa', *Cahiers d'études africaines*, VI (1961) 317. See also G. Greco, 'Appunti per una Tipologia della Clientela', *Quaderni di Sociologia*, II (1972) 178–97, esp. 180–1.

11. George N. Foster, 'The Dyadic Contract: A Model of the Social Structure of a Mexican Peasant Village', *American Anthropologist*, XXIII (Dec 1961) 1173–92.

12. As is properly emphasised by John Duncan Powell in 'Peasant Society and Clientelist Politics', *American Political Science Review*, LXIV (June 1970) 412.

13. J. A. Pitt-Rivers, *The People of the Sierra* (London: Weidenfeld and Nicolson, 1954) p. 189.

14. See Greco's reflections in *Quaderni di Sociologia*, II, 183; and Jeremy Boissevain, 'Maltese Village Politics and Their Relation to National Politics', *Journal of Commonwealth Studies*, I (Nov 1962) 211–23.

15. Greco, *Quaderni di Sociologia*, II, 191.

16. See F. Chevalier, ' "Caudillos" and "caciques" en Amérique: contribution à l'étude des liens personnels', in *Mélanges offerts à Marcel Bataillon par les hispanistes français* (Bordeaux, 1962) pp. 30–47.

17. See 'Patron – Client Relations: Concept and Terms', *Journal of Peasant Studies*, I (July 1974) 507.

18. See esp. Carl Herman Lande, *Southern Tagalog Voting 1946–1963: Political Behaviour in a Philippine Region* (DeKalb, Ill: Northern Illinois University Center for Southeast Asian Studies, 1973) pp. 3–4; and T. C. Nowak and K. A. Snyder, 'Clientelist Politics in the Philippines: Integration or Instability?', *American Political Science Review*, LXVII (Sep 1974) 1147–8.

19. As J. F. Medard very properly writes in his 'Le Rapport de clientèle: du phénomène social à l'analyse politique', *Revue française de science politique*, XXVI (Feb 1976) 103–31.

20. Gilhodes, *Politique et violence*, p. 86.

21. P. A. Allum, *Politics and Society in Post-War Naples* (Cambridge: Cambridge University Press, 1973) pp. 16 and 19.

22. A. F. Montenegro, 'As Eleiçoes Cearenses de 1962', *Revista Brasileira de Estudos Politicos*, XVI (Jan 1964) 89.

23. We refer to a series of studies devoted by the *Revista Brasileira de Estudos Politicos* to this type of election, esp. Orlando M. Carvalho, *Ensaios de Sociologia Eleitoral* (Belo Horizonte: Ediçoes de Revista Brasileira de Estudos Politicos) pp. 30–51, and the articles on the 1962 Sergipe and Alagoas elections in the Jan 1964 issue of the *Revista*.

24. Luigi Graziano, 'Clientela e Politica nel Mezzogiorno', in Paolo Farneti et al.,

Il Sistema Politico Italiano (Bologna: Il Mulino, 1974) p. 212.

25. Greco, *Quaderni di Sociologia*, II, 183.
26. Powell, in *American Political Science Review*, LXIV, 411.
27. This expression is taken from James C. Scott, 'Corruption, Machine Politics and Political Change', *American Political Science Review*, LXIII (Dec 1969) 1156.
28. As stressed by Myron Weiner in *The Politics of Scarcity: Public Pressure and Political Response in India* (Chicago: Chicago University Press, 1962).
29. Maria-Antonietta Macciochi, *Lettres de l'intérieur du parti* (Paris: Maspéro, 1970) pp. 21–8.
30. Gilhodes, *Politique et violence*, p. 127.
31. On the state industries and their clientele network in contemporary Italy, see Graziano, in Farneti et al., *Il Sistema Politico Italiano*, p. 234 and Allum, *Politics and Society*, p. 161. Paul Littlewood has studied a case of clientelism through control of the 'school coffers' in a small town that helped to provide work for unemployed teachers; see his 'Strings and Kingdoms: The Activities of a Political Mediator in Southern Italy', *Archives européennes de sociologie*, XV (1974) 35–51.
32. See André Siegfried, *Tableau politique de la France de l'ouest sous la Troisième République*, 2nd edition (Paris: Colin, 1964) p. 370. See also P. Bouju and J. Tudesq's pieces on notables in French political life in CERVL, *Les Facteurs locaux et la vie politique nationale* (Paris: Pedone, 1972) pp. 21 and 345.
33. For this perception of the limited good and its political implications, see Carl H. Lande, 'Networks and Groups in Southern Asia: Some Observations on the Group Theory of Politics', *American Political Science Review*, LXVII (Mar 1973) 119–20.
34. See Benno Galjart, 'Class and Following in Rural Brazil', *America Latina*, VI (July – Sep 1964) 3– .
35. On Colombia, see Steffen W. Schmidt, 'Bureaucrats as Modernizing Brokers: Clientelism in Colombia', *Comparative Politics*, VI (Apr 1974) 437. Galjart also deals with neo-clientelism in his 'Old Patron and New: Some Notes on the Consequences of Patronage for Local Development Projects', *Sociologia Ruralis*, VII (1967) 335–45. On the persistence of patronage relations in South-East Asia, one can also consult James C. Scott and Ben Kerkvliet, 'The Politics of Survival: Peasant Response to Progress in South-East Asia', *Journal of Southern Asian Studies*, IV (Sep 1973) 241–68.
36. Alex Weingrod, 'Patrons, Patronage and Political Parties', *Comparative Studies in Society and History*, X (July 1968) 379–99.
37. Graziano, in Farneti et al., *Il Sistema Politico Italiano*, p. 224.
38. A characteristic feature of authoritarian contexts might be seen in this episode. Social *domination* would imply the rejection of channels of communication, but *influence* following from competitive elections and open pluralist systems would derive from electors' gratitude to the person who had obtained a railway or a road for them. The latter is the source of the numerous roads and railways that, to this day, are built in France and Italy for electoral purposes.
39. Schmidt, in *Comparative Politics*, VI, 440.
40. Antonio Octavio Cintra, *A Politica Traditional Brasileira: Une Interpretacão das Relacões Entre o Centro e a Periferia*, Cadernos de Departamento de Ciencias Politicas, Universidade de Minas Gerais (Mar 1974) p. 80.
41. Ibid., pp. 63–6.

42. Antonio Callado, *Os Industriais de Sèca e os Galileus de Pernambuco: Aspectos da Luta Pela reforma Agraria no Brasil* (Rio de Janeiro: Civilizaçao Brasileira, 1960) p. 26.
43. As ir Iran, according to P. Vieille in 'État et Féodalité en Iran', *L'Homme et la Société*, XVII (July – Sep 1970) 259–60.
44. Weingrod, *Comparative Studies in Society and History*, X, 379–80.
45. To use the terminology of Benjamin N. Colby and Pierre L. Van den Bergh in 'Ethnic Relations in Southeastern Mexico', *American Anthropologist*, LXIII (Aug 1961) 778.
46. W. F. Wertheim, 'From Aliran Towards Class Struggle', paper prepared for the International Conference on Asian History at Kuala Lumpur, Aug 1968, published in *Pacific Viewpoints*, X (Sep 1969) 1–17.
47. According to René Lemarchand in 'Political Clientelism and Ethnicity in Tropical Africa: Competing Solidarities in Nation-Building', *American Political Science Review*, LXVI (Mar 1972) 70 and 86.
48. The following analysis of 'bossism' draws heavily on the study in Jean-Louis Seurin, *La Structure interne des partis politiques américains* (Paries: Colin 1953) and H. F. Gosnell, *Machine Politics: Chicago Model* (Chicago: Chicago University Press, 1937).
49. David Rock, 'Machine Politics in Buenos Aires and the Argentine Radical Party, 1912–1930', *Journal of Latin American Studies*, IV (1972) 233–56.
50. See Lemarchand, in *American Political Science Review*, LXVI (esp. on the Ivory Coast's single party); and Joel D. Barkan, *Bringing Home the Pork: Legislator Behavior, Rural Development and Political Change in East Africa*, University of Iowa, Center for Comparative Legislative Research, Occasional Paper no. 9 (Aug 1975).
51. Joseph La Palombara, *Clientela e Parentela: Studio sui Gruppi d'Interesse in Italia* (Milan: Edizioni di Comunita, 1967) esp. p. 241.
52. Geneviève Bibes, *Le Système Politique Italien* (Paris: Presses Universitaires de France, 1974) pp. 4–5.
53. Graziano, in Farneti et al., *Il Sistema Politico Italiano*, p. 231; and Allum, *Politics and Society*, pp. 161–5.
54. According to the very critical interpretation in Guiseppe Tamburrano, *L'Iceberg Democristiano: Il Potere in Italia Oggi, Domani* (Milan: Sugarco Edizioni, 1974) pp. 122–30.
55. J. C. Scott, 'Patron – Client Politics and Political Change in South-East Asia', *American Political Science Review*, LXVI (Mar 1972) 102.
56. W. P. Wertheim, 'Patronage, Organisation Verticale et Populisme', unpublished MS., Paris, 1968, p. 9.
57. Scott, in *American Political Science Review*, LXIII, 1144.
58. The subproletarians of the Neapolitan *vicolo*, considering the election campaign as a time for bargaining, asked a Communist candidate who was exposing the misdeeds of capitalism to them for some pastry goodies or olive oil. In the logic of their situation, their peers who have nothing to give have no governing vocation. 'If beggars are put in the place of the rich, what benefit can be drawn from them', think the clientelised masses in a Naples that is still monarchist in the 1960s. See Macchioci, *Lettres de l'intérieur du parti*, pp. 90–115.

CHAPTER 3

1. Cf. Juan Linz on 'Totalitarian and Authoritarian Regimes' in *The Handbook of Political Science*, ed. Fred I. Greenstein and Nelson W. Polsby, vol. III: 'Macropolitical Theory' (Reading, Mass.: Addison-Wesley, 1975) pp. 175–411, which contains a detailed presentation of the typology of non-democratic regimes on which this paper builds.

2. Karl Dietrich Bracher, Wolfgang Sauer and Gerhard Schulz, *Die national-sozialistische Machtergreifung* (Cologne: Westdeutscher Verlag, 1960).

3. Ibid., p. 89.

4. Edward N. Peterson, *The Limits of Hitler's Power* (Princeton, N. J.: Princeton University Press, 1969).

5. Renzo De Felice, *Mussolini il Fascista*, vol. I: 'La Conquista del Potere, 1921–1925' (Turin: Einaudi, 1966); and vol. II: 'L'Organizzazione dello Stato Fascista, 1925–1929' (Turin: Einaudi, 1968). Idem, *Mussolini il Duce* vol. I: 'Gli Anni del Consenso, 1929–1936' (Turin: Einaudi, 1974).

6. De Felice, *Mussolini il Fascista*, vol. I, pp. 564–88. On the Popolari in the election, see Gabriele de Rosa, *Storia del Partito Popolare* (Bari: Laterza, 1958) pp. 424–47.

7. See, for example, Sandor Brunauer, *Communist Use of the Franchise in Hungary* (New York: Mid-European Studies Center, 1954); and Mihai Fătu, *Un Vot Decisiv (Noiembrie 1946)* (Bucharest: Institutl de Studii Istorice Si Social-Politice de Pe Lingă CC al PCR, 1972).

8. De Felice, *Mussolini il Fascista*, vol. I, p. 569ff.

9. Ibid., p. 572.

10. Ibid., p. 584.

11. Ibid., p. 585.

12. For example, in Yugoslavia the percentage of eligible voters actually voting changed with 'detotalitarianisation' as follows: 1945, 88·7; 1950, 91·9; 1953, 89·4; 1958, 94·1; 1963, 95·5; 1965, 93·6; 1967, 88·1; 1969, 87·0. Data from *Statisticki Godisnjak* for each year, quoted in an unpublished paper by Susan McCarthy.

13. J. L. Talmon, *The Origins of Totalitarian Democracy* (New York: Praeger, 1961).

14. Linz, in *The Handbook of Political Science*, vol. III, ed. Greenstein and Polsby, pp. 191–2.

15. James R. Townsend, *Political Participation in Communist China* (Berkeley, Calif.: University of California Press, 1972); and Richard R. Fagen, *The Transformation of Political Culture in Cuba* (Stanford, Calif.: Stanford University Press, 1969).

16. But see Hermann-Otto Leng, *Die allgemeine Wahl im bolschewistischen Staat. Theorie – Praxis – Genesis* (Meisenheim am Glan: Anton Hain, 1973).

17. Max E. Mote, *Soviet Local and Republic Elections: A description of the 1963 Elections in Leningrad Based on Official Documents, Press Accounts, and Private Interviews* (Stanford, Calif.: Hoover Institution, 1965).

18. On the 1934 plebiscitarian election, see Bracher et al., *Die nationalsozialische Machtergreifung*, pp. 348–368.

19. See Charles L. Taylor and Michael C. Heidean, *World Handbook of Political and Social Indicators* (New Haven: Yale University Press, 1972) pp. 54–8.

20. Leng, *Die allgemeine Wahl*, p. 148.

21. De Felice, *Mussolini il Fascista*, vol. II, pp. 437–9, and *Mussolini il Duce*, vol. I pp. 311–13, for the 1934 plebiscite.

22. See, for example, Peter B. Maggs, 'Negative Votes in Soviet Elections', in *Res Baltica. A Collection of Essays in Honor of the Memory of Dr Alfred Bilmanis (1887–1948)*, ed. Adolf Sprudzs and Armins Rusis (Leyden: A. W. Sijthoff, 1968) pp. 146–51.

23. Carl Schmitt, *Die geistesgeschichtliche Lage des heutigen Parlamentarismus* (Berlin: Duncker Humblot, 1926; repr. 1969) p. 22.

24. Georg Simmel, 'Superordination and Subordination', in *The Sociology of Georg Simmel*, trans. and ed. Kurt H. Wolff (Glencoe, NY: Free Press, 1950) pp. 242–4.

25. Bracher et al., *Die nationalsozialistische Machtergreifung*, p. 353.

26. Ibid., p. 349.

27. Zbigniew Pelczynski, 'Poland 1957', in *Elections Abroad*, ed. D. E. Butler (London: Macmillan, 1959) pp. 119–79.

28. Susan Beth Kaufman, 'Decision-making in an authoritarian regime: the politics of profit-sharing in Mexico', Ph.D. dissertation, Columbia University, 1970.

29. See Juan J. Linz, 'Some Notes Toward a Comparative Study of Fascism in Sociological and Historical Perspective', in *A Readers' Guide to Fascism*, ed. Walter Laqueur (Berkeley, Calif.: University of California Press, 1976) pp. 3–121, and 'Conditions for and against Fascism in Inter-War Europe', to be published in *Who were the Fascists?*, ed. Stein Larsen et al., (Oslo: Universitetsforlaget).

30. See Bela Vago, *The Shadow of the Swastika. The Rise of Fascism and Anti-Semitism in the Danube Basin, 1936–1939* (Farnborough, Hants: Saxon House, 1975); and Tönu Perming, *The Collapse of Liberal Democracy and the Rise of Authoritarianism in Estonia*, Sage Professional Papers, Contemporary Political Sociology Series, no. 06–010 (London, 1975).

31. Jozo Tomasevich, *Peasants, Politics and Economic Change in Yugoslavia* (Stanford, Calif.: Stanford University Press, 1955) pp. 240–7.

32. For example, in Romania, where elections in the inter-war years assured an absolute majority of votes and over three-quarters of the seats to the government party, the reported participation ranged between 77·1 per cent (1927) and 67·9 per cent (1933).

33. See J. J. Linz, 'Opposition in and under an Authoritarian Regime: the Case of Spain', in *Regimes and Oppositions*, ed. Robert A. Dahl (New Haven: Yale University Press, 1973) pp. 171–259.

34. See Miguel Martínez Cuadrado, 'Representación. Elecciones. Referéndum', in *La España de los Años 70*, ed. Manuel Fraga Iribarne, vol. III: 'El Estado y la Política, tomo I', pp. 1371–1439 (Madrid: Moneda y Crédito, 1974); Guy Hermet, 'Electoral Trends in Spain: An Appraisal of the Polls Conducted Under the Franco Regime', *Iberian Studies*, III, no. 2 (1974) 55–9; Jorge Solé Tura, 'Elecciones Municipales y Estructura del Poder Político en España', in *Estudios de Ciencia Política y Sociología. Homenaje al Profesor Carlos Ollero* (Madrid: Carlavilla, 1972) pp. 786–99; and José Vidal Beneyto, *Elecciones Municipales y Referéndum*, (Madrid: Cuadernos de Ciencia Social, 1966); and *Les Eleccions Municipals a Barcelona del 16 d'Octubre 1973. Assaig de Sociologia Electoral* (Barcelona: Department de Dret Polític, Facutat de Dret, 1975).

35. Raimund Rämisch, 'Der berufständische Gedanke als Episode in der

nationalsozialistischen Politik', *Zeitschrift für Politik*, IV (1957) 263–72.
36. See Philippe C. Schmitter, *Corporatism and Public Policy in Authoritarian Portugal*, Sage Professional Papers, Contemporary Political Sociology Series, no. 06–011 (London, 1975) pp. 24–37; and Harry M. Makler, 'The Portuguese Industrial Elite and its Corporative Relations: A Study of Compartmentalization in an Authoritarian Regime', in *Economic Development and Cultural Change*, vol. XXIV, no. 3 (Apr 1976) 495–526.
37. Juan J. Linz and Amando de Miguel, *Los Empresarios ante el Poder Público* (Madrid: Instituto de Estudios Políticos, 1966) esp. ch. 6 on formal and informal leadership in the business community.
38. See, for example, Jose Maria Maravall, 'Students and Politics in Contemporary Spain', *Government and Opposition*, XI, no. 2 (Spring 1976) 156–79.
39. This analysis is based on personal observation during the pre-election period in high government offices in Madrid.
40. Juan j. Linz, 'From Falange to Movimiento-Organización: The Spanish Single Party and the Franco Regime, 1936–1968', in *Authoritarian Politics in Modern Society*, ed. S. P. Huntington and C. H. Moore (New York: Basic Books, 1970) pp. 128–203.
41. Good examples of the kind of thinking involved and the intra-party debates on the issue can be found in Palmiro Togliatti, *Lectures on Fascism* (New York: International Publishers, 1976) in the chapters on Fascist trade unions and the Dopolavoro.
42. See De Felice, *Mussolini il Fascista*, vol. II, pp. 471–3, on the divergent positions of the opposition at the time of the 1929 plebiscite.
43. Alfred Stepan, *The State and Society: Peru in Comparative Perspective* (Princeton, NJ: Princeton University Press, forthcoming).
44. Marcus Faria Figueiredo and Peter McDonough, *Towards a Theory of Political Control: Coercion and Cooptation in Brazil*, a paper of the Center for Political Studies, Institute for Social Research, The University of Michigan (Ann Arbor, 1975).
45. *Os Partidos e as Eleições no Brasil*, ed. Fernando Henrique Cardoso and Bolívar Lamounier (Rio de Janeiro: Paz e Terra, 1975), and the special issue of *Revista Brasileira de Estudos Políticos*, 43, July 1976, with articles on the 1974 election in different states and cities in Brazil.
46. Walter F. Weiker, *Political Tutelage and Democracy in Turkey. The Free Party and its Aftermath* (Leiden: E. J. Brill, 1973); and Kemel H. Karpat, *Turkey's Politics: The Transition to a Multiparty System* (Princeton, NJ: Princeton University Press, 1959).
47. Quoted by Carlos Estevam Martins in his 'O Balanço da Campanha', in *Os Partidos e as Eleições no Brasil*, ed. Cardoso and Lamounier, pp. 77–125. See p. 115.

CHAPTER 4

1. We borrow the concept of the system of inequality and domination from G. Balandier, *Anthropo-logiques* (Paris: Presses Universitaires de France, 1974) ch. 3.
2. See ch. 2 above, and R. Lemarchand, 'Les Relations de clientèle comme agent de contestation – le cas du Rwanda', *Civilisations*, XVIII, no. 4 (1968) 555.
3. Following Lemarchand (in *Civilisations*, XVIII, no. 4; 554, note 2), I use the term

'clientage' for an institution, 'clientele' for a model of relation, and 'clients' for political actors.

4. Balandier, *Anthropo-logiques*, chs 1 and 2, and *Anthropologie politique* (Paris: ch. 3; C. Meillassoux, *Femmes, greniers et capitaux* (Paris: Maspéro, 1975); P. P. Rey, *Colonialisme, neo-colonialisme et transition au capitalisme* (Paris: Maspéro, 1971); C. Tardits, 'Stratification sociale et parenté chez les Bamoun', *L'Homme*, v, nos 3–4 (1965), and 'Parenté et pouvoir politique chez les Bamoun', *L'Homme*, XIII, nos 1–2 (1973).

5. J. F. Medard, 'Les Rapports de clientèle: du phénomène social à l'analyse politique', *Revue française de science politique*, XXVI, no. 1 (Feb 1976) 106–7.

6. A. Wirz, 'La Rivière du Cameroun: commerce pré-colonial et contrôle du pouvoir en société lignagère', *Revue française d'histoire d'outre-mer*, LX, no. 219 (1973) pp. 188 ff.; and P. Laburthe-Tolra, *Minlaaba histoire et société traditionnelle chez les Beti du sud Cameroun* (Paris, 1974) p. 858. For lack of sufficient documentation, I cannot evoke the evolution of the clientages at this period in Bamiléké country.

7. For a fuller discussion of *cadets sociaux*, translated here as 'social inferiors', see esp. Rey, *Colonialisme*; Meillassoux, *Femmes, greniers et capitaux*; *L'Anthropologie économique courants et problèmes*, ed. F. Pouillon (Paris: Maspéro, 1976); and M. Augé, *Théorie des pouvoirs et idéologie* (Paris: Hermann, 1975).

8. Laburthe-Tolra, *Minlaaba*, pp. 859ff.; and R. Gouellain, *Douala, ville et histoire*, (Paris: Institut d'Ethnologie, 1975) pp. 102ff.

9. Wirz, in *Revue française d'histoire d'outre-mer*, LX, no. 219, 191ff.; Gouellain, *Douala*, p. 100ff.; Laburthe-Tolra, *Minlaaba*, p. 863.

10. Wirz, in *Revue française d'histoire d'outre-mer*, LX, no. 219, pp. 193–4.

11. J. D. Powell, 'Peasant Society and Clientelist Politics', *American Political Science Review*, LXIV (June 1970) pp. 411–25, and R. Lemarchand and K. Legg, 'Political Clientelism and Development: A Preliminary Analysis', *Comparative Politics*, IV, no. 2 (Jan 1972) pp. 158–9, give an account of this change of scale. As far as I know, the change of kind of domination has never been systematically studied.

12. It would be suitable to vary this general picture infinitely. As for the Duala, they constitute a downright exception to the process just described; the authority of the aristocracy over the community does not seem to have been really changed. Cf. Gouellain, *Douala*.

13. The return to direct administration was accomplished sometimes to the benefit of the chiefs of the canton of administrative origin and without traditional decree (for instance, the canton of Ndoukoula in Toupouri country, and of the canton chiefs in Massa country), and sometimes to the profit of the ancestral chiefs, who then added the title of chief of canton to their customary functions (for example, the canton of Muturua in Guiziga country). Sources: J. Guillard, *Golonpoui* (Paris: Mouton, 1965); I. de Garine, *Les Massa du Cameroun* (Paris: Presses Universitaires de France, 1964); G. Pontie, *Les Guiziga du Cameroun septentrional* (Paris: ORSTOM, 1973).

14. Sources relating to the Bamiléké country: J. Hurault, *La Structure sociale des Bamiléké* (Paris: Mouton, 1962), and 'Essai de synthèse du système social des Bamiléké', *Africa*, XL, no. 1 (Jan 1970); C. Tardits, *Les Bamiléké de l'ouest Cameroun* (Paris: Berger Levrault, 1960); R. Delarozière, 'Les institutions politiques et sociales des populations dites Bamiléké', *Études camerounaises*,

xxvii–xxviii (Sep – Dec 1949).

15. Formerly presented as polemic assertions, the profusion of frauds committed by the administration to the detriment of the UPC, bringing about their electoral defeats, are today recognised by virtually all the historians. See esp. R. Joseph, 'Ruben Um Nyobé and the "Kamerun" Rebellion', *African Affairs*, LXXIII, no. 293 (Oct 1974) 432.

16. See Ch. 2 above.

17. Powell, in *American Political Science Review*, LXIV, 416.

18. A remarkable documented account of this period is in R. Joseph, 'National Politics in Postwar Cameroun: The Difficult Birth of the UPC', *Journal of African Studies*, II, no. 2 (Summer 1975) 201–29.

19. Description of the Efoula-Meyong in G. Balandier, *Sociologie actuelle de l'Afrique noire*, new edition (Paris, 1971) p. 236; and in P. Alexandre and J. Binet, *Le groupe dit Pahouin (Fang, Boulou, Beti)* (Paris: Presses Universitaires de France, 1958) ch. 5.

20. A thesis upheld notably by Balandier, in his *Sociologie actuelle*, and by Joseph, in *Journal of African Studies*, II, no. 2, 228.

21. Interviews with P. Alexandre, Paris, 1970–5.

22. C. Assale, quoted in Victor T. Levine, *The Camerouns from Mandate to Independence* (Berkeley, Calif.: University of California Press, 1964) p. 151.

23. J. F. Bayart, 'Le Régime politique camerounais 1958–1972', doctoral thesis, Fondation Nationale des Sciences Politiques, Paris, 1975, p. 22ff.

24. This is the conclusion suggested particularly by the account in Gouellain, *Douala*, of the history of the Duala, and put forward from 1966 by M. L. Kilson about Sierra Leone, in *Political Change in a West African State: A study of the Modernization Process in Sierra Leone* (Cambridge, Mass.: Harvard University Press, 1966).

25. It may seem premature to speak of the clientelist state (Powell, in *American Political Science Review*, LXIV, 415ff.) or of *caciquismo* in connection with the Cameroun of 1958; the colonial administration was still all-powerful. It is, however, indisputable that political figures such as C. Assale, G. Medou, A. Mbida, D. Kemajou, M. Djoumessi and C. Okala were near to the Latin American model of the *cacique* and that their political action brought about the emergence of a clientelist state, from now onwards written into the reality of the country. Moreover, the politics of patronage of the colonial administration or of an *Aujoulat* (metropolitan 'governor' of the political, autochthonous and legalist elite) contributed actively to it. Cf. A. Ugalde, 'Contemporary Mexico: From Hacienda to PRI, Political Leadership in a Zapotic Village', in *The Caciques*, ed. R. Kern (Albuquerque: University of New Mexico Press, 1973) p. 124.

26. Joseph, in *African Affairs*, LXXIII, no. 293, 441ff. The 'traditional' (that is, administrative) chiefs in particular were subject to the judgements of the popular tribunals.

27. W. R. Johnson, *The Cameroun Federation: Political Integration in a Fragmentary Society* (Princeton, NJ: Princeton University Press, 1970) p.153ff.

28. Ibid., p. 156.

29. Remark made in J. Hurault, *Essai de Synthèse*, pp. 21–2.

30. I analyse these dimensions of the regime in an article to appear in *Cahiers d'études africaines*.

31. 'The Party has a tendency to become . . . a recruiting office', warned Mr. Moussa Yaya, Secretary-General of the Union Camerounaise, in 1960. See 'Rapport du secrétaire général du comité directeur', *IIIe Congrès du parti politique de l'Union camerounaise tenu à Maroua les 22 – 25 septembre 1960* (Alençon: Impr. Alençonnaise, 1960).

32. Report of the Political Secretary, *Procès verbal des travaux du premier congrès extraordinaire de l'Union nationale camerounaise tenu à Yaoundé les 2 au 3 juin 1972*, mimeo., 1972, p. 74. *Luttes d'influence* ('struggles of influence') is probably the most commonly used expression in the political vocabulary of Cameroun: there is not a report that does not deplore such struggles, nor a speech that does not beseech their disappearance.

33. See the excellent case-study in R. E. Ritzenthaler, 'Anlu: A Women's Uprising in the British Cameroons', *African Studies*, xix, no. 3 (1960) 151 -6.

34. N. Poulantzas, *La Crise des dictatures européennes (Portugal, Grèce, Espagne)* (Paris: Maspéro, 1975) pp. 83 – 5.

35. Reply of Mr. Ayissi Mvodo on the afternoon of 25 Nov, in *Procès verbal du IIIe conseil national de l'UNC tenu à Yaoundé du 25 au 27 novembre 1973*, mimeo., 1973.

36. Circular no. 2 of the CDP, dated 12 Oct 1966. Scrutiny of the section reports to the congress of Garoua (1969) shows that certain presidents are loath to apply this measure and continue to confuse adherents of the UNC and adherents of OFUNC and JUNC (notably in the case of the sections of Wouri and Lékié). Elsewhere, the collection of subscriptions remains in the hands of those responsible in the UNC, who are supposed to bring about cancellations to the advantage of OFUNC; the staff of the women's organisation reproach those of the party with not turning over to them the total sums to which they have the right.

37. S. Amin, *L'Accumulation à l'échelle mondiale. Critique de la théorie de sous-développement* (Paris: Anthropos, 1971); and P. P. Rey, *Les Alliances de classes*, (Paris: Maspéro, 1973).

38. Unfortunately, it is impossible to know or even to evaluate the percentage of the abstentions, because of the systematic manipulation of the results and, indeed, the complete lack of electoral rolls.

39. See, for example, Pontie, *Les Guiziga*, pp. 159ff. and 199ff.; Guillard, *Golonpoui*, p. 145ff.; de Garine, *Les Massa*, pp. 105 –6, 125ff., 138ff., 145ff., and 210ff.; Laburthe-Tolra, *Minlaaba*, p. 854; and Tardits, *Les Bamiléké*, p. 35.

40. See, for example, Laburthe-Tolra, *Minlaaba*, p. 837.

41. J. C. Scott, 'Patron – Client Politics and Political Change in South-East Asia', *American Political Science Review*, LXVI (Mar 1972) 111ff. A more thorough investigation would be necessary to state this point precisely. But Powell, in *American Political Science Review*, LXIV, 416, seems to me to be in the right when he notes that factionalism does not necessarily strengthen the client's position.

42: W. P. Wertheim, 'Patronage, organisation verticale et populisme', unpublished MS., Paris, 1965; quoted in ch. 2 above (see ch. 2, note 56).

CHAPTER 5

1. The authors wish to acknowledge the support of a grant from the Agency of International Development to the Comparative Legislative Research Center

at the University of Iowa, and the support of a grant from the Rockefeller Foundation for making possible the research reported in this article. The views expressed in the article are solely those of the authors and should not in any way be attributed to the supporting agencies.

2. Kenya has been a *de facto* one-party state since Nov 1964, when the Kenyan African Democratic Union dissolved itself and its members joined the ruling party, the Kenya African National Union. Between 1966 and 1969, KANU was challenged by the Kenya Peoples Union, but after the election of 1966 the opposition party held only nine out of 158 seats in the National Assembly, and these representatives were subsequently detained. Although KPU was banned in 1969, and the government has periodically threatened any prospective organisers of a new opposition party, Kenya's Constitution does not specify that the country is a one-party state. President Jomo Kenyatta, moreover, has explicitly stated that, unlike many other African states, Kenya will not amend its Constitution to include such a provision.

3. See, for example, Hyden and Leys, 'Elections and Politics in Single Party Systems: The Case of Kenya and Tanzania', *British Journal of Political Science*, II, no. 4 (Oct 1972) 389–420.

4. S. P. Huntington, 'Political Order and Political Decay', in his *Political Order in Changing Societies* (New Haven: Yale University Press, 1968) pp. 1–92.

5. *Employment, Incomes and Equality: A Strategy for Increasing Productive Employment in Kenya* (Geneva: International Labour Office, 1971); and Colin Leys, *Underdevelopment in Kenya* (Berkeley, Calif.: University of California Press, 1975).

6. Hyden and Leys, in *British Journal of Political Science*, II, 389–420; *One Party Democracy: The 1965 Tanzanian General Elections*, ed. Lionel Cliffe (Nairobi: East African Publishing House, 1967); *Socialism and Participation: Tanzania's 1970 National Elections* (Dar es Salaam: Tanzania Publishing House, 1974).

7. At its peak in 1959, the number of permanent European residents in Kenya who regarded the country as 'home' was slightly more than 60,000 or about 1 per cent of the population. The number of permanent residents of Indian and Pakistani origin was approximately 120,000.

8. Consistent with British policy in other British colonies, the colonial government progressively enlarged the Legislative Council and transformed it into an elected parliament as Kenya moved toward independent rule. Elections were held for six additional seats in 1958, nineteen more in 1961, and eighty-four more in 1963, the last election before independence. Kenya thus became independent in December 1963 with a House of Representatives consisting of 117 members who were directly elected from single-member constituencies, and fourteen indirectly elected or appointed members (overall total 131). A Senate of forty-one members, also elected from single-member districts, was established in 1963, under a provision of the Constitution on which Britain granted independence. The House of Representatives and Senate were merged in 1966 into a unicameral National Assembly consisting of 158 directly elected members and twelve nominated by the President (overall total 170).

9. For an expanded discussion of how this process evolved, see J. D. Barkan and J. J. Okumu, 'Alternative Linkage Agents for Declining Parties: Legislators in Kenya', in *Political Parties and Linkages*, ed. Kay Lawson (New Haven: Yale University Press, forthcoming).

10. For details on this important election see G. Bennett and Carl G. Rosberg Jr,

The Kenyatta Election (London: Oxford University Press, 1961).
11. Kenya is divided into eight provinces and forty-four districts, which are in turn divided into locations and sub-locations. These administrative units are respectively run by eight provincial commissioners, forty-four district commissioners assisted by two or three district officers, and a large number of chiefs and sub-chiefs, who represent the central government at the location and sub-location level but are long-term residents of the areas in which they serve. Kenyatta depends heavily on this administrative apparatus, perhaps more than on the civil service located in Nairobi, and is in daily contact with the provincial commissioners. For this reason, the President is occasionally humorously referred to as 'the last of the colonial governors'.
12. Henry Bienen, *Kenya: The Politics of Participation and Control* (Princeton, NJ: Princeton University Press, 1974) p. 75.
13. In referring to these linkages as being clientelist in type, we conceive of a hierarchy of personal relationships between unequal partners based on reciprocity, and from which the subordinant partner can voluntarily withdraw. Our conception of clientelist linkage structures is therefore consistent with most of the contemporary literature on clientelism and politics. For a discussion of the pyramiding of patron – client ties into linkage chains, see J. C. Scott, 'Patron – Client Politics and Political Change in South-East Asia', *American Political Science Review*, LXVI (Mar 1972) 91 – 113.
14. For these reasons Kenyatta increased the number of assistant ministers, following the 'Little General Election' of 1966. The elections, which were specially called when twenty-nine KANU MPs resigned from the party to form the Kenya Peoples Union, were extremely divisive and posed the most significant challenge to Kenyatta's authority since independence. For details of this election see Cherry Gertzel, *The Politics of Independent Kenya* (Evanston, Ill.: Northwestern University Press, 1970) pp. 74 – 124.
15. Containment of local leaders is a major objective of Kenyatta's clientelist system. While aspirants to political office are given free rein to organise constituency, and even district, ethnic machines, those who attempt to organise rival clientelist networks which include all of a major ethnic group, and especially several ethnic groups, are considered a threat and are harshly dealt with. Such was the background to the detention of Oginga-Odinga in 1969, the assassination of J. M. Kariuki in 1975, and the detention of John Seroney, Martin Shikuku, and Chelegut Mutai in 1976.
16. One of the more interesting aspects of the Kenyan National Assembly is that while it has never been a policy-making body, it has been a lively forum for public debate in the Westminster tradition. In the context of the no-party state, this has meant that backbenchers often play the role of the loyal opposition. Since July 1975, however, Kenyatta has sought to stifle debate in the Assembly as a result of the Assembly's adoption of a highly critical and controversial report by the commission of inquiry on the assassination of J. M. Kariuki.
17. Kenya has experienced four major crises since independence and survived them all: an army mutiny in 1964; the formation of the Kenya Peoples Union in 1966, and the 'Little General Election' in the same year; the assassination of Tom Mboya and the banning of the KPU in 1969; and the assassination of J. M. Kariuki in 1975. In addition to these specific periods of crisis, it is generally

acknowledged that material inequities in Kenya have increased, even though the country has experienced a rapid rate of economic growth, and that these inequities constitute a potential source of social unrest.

18. Immanuel Wallerstein, 'The Decline of the Party in Single-Party African States', in *Political Parties and Political Development*, ed. Joseph La Palombara and Myron Weiner (Princeton, NJ: Princeton University Press, 1966) pp. 201–16; Aristide R. Zolberg, *Creating Political Order* (Chicago: Rand McNally, 1966).

19. Huntington, *Political Order in Changing Societies*, pp. 397–461, esp. pp. 433–8.

20. The constituencies which served as the research sites for the surveys were selected on the basis of ethnic composition, level of economic development, and proximity to the capital, Nairobi. While they do not, strictly speaking, constitute a random sample of Kenya's 158 electoral districts, the total population interviewed in these districts is highly representative of the Kenyan population as a whole. 300 adults were interviewed in each constituency. Sampling within the constituencies was accomplished by first selecting at random, with the aid of aerial photographic maps, thirty sampling plots a quarter of a mile in diameter. Ten respondents were then selected within each plot, according to quota criteria derived from the 1969 census for the area.

21. Other events in this period include the 1966 election, the disqualification of KPU candidates in the town-council elections of Aug 1968, and the assassination of Tom Mboya in July 1969.

22. In some cases the challenger was disqualified, as in the constituency of Mbiyu Koinange, the Minister of State. In others, Kenyatta's associates ran unopposed, as did Daniel Arap Moi, the Vice-President. In still others, irregularities occurred in the counting of the vote, as was allegedly the case in the Nairobi constituency of Mwai Kibaki, Kenya's brilliant Minister of Finance. (Perhaps in response to this incident, Kibaki stood in a different constituency in 1974 and won more than 90 per cent of the vote on a legitimate count.)

23. For details of the 1969 elections, see Hyden and Leys, in *British Journal of Political Science*, II, no. 4, 396–405.

24. Not all of Kenya's ethnic groups are territorially divided on the basis of clan. Some groups have no clan structure. While in others, such as the Kikuyu, the traditional land-tenure system has broken down so that the members of any one clan are dispersed over a wide area and intermix with the members of others. In such cases, electoral conflict within constituencies tends to be between leaders who represent different sets of administrative locations and sub-locations.

25. In its only controversial decision, the KANU executive refused to permit Oginga-Odinga, the former leader of KPU, to stand for election in his former constituency of Bondo as a candidate for KANU, to which he had sworn allegiance. More significant perhaps, was the executive's decision to permit two of the government's most severe critics, J. M. Kariuki and Martin Shikuku, to seek re-election. Both were re-elected by a wide margin.

26. That members of peasant societies are more aware of the activities of their political leaders than members of industrial societies should not be surprising when one remembers that the activities of such leaders are likely to be more visible in the former, owing to the less complex social structure of the

community. For more on this misconception see Fred Hayward, 'A Reassessment of Conventional Wisdom About the Informed Public: National Political Information in Ghana', *American Political Science Review*, LXX, no. 2 (June 1976) 433–451.

27. For a more extensive presentation of this model, see Joel D. Barkan, 'Further Reassessment of the Conventional Wisdom: Political Knowledge and Voting Behavior in Rural Kenya', *American Political Science Review*, LXX, no. 2 (June 1976) 452–5.

28. The reader will note that the high correlation coefficient for the relationship between the vote received by incumbents and the evaluation scores washes out upon controlling for the number of candidates in the race. That is, of course, what should occur if the respondents' evaluations determined the size of the election fields, which in turn determined the levels of the incumbents' vote. This *indirect* effect of the aggregate evaluation scores on the incumbents' vote can be seen by computing the coefficient for the path, which is 0·52 (−0·8 × −0·64). For a discussion of effect coefficients, see Michael Lewis-Beck and Lawrence B. Mohr, 'Evaluating Effects of Independent Variables', *Political Methodology*, Winter 1976.

29. Scott, in *American Political Science Review*, LXVI, 111–13.

CHAPTER 6

1. Bismarck U. Mwansasu, 'Presidential Elections: An In-Depth Analysis', *Daily News* (Dar es Salaam), 19 Nov 1975.

2. On the elections held in 1965 and 1970, see *One Party Democracy: The 1965 Tanzanian General Elections*, ed. Lionel Cliffe (Nairobi: East African Publishing House, 1967); William Tordoff, 'The 1965 general election', in *Government and Politics in Tanzania* (Nairobi: East African Publishing House, 1967) 31–53; The Election Study Committee, University of Dar es Salaam, *Socialism and Participation: Tanzania's 1970 National Elections* (Dar es Salaam: Tanzania Publishing House, 1974); G. Hyden and C. Leys, 'Elections and Politics in Single Party Systems: The Case of Kenya and Tanzania', *British Journal of Political Science* II, no. 4 (Oct 1972) 389–420; J. S. Saul, 'The Nature of Tanzania's Political System: Issues Raised by the 1965 and 1970 Elections', *Journal of Commonwealth Political Studies*, X, nos 2 and 3 (1972) 113–29 and 198–221; and D. Martin, 'La Houe, la maison, l'urne et le maître d'école; Les Elections en Tanzanie, 1965–1970', *Revue française de science politique*, XXV, no. 4 (1975) 677–716.

3. In 1965 there were 801 candidates for 107 seats and in 1970 there were 1278 for 120 seats (direct election only).

4. The approximate character of the figures given in this study, including those in Table VI.1, cannot be emphasised too strongly. For 1975, they were calculated from the results given in the *Daily News* from 27 to 31 Oct 1975. These results were not identical from day to day, nor do their totals always correspond to the sum of the partial results presented. In the most discrepant cases, I have tried to estimate a 'realistic' average, thereby ending up with results that sometimes differ from those used by Bismarck Mwansasu in his *Daily News* articles (6, 19 and 21 November). For 1970 and 1965, I took the figures used in the works cited in note 2 above. Minor inconsistencies in the

figures cited in this paper reflect differences in the sources.

5. The adoption of a national electoral manifesto around which candidates had to build their appeals undoubtedly brought a greater homogeneity to their campaigns, since it prohibited discussion of the respective merits of campaign symbols, as well as the use of personal arguments. There were nevertheless cases of clandestine individual campaigns and attempts at corruption, as in Sumbawanga (Morogoro) and especially in Dodoma. There the 'war of the reverends', pitting the Rev. Simon Chiwanga, the Minister of Education, against the Rev. Severino Supa, obliged the Party's central leadership to intervene and suspend election meetings for three days. See *Daily News*, 11 Sep and 16 Oct 1975.

6. See B. U. Mwansasu, 'Consolidating Our One-party System', *Daily News*, 6 Nov 1975.

7. See Jon R. Moris, 'The Voter's View of the Elections', in the Election Study Committee, *Socialism and Participation*.

8. See H. U. E. Thoden van Velzen and J. J. Sterkenburg, 'Stirrings in the Tanzanian National Assembly', and 'The Party Supreme', in *Socialism in Tanzania*, ed. L. Cliffe and J. S. Saul, vol. 1: 'Politics' (Nairobi: East African Publishing House, 1972) 228–53 and 257–64.

9. Witness the reactions to the speech the President made after being nominated once again to be the candidate in the presidential elections. In this short speech, he asserted that he had hesitated to accept a new mandate and wondered for how long it was good for a country to keep the same man at its head. See esp. the readers' letters in the *Daily News*, Oct and Nov 1975.

10. See 'Some Aspects of Liberation', a speech made at Oxford by Julius K. Nyerere, in *Daily News*, 20 Nov 1975.

11. See Juma Habari, 'Tanzania Among Worst Hit by Inflation', *African Development*, Dec 1975.

12. In 1975, in order to finance indispensable cereal and petrol imports, it was estimated that Tanzania would have to spend the revenues anticipated from the export of coffee, cotton and sisal, the three products bringing most foreign currency into the country. See the 1975/6 budget presentation, *Daily News*, 17–18 June 1975.

13. See 'Tanzania Economic Survey', *African Development*, Dec 1975.

14. See J. K. Nyerere, 'The Arusha Declaration and TANU's Policy on Socialism and Self-Reliance', in *Ujamaa: Essays on Socialism* (Dar es Salaam: Oxford University Press, 1968).

15. *Daily News*, 16 Aug 1974.

16. On the problems of economic dependence, see Justinian Rweyemamu, *Underdevelopment and Industrialization in Tanzania: A Study of Perverse Capitalist Industrial Development* (Nairobi: Oxford University Press, 1973); *The Silent Class Struggle* (Dar es Salaam: Tanzania Publishing House, 1974). For the year 1975/6, see Jamhuri Ya Muungano Wa Tanzania, *Mpango wa Maendeleo wa Mwaka 1975–76* (Dar es Salaam: Printpak Tanzania Ltd, n.d.).

17. Tanganyika African National Union, *Mwongozo wa TANU* (Dar es Salaam: National Printing Co., 1971). An English translation was published in the *Nationalist* (Dar es Salaam) 22 Feb 1971.

18. J. K. Nyerere, *Decentralization* (Dar es Salaam: The Government Printer, 1972).

19. See *Daily News*, 22 Jan, 1 2 and 3 Apr and 28 Nov 1974.
20. See *Daily News*, 11 March 1975 and 3 June 1975; and *Gazette of United Republic of Tanzania*, LVI, no. 24 (1975).
21. See Martin, in *Revue française de science politique*, XXV, no. 4.
22. Nyerere, 'Some Aspects of Liberation', in *Daily News*, 20 Nov 1975. He had already warned on a tour in the Shinyanga region, 'The people are ready for revolution, but the leaders do not mobilize the people in development activities. . . . ' TANU and government leaders 'are far from being experts in planning development projects and implementing them', they are 'only experts in organizing meetings and writing reports'. See *Daily News*, 15 Oct 1975.
23. *Daily News*, 20 Jan 1974.
24. *Daily News*, 1, 2 and 3 Apr 1974.
25. *Daily News*, 7 Nov 1973.
26. *Daily News*, 15 Nov 1973.
27. In French in the text.
28. *Daily News* editorial, 5 Oct 1974.
29. 'There must be a deliberate effort to build equality between the leaders and those they lead. For a Tanzanian leader, it must be forbidden to be arrogant, extravagant, contemptuous and oppressive. The Tanzanian leader has to be a person who respects people, scorns ostentation and who is not a tyrant. He should epitomize heroism, bravery and be a champion of justice and equality' – TANU, *Mwongozo wa TANU*.
30. Henry Mapolu, 'The Workers' Movement in Tanzania', *Maji Maji*, no. 12 (Sep 1973) 39. See also 'Power to the Toilers', *Daily News*, 24 June 1973; 'Can We Afford Labour Unrests', *Sunday News*, 24 Feb 1974; and Paschal B. Mihyo, 'Labour Unrest and the Quest for Workers' Control', *Maji Maji*, no. 17 (Aug 1974).
31. This bridge, which is situated on Bagamayo Road, is the principal means of access to the capital for those people who live on the coast north of Centertown. Here are found not only a good number of embassies but also the President's personal residence.
32. See again the similar diagnosis made by President Nyerere in 'Some Aspects of Liberation', a speech given on the occasion of his visit to Lourenço Marques (Maputo), in *Daily News*, 2 October 1975.
33. See Saul, in *Journal of Commonwealth Political Studies*, X, nos 2 and 3; and Hyden and Leys, in *British Journal of Political Science*, II, no 4.
34. 'The officials decided that people should move immediately and so the police, T. P. D. F. [Tanzania People's Defence Force], National Service and Militiamen were mobilized to move the people. People were ill-treated, harassed, punished in the name of TANU, under socialism and those who questioned it were told, "This is Nyerere's order", usually followed with a hysteric rebuke, "Wewe ni mpinzani mkubwa Wa Tanu na Rais" ("You are a great opponent to the Party and the President")' – R. R. Matango, 'Operation Mara. The Paradox of Democracy', *Maji Maji*, no. 20 (Jan 1975). Similarly in the Rufiji district: 'Private and government vehicles, party and government leaders, Policy and People's militia in Rufiji district have since last Sunday been moving people from their scattered villages to development villages' – *Sunday News*, 15 Sep 1974.

35. Perhaps this increase was a side-effect of the 'war of the reverends'.
36. In 1965 Paul Bomani was defeated; in 1970 it was Bhoke Munanka's turn. In 1975, no outgoing MP was re-elected in the whole region. Two of the new MPs had taken no part in the 1970 election races; one, Francis Masanja, had come third at the District Conference of that year; another, Machemba Madaha, had been nominated but was later beaten by Paul Bomani.
37. Ganja Geneya, 'Sukumuland; Traditional Values and Modern Leadership', in *One Party Democracy*, ed. Cliffe, p. 189.
38. James R. Finucane, *Rural Development and Bureaucracy in Tanzania: The Case of the Mwanza Region* (Uppsala: Scandinavian Institute of African Studies, 1974) p. 49.
39. See Andrew G. Maguire, *Toward Uhuru in Tanzania: The Politics of Participation* (Cambridge: Cambridge University Press, 1969).
40. In Apr 1968, thirteen people who had not paid their taxes were found dead in a cell at Ilala prison.
41. Finucane, *Rural Development*, p. 157.
42. Ibid., p. 68.
43. 'There is still perhaps a tendency for the Sukuma to identity those factors which affect their wellbeing – the rain, cotton, prices, etc. – with those in authority over them, and this was a significant factor which influenced Sukuma attitudes in the (1965) elections' – Geneya, in *One Party Democracy*, ed. Cliffe, p. 189.
44. This is the central theme of Finucane's study. On this point, see also *Building Ujamaa Villages in Tanzania*, ed. J. Harris Proctor (Dar es Salaam: Tanzania Publishing House, 1971).
45. TANU, *Ilani ya Uchaguzi Kwa Ajili ya Uchaguzi wa 1975* (Dodoma: Makao Makuu ya Chama, n.d.) p. 2. English translation given in *Daily News*, 8 Oct 1975.
46. *Daily News*, 4 Oct 1975. Note also: 'To avoid the danger of having MPs who are ignorant of Party policies, TANU has decided that all candidates should be subject to a crucial test before the very people they want to serve by being given a uniform manifesto on which they will be required to propound at election campaign meetings' – *Daily News* editorial, 16 Sep 1975.
47. TANU, *Ilani*, pp. 2–3.
48. Ibid., p. 5.
49. *Daily News*, 21 July 1975.
50. With the adoption of the new Leadership Code, the setting up of political-education sessions for new members, and the demand by the party's youth organisation that it be allowed to give opinions on the political quality of people who wish to join the party, it may seem that TANU is quietly being transformed into an *avant-garde* party. Undoubtedly, however, this is a battle that has still to be won.
51. TANU, *Ilani*, pp. 4–5.
52. *Daily News*, 2 Apr 1975.
53. Martin, in *Revue française de science politique*, xxv, no. 4, 712–13.

CHAPTER 7

1. Even if its practice remained formal. See R. Binder, 'Syrian Deputies and Cabinet Ministers, 1919–1959', *Middle East Journal*, XVI (Autumn 1962) 407–29 and XVII (Winter 1963) 35–54.
2. On this period see Amos Perlmutter, 'From Obscurity to Rule: The Syrian Army and the Ba'ath Party', *Western Political Quarterly*, XXII (Dec 1969) 827–45.

3.
Registered	2,031,306	
Turnout	1,935,803	95·8 per cent
Yes	1,919,609	99·2 per cent
No	15,480	0·8 per cent
Blanks	714	

4. See J. Donohue, 'La Nouvelle constitution syrienne et ses détracteurs', *Travaux et Jours*, XLVII (Apr–June 1973) 93–111.

5.
Registered	2,345,625	
Turnout	2,085,261	88·9 per cent
Yes	2,035,215	97·6 per cent
No	48,825	2·3 per cent
Blanks	3,221	0·2 per cent

6. See Simon Jargy, 'La Syrie d'hier et d'aujourd'hui', *Orient*, XX (1964) 67–76.
7. See G. Torrey, 'Aspects of the Political Elite in Syria', in *Political Elites in the Middle East*, ed. G. Lenczowski (Washington, DC: American Enterprise Institute for Public Policy Research, 1975) pp. 151–63.
8. Members of the People's Council, 16 Feb 1971 to 22 Feb 1973: Ba'athists 85, SUO 12, UAS 12, ASM 8, Communists 8, representatives of popular organisations (trade unions, etc.) 48.

CHAPTER 8

1. For sources other than Portugal, see *International Guide to Electoral Statistics*, ed. Stein Rokkan and Jean Meyriat (The Hague: Mouton, 1969).
2. B. M. Russett et al., *World Handbook of Political and Social Indicators* (New Haven: Yale University Press, 1964) p. 83.
3. Similar clauses restricted one's eligibility to be a candidate for the National Assembly, with the replacement of the phrase 'contrary . . . to social discipline' by 'contrary . . . to the fundamental principles of established order'. These exclusions were used extensively and selectively. For an excellent discussion of the details of the electoral code, see José de Magalhães Godinho, *A Legislação Eleitoral e Sua Crítica* (Lisbon: Prêlo, 1969).
4. For a discussion of this, see my 'Liberation by *Golpe*: Retrospective Thoughts on the Demise of Authoritarian Rule in Portugal', in *Armed Forces and Society*, II, no. 1 (Fall 1975) 5–33.
5. On this topic, see Douglas Wheeler, 'Portuguese Elections and History', unpublished MS., University of New Hampshire, 1974.
6. Hugh Kay, *Salazar and Modern Portugal* (London: Eyre and Spottiswoode, 1970) p. 32.

7. For an analysis of its functioning see my *Corporatism and Public Policy in Authoritarian Portugal*, Sage Professional Papers, Contemporary Political Sociology Series, no. 06–011, vol. 1 (1975).

8. As Salazar himself once said, 'In truth, the regime we have lived in since 28 May [1926] has been impermeable to the political hysteria running around the world and this is why the opposition is always referring to our "immobilism"' – radio speech (5 Nov 1965) as reported in Oposiçao Democratica, *Campanha Eleitoral de 1965* (n.d.) p. 103.

9. Ibid., p. 101.

10. This becomes abundantly clear from reading his *Depoimento* (Rio: Distribuidôra Record, 1974) pp. 47–66 and 88–90.

11. Mário Soares, *Le Portugal baillonné* (Paris: Calmann-Levy, 1972) p. 255.

12. António de Figueiredo, *Portugal and its Empire: The Truth* (London: Victor Gollancz, 1961) p. 80. For more on the incidents upon which this observation was based (the 1945 campaign of Cunha Leal and the 1949 campaign of Norton de Mattos) see Soares, *Le Portugal baillonné*, pp. 51–3, 70–3.

13. K. Coleman and J. Wanat, 'Models of Political Influence on Federal Budgetary Allocations to Mexican States', paper delivered at the American Political Science Association meeting at New Orleans, 4–8 Sep 1973.

14. That is, in polities lacking a single mass party and extensive electoral mobilisation: the hypothesis it is not meant to be applicable to the non-competitive, non-free and insignificant elections characteristic of state socialist systems.

15. See my *Corporatism and Public Policy in Authoritarian Portugal* for an elaboration of this point.

16. *Depoimento*, p. 48.

17. See Hermínio Martins, 'Portugal' in *European Fascism*, ed. S. J. Woolf, (London: Weidenfeld and Nicolson, 1968) pp. 319–22.

18. 'The Social Origins, Economic Needs and Political Imperatives of Authoritarian Rule in Portugal', paper presented at the conference on 'Crisis in Portugal: Political, Military and Social Aspects of the MFA Revolution', University of Toronto, Toronto, 16–17 Apr 1976.

19. See the testimony by Caetano in *Depoimento*, pp. 57–66, 84–90, where he attempts to make them responsible for the failure of his 'decompression' strategy. See also Soares, *Le Portugal baillonné*, pp. 240–6, 271 et seq. For the frustrated testimony of one of the principal liberals involved, see Francisco Sá Carneiro, *Uma Tentativa de Participação Política* (Lisbon: Moraes Editores, 1971).

20. Antonio Alçada Baptista, *Documentos Políticos* (Lisbon: Moraes Editores, 1970) pp. 39–40, 73–5.

21. *Para um Dossier da 'Oposição Democrática'*, 2nd ser., ed. Serafin Ferreira and Arsénio Mota (Oporto, 1969) p. 484.

22. Baptista, *Documentos Políticos*, p. 13.

23. Soares, *Le Portugal baillonné*, p. 279.

24. To a certain extent, this potential for 'functional transformation' was recognised by the regime, which when faced with this possibility, reacted with 'appropriate' adjustments. After the 1958 presidential election, in which Humberto Delgado received a recognised (but probably fraudulent) 25 per cent of the votes and it appeared that the effort might carry over into the next

election, Salazar responded by making elections for that office indirect. In 1965 Delgado was assassinated in Spain near the Portuguese border.

25. Of course, in any given election, not all of these quasi-parties may have been actually available for voter choice. Specifically, the propensity for the opposition party (or parties) to withdraw just prior to the election frequently deprives us of any opportunity to measure empirically its (their) strength and distribution across units. Presumably, most of these withdrawn opponents swelled the ranks of the abstention party, if they were previously registered but did not vote, while some may have contributed to raising the totals for the disenfranchised party, to the extent they failed to register or were impeded from doing so. It can be presumed that none of these are likely to have voted for the regime-supporting party.

26. Prior to 1945, the entire country voted as a single constituency, making impossible any sort of ecological analysis by territorial sub-units. Perhaps, with the change in regime, it may become possible to disinter such breakdowns from official records, as well as to recover the district-level results for the 1945–1965 elections (so far as I know, these results have not yet become publicly available).

27. The specific formula for this vitality index is: (rate of fertility × population aged 20–39)/(rate of mortality × ratio of the population over 60 to the population under 20). The source is L. Morgado Cândido, *Aspectos Regionais da Demografia Portuguesa* (Lisbon: Fundação Calouste Gulbenkian, 1969) p. 227.

28. Naturally, this is a bit of an exaggeration in that the base figure (age-eligible population) did include some twenty-year-olds not yet formally eligible, many women who had just received the franchise, and, of course, many aged, infirm, and so on.

29. Horta is the extreme outlier in the scatterplot. According to the official data, 61 per cent of the age-eligible population in 1969 and 47 per cent in 1973 voted UN – ANP. The nearest figures for any other district were 37 and 41 per cent (Bragança), suggesting either the presence of an astonishingly effective local machine or the existence of vote fraud on a substantial scale.

30. *Corporatism and Public Policy in Authoritarian Portugal*, p. 58.

31. Schmitter, in *Armed Forces and Society*, II, no. 1, 5–33.

CHAPTER 9

1. H. McClosky and J. E. Turner, *The Soviet Dictatorship* (New York, 1960) pp. 324–32; M. Fainsod, *How Russia is Ruled* (London, 1963) pp. 381–2; G. B. Carson, *Electoral Practices in the USSR* (London, 1956) esp. pp. 85–100.

2. M. E. Mote, *Soviet Local and Republic Elections* (Stanford, Calif.; 1965); L. G. Churchward, 'Soviet Local Government Today', *Soviet Studies*, XVII, no. 4 (Apr 1966) 431–52; H. R. Swearer, 'The Functions of Soviet Local Elections', *Midwest Journal of Political Science*, V, no. 2 (May 1961) 129–49; R. A. Clarke, 'The Composition of the USSR Supreme Soviet, 1958–66', *Soviet Studies*, XIX, no.1 (July 1967) 53–65; R. J. Hill, 'Patterns of Deputy Selection to Local Soviets', *Soviet Studies*, XXV, no. 2 (Oct 1973) 196–212, and 'The CPSU in a Soviet Election Campaign', *Soviet Studies*, XXVIII, no. 4 (Oct

1976) 590–8; E. M. Jacobs 'Soviet Local Elections: What they are and What They are Not', *Soviet Studies*, XXII, no. 1 (July 1970) 61–76; J. M. Gilison, 'Soviet Elections as a Measure of Dissent: the Missing One Percent', *American Political Science Review*, LXII, no. 3 (Sep 1968) 814–23.

3. Z. Pelczynski, 'Poland 1957', in *Elections Abroad*, ed. D. Butler (London, 1959) pp. 119–79; J. Wiatr, 'Elections and Voting Behavior in Poland', in *Essays on the Behavioral Study of Politics*, ed. A. Ranney (Urbana, Ill., 1962) pp. 236–51; J. Ptakowski, 'Parliamentary Elections in Poland', *East Europe*, Aug 1965, 16–18; F. Dinka and M. J. Skidmore, 'The Functions of Communist One-Party Elections: The Case of Czechoslovakia 1971', *Political Science Quarterly*, Sep 1973, 395–422; D. Rusinow, 'Yugoslav Elections 1969' (3 parts), *American Universities Fieldstaff Reports*, Southeast Europe Series, XVI, nos 4–6. Useful detailed reports and analyses of elections in Poland, Hungary, Czechoslovakia, Bulgaria and Romania are to be found in the *Situation* and *Background Reports* of Radio Free Europe.

4. Soviet and East European literature on elections continues to be dominated legal and procedural studies; though a few critical Soviet analyses have appeared, Poland is still exceptional in its detailed election studies, of which full use is made throughout. Wherever possible, English language references are given for Soviet and East European material.

5. See, for example, V. M. Chkhikvadze, *The Soviet Form of Popular Government* (Moscow, 1972) p. 79; A. Bezuglov, *Soviet Deputy* (Moscow, 1973) pp. 16–18; L. G. Churchward, *Contemporary Soviet Government* (London, 1968) p. 103.

6. Carson, *Electoral Practices*, pp. 1–48.

7. See C. A. McCartney and A. N. Palmer, *Independent Eastern Europe* (London, 1962) pp. 165, 216, 220–1, 375, 377, 394– even Romania in 1928 and Bulgaria in 1938 had competitive elections. For Poland, see A. Polonsky, *Politics in Independent Poland 1921–39* (Oxford, 1972) pp. 60–1, 247–51, 321–3. For Czechoslovakia, see P. E. Zinner, *Communist Strategy and Tactics in Czechoslovakia 1918–48* (London, 1963) pp. 63–5, 183–6.

8. See H. G. Skilling, *The Communist Governments of Eastern Europe* (Toronto, 1966) pp. 65–6; Q. Schmidt, 'The New Electoral Law in Hungary's Electoral System', *Hungarian Law Review*, no. 2 (1967) 32. The extremely sceptical Czechoslovak attitudes to elections in 1968 must be attributed in part to their traditions of competitive elections; see J. A. Piekalkiewicz, *Public Opinion Polling in Czechoslovakia 1968–69* (New York, 1972) pp. 171–98.

9. See Skilling, *Communist Governments*, pp. 111–23. Analysis of these countries' political traditions and political cultures can be found in *Political Culture and Political Change in Communist States*, ed. A. H. Brown and J. Gray (London, 1977).

10. A. K. Makhnenko, *The State Law of the Socialist Countries* (Moscow, 1976) pp. 274–5; Carson, *Electoral Practices*, pp. 9–48. For Hungary, see Schmidt, in *Hungarian Law Review*, no. 2, 25–31; and F. A. Vali, *Rift and Revolt in Hungary* (London, 1962) pp. 32, 40. For Czechoslovakia, see Zinner, *Communist Strategy*, p. 226; and J. Houser, in *Pravnik*, 1972, 1044–9. For Poland, see Z. Jarosz, *System wyborczy PRL* (Warsaw, 1969) pp. 15–16; and Wiatr, in *Essays on the Behavioral Study of Politics*, ed. Ranney, p. 236, for the term 'semi-civil-war elections'.

11. Carson, *Electoral Practices*, pp. 49–80 (USSR); Schmidt, in *Hungarian Law*

Review, no. 2, 32–3, and Vali, *Rift and Revolt*, p. 57 (Hungary); Houser, in *Pravnik*, 1972, 1050 (Czechoslovakia); Jarosz, *System wyborczy PRL*, pp. 17–19, and Wiatr, in *Essays on the Behavioral Study of Politics*, ed. Ranney, p. 237 (Poland). Wiatr calls these 'safe' elections.

12. In the Soviet Union, hopes that the new laws meant a real freeing of elections were dispelled by police intervention to ensure only one candidate per seat. See Carson, *Electoral Practices*, pp. 52, 63.

13. See Swearer, in *Midwest Journal of Political Science*, v, no. 2, 141–3, and Bezuglov, *Soviet Deputy*, pp. 147–8 (USSR); L. Janicki, *Ustroj polityczny NDR* (Poznan, 1964) pp. 101–3 (East Germany); Schmidt, in *Hungarian Law Review*, no. 2, 35 (Hungary).

14. They figured in the Harich group demands in East Germany in 1956 – see D. Childs, *East Germany* (London, 1969) p. 38; and in Hungary in 1956 – see *Hungarian Revolution*, ed. M. J. Laski (London, 1957) pp. 48, 51. For Polish developments, see Pelczynski, in *Elections Abroad*, ed. Butler, pp. 125–33; for Yugoslavia, see F. Singleton, *Twentieth Century Yugoslavia* (London, 1976) pp. 145–7, and *Yugoslav Survey*, Oct – Dec 1963, 2125–38.

15. For the USSR, see V. M. Chkhivadze, *The State, Democracy and Legality in the USSR* (Moscow, 1972) pp. 148–58; and the 1972 statute on the deputy's status as outlined in *Pravda*, 21 Sep 1972, trans. in *Current Digest of the Soviet Press*, 1972, no. 39, 6–7. For Poland, see Radio Free Europe, *Polish Background Report*, 3 Nov 1972; for Czechoslovakia, G. Golan, *The Czechoslovak Reform Movement* (London, 1971) pp. 178–84; for Hungary, W. F. Robinson, *The Pattern of Reform in Hungary* (New York, 1973) pp. 216–21.

16. Bezuglov, *Soviet Deputy*, pp. 1–32; and J. Grospic, in *Pravnik*, 1971, 777. For an interesting Soviet analysis of interests, see Y. S. Zavaylov, 'Politic heskiye interesy i ikh osushchestvleniye v SSSR', *Sovetskoe gosudarstvo i pravo*, 1973, no. 1, 27–34.

17. For a useful review of Soviet proposals, see R. J. Hill, 'Soviet Literature on Electoral Reform: A Review', *Government and Opposition*, Autumn 1976, pp. 482–95. An account of Czechoslovak attempts at reform is in Golan, *The Czechoslovak Reform Movement*, pp. 185–8.

18. See Childs, *East Germany*, p. 90; Robinson, *The Pattern of Reform in Hungary*, pp. 249–50 and 266–69; Radio Free Europe, *Romanian Background Report*, 16 Jan 1975; Rusinow, in *American Universities Fieldstaff Reports*, SE Europe Series, XVI, no. 4, 12–13 (Yugoslavia); S. Gebert, 'Wspolna ordynacja wyborcza do Sejm i rad narodowych', *Panstwo i Prawo*, 1976, nos 1–2, 112–26 (Poland).

19. *The Secret Vysocany Congress*, ed. J. Pelikan (London, 1972) pp. 234–37.

20. Non-Communist parties exist in Czechoslovakia, Poland, East Germany and Bulgaria. See Skilling, *Communist Governments*, pp. 65–6; Makhnenko, *State Law*, pp. 162–8. For the concept of 'hegemonic party' see J. Wiatr, 'Political Parties, Interest Representation and Economic Development in Poland', *American Political Science Review*, LXIV, no. 4 (Dec 1970) 1239–45.

21. M. Saifulin, *The Soviet Parliament* (Moscow, 1967) p. 31; Houser, in *Pravnik*, 1972, p. 1054. According to Mote (*Soviet . . . Elections*, p. 29) there have been only one or two instances of two candidates at village level.

22. A. I. Kim, Sovetskoe izbiratelnoe pravo (Moscow, 1965) p. 185; Chkhivadze, *The Soviet Form of Popular Government*, p. 85.

23. See R. J. Hill, in *Government and Opposition*, Autumn 1976, p. 486; R.

Medvedev, *On Socialist Democracy* (London, 1975) p. 144. The 1967 Czechoslovak election law introduced an excess of one-third to one-half of candidates over seats, but was rescinded in 1971; see Golan, *The Czechoslovak Reform Movement*, pp. 185–8.

24. See, for instance, the Soviet Communist Party call to electors in *Pravda* 7 May 1966; trans. in *Current Digest of the Soviet Press*, 1966, no. 18, 31–2.

25. See V. M. Chkhivadze, *Soviet State and Law* (Moscow, 1969) pp. 140–1; *Partiinaya zhizn*, 1976 no. 8, 6; and Czechoslovak election law of 1971, in *Sbirka zakonu*, 6 July 1971.

26. For Soviet election campaigns, see Mote, *Soviet . . . Elections*, pp. 44–65; Churchward, in *Soviet Studies*, XVII, no. 4, 447–8; J. M. Gilison, *British and Soviet Politics: A Study in Legitimacy and Convergence* (London 1973) pp. 69–71. For the Czechoslovak campaign of 1971, see Dinka and Skidmore, in *Political Science Quarterly*, Sep 1973, 403–6.

27. See, for instance, *Partiinaya zhizn*, 1966, no. 10, 9; *Vedomosti Verkhovnogo Soveta RSFSR*, 9 Feb 1969, trans. in *Current Digest of the Soviet Press*, 1969, no. 21, 25–6.

28. See *Zeri i popullit*, 8–9 Oct 1974, in *ABSEES*, VI, no. 1 (June 1975) 128 (Albania); Radio Free Europe, *Czechoslovak Situation Report*, 27 Oct 1976. J. M. Gilison (in *American Political Science Review*, LXII, no. 3, 820) takes absenteeism as an indicator of individual dissent.

29. See Swearer, in *Midwest Journal of Political Science*, V, no. 2, 146; and Mote *Soviet . . . Elections*, pp. 77–81. For criticism, see Y. Sabanov, quoted by Hill, in *Government and Opposition*, Autumn 1976, 487–8. In one survey conducted in Czechoslovakia in 1968 no. respondents (487) secrecy of the ballot was thought to be one of the most important conditions for an improvement in elections; see Piekalkiewicz, *Public Opinion Polling in Czechoslovakia*, p. 172.

30. Gilison, in *American Political Science Review*, LXII, no. 3, 820 – 2; Jacobs, in *Soviet Studies*, XXII, no. 1, pp. 70–6.

31. See Bezuglov, *Soviet Deputy*, pp. 143–52; Makhnenko, *State Law*, p. 287; and, for Czechoslovakia, J. Chovanec, *Zastupitelska soustava CSSR* (Prague, 1974) p. 116.

32. See V. K. Grigoriev, *Vybory v mestniye Sovety deputatov trudyashchikhsya* (Moscow, 1969) pp. 36–40; Kim, *Sovetskoe izbiratelnoe pravo*, pp. 172–80; and, for Czechoslovakia, see Chovanec, *Zastupitelska soustava CSSR*, pp. 105, 116.

33. Western accounts (see Swearer, in *Midwest Journal of Political Science*, V, no. 2, 137–8, and Clarke, in *Soviet Studies* XIX, no. 1, 60–3) are confirmed by Soviet sources (see Y. Shabanov, quoted by Hill, in *Soviet Studies*, XXVIII, no. 4, 594–5). In Czechoslovakia the process is similar, though the National Front provides an institutional forum for local officials' negotiations (see Chovanec, *Zastupitelska soustava CSSR*, p. 116).

34. See Swearer, in *Midwest Journal of Political Science*, V, no. 2, 140–1; Mote, *Soviet . . . Elections*, pp. 26–9; Churchward, in *Soviet Studies*, XVII, no. 4, 447–9. For critical comment on similar Czechoslovak practice, see V. Klokocka, *Volby v pluralitnich demokraciich* (Prague, 1968) p. 249.

35. A. Aimbetov, M. Baimakhanov and M. Imasev, *Problmy sovershenstvovaniya organizatsii i deyatelnost mestnykh Sovetov* (Alma-Ata, 1967) pp. 90–1; Mote, *Soviet . . . Elections*, pp. 57–60; Swearer, in *Midwest Journal of Political*

Science, v, no. 2, p. 143.

36. See proposals by A. I. Kim, Y. Shabanov and A. V. Moshak cited by Hill in *Government and Opposition*, Autumn 1976, 489–92.

37. Aimbetov et al., *Problmy*, pp. 91–2; Kim, *Sovetskoe izbiratelnoe pravo*, pp. 180–1. For official Soviet concern see *Partiinaya zhizn*, 1971, no. 8, 19; 1973, no. 9, 14. In 1967, a sample of 1248 local councillors in East Bohemia (Czechoslovakia) thought that voters should have more chance to discuss candidates; see *Problemy Rad Narodowych*, 1969, no. 14, 77. For more radical Czech criticism, see Klokocka, *Volby*, p. 249.

38. Aimbetov et al., *Problmy*, pp. 91–2; Y. Shabanov, quoted by Hill, in *Soviet Studies* XXVIII, no. 4, 595.

39. Medvedev (*On Socialist Democracy*, pp. 372–3) gives an instance of this happening at Tartu University in Estonia. The phrase is T. H. Rigby's; see his 'Hough on Political Participation in the Soviet Union', *Soviet Studies*, XXVIII, no. 2 (Apr 1976) 260.

40. Poland, Hungary and Yugoslavia are generally regarded as politically the most pluralist Communist Party states, and even Romania and East Germany can be ranked above the USSR and Bulgaria. Czechoslovakia is the exception which proves the rule, as only armed intervention prevented the introduction of a radical version of limited-choice elections. For a general discussion of pluralism, see G. Ionescu, *The Politics of the European Communist States* (London, 1967).

41. See K. Sontheimer and W. Bleek, *The Government and Politics of East Germany* (London, 1975) p. 80; B. A. Strashun, 'Razvitie izbiratelnogo prava sotsialisticheskikh stran, *Sovetskoe gosudarstvo i pravo*, 1973, no. 7, 47; K. Nowak, 'Wybory do Izby Ludowej i okregowych przedstawicielstw w NRD', *Przeglad zachodny,* 1967, no. 6, 296–9. The post-1965 system is only slightly different from the old one of substitute deputies – current throughout Eastern Europe in the early 1950s – under which 'surplus' candidates could never be elected to full office; see Makhnenko, *State Law*, pp. 293–5.

42. See Pelczynski, in *Elections Abroad*, ed. Butler, pp. 131–2; Wiatr, in *Essays on the Behavioral Study of Politics*, ed. Ranney, p. 241; Gebert, in *Panstwo i Prawo*, nos 1–2, 115. The 1956 law stipulated that there should be an excess of at least two-thirds of candidates for all elections; in 1957 this was reduced to a half and made optional for parliamentary elections. In 1976 it was again made obligatory for all elections.

43. Under the complex and oft-changing Yugoslav system of the 1950s and 1960s, direct elections were held only to communal assemblies and the general representative chambers at higher levels, all others being elected indirectly; see Rusinow, in *American Universities Fieldstaff Reports*, SE Europe Series, XVI, no. 4, 4–10. Under the delegation system introduced in 1974, only the local delegations are directly elected; see Singleton, *Twentieth Century Yugoslavia*, pp. 274–5, and Makhnenko, *State Law*, pp. 283–4. In Hungary, the Budapest Council and all regional councils are indirectly elected.

44. See *Yugoslav Survey*, Nov 1967, 17; Jarosz, *System wyborczy PRL*, pp. 218–19 (Poland); Radio Free Europe, *Romanian Situation Report*, 21 Feb 1975. Nowak, in *Przeglad zachodny*, 1967, no. 6, 299, gives 20 per cent as the excess for the 1967 elections in East Germany. In Hungary the largest excess was the 10 per cent recorded in the 1971 elections (see Radio Free Europe, *Hungarian*

Background Report, 13 June 1975). These figures are far lower than the seven-to-one ratio in the comparable Tanzanian elections of 1965; see A. J. Milnor, *Elections and Political Stability* (Boston, Mass., 1969) p. 163.

45. Notably in 1967 and 1969; see Rusinow, in *American Universities Fieldstaff Reports*, SE Europe Series, xvi, no. 4, 3, and no. 6, 2. For the official line in Hungary, for instance, see Kadar, *Nepszabadsag*, 21 Apr 1971; quoted in Radio Free Europe, *Hungarian Background Report*, 24 May 1971.

46. In the Hungarian elections of 1971 some provincial party officials were placed in contested seats (this was not repeated in 1975); see Radio Free Europe, *Hungarian Background Report*, 31 Mar 1971, and 13 June 1975. In Romania in 1975, one or two government officials did fight seats; see Radio Free Europe, *Romanian Situation Report*, 14 Mar 1975.

47. See Radio Free Europe, *Hungarian Background Report*, 13 June 1975, and *Polish Background Report*, 17 Mar 1972. For an analysis of these 'core' deputies in the Soviet context, which is also valid for Eastern Europe, see R. J. Hill, 'Continuity and Change in Supreme Soviet Elections', *British Journal of Political Science*, ii, no. 1 (Jan 1972) 49–57.

48. See Radio Free Europe, *Hungarian Background Report*, 13 June 1975, and *Polish Background Report* 17 Mar 1972. Polish evidence is by far the best here; see S. Bereza, 'Wybory do dzielnicony rady narodowy Warszawa-Ochota', *Studia socjologiczno-politiczne*, 1959, no. 2, 163; and W. Skrzydlo, 'Wybory do rad narodowych 1965 w swietle ordynacej wyborczy i praktyki, *Problemy Rad Narodowych*, 1966 no. 7, 122.

49. For detailed analyses of the Polish campaigns of 1957 and 1958, see Pelczynski, in *Elections Abroad*, ed. Butler, pp. 148–68 and J. Wiatr, 'Niektore zagadnienia opinii publiczne w swiatle wyborow 1957–58', *Studia socjologiczno-politiczne*, 1959, no. 4, esp. 107, 144. For the 1965 elections, see S. Gebert, 'Prawo i praktyka wyborcza w swietle doswiadczen z wyborow do rad narodowych', *Problemy Rad Narodowych*, 1966, no. 7, 70–3. For Hungary in 1971, see Radio Free Europe, *Hungarian Background Report*, 25 Feb 1971.

50. A poll taken in Lodz during the 1958 elections found that two-thirds of the 352 respondents could not name any candidate; in 1961 a similar poll in Lodz found that the figure had fallen to one-third. See Z. Gostowski, 'Popular Interest in Activity of People's Councils, Lodz 1958', *Public Opinion Quarterly*, Fall 1959, 375, and 'Analysis of the Panel Effect in the Study of an Election Campaign in Poland', *Polish Sociological Bulletin*, 1967, no. 1, 50–1.

51. See Rusinow on the 1969 Yugoslav elections, in *American Universities Fieldstaff Reports*, SE Europe Series, xvi, no. 4, 14–15, and no. 6, 7. For conflicts in Poland in 1957, see Pelczynski, in *Elections Abroad*, ed. Butler, pp. 154–7. For the milder debates in Hungary in 1971, see Radio Free Europe, *Hungarian Background Report*, 24 May 1971.

52. In Hungary and Yugoslavia, recall follows the same procedure as elections; see Makhnenko, *State Law*, p. 287, and, for variations, O. Bihari, *Socialist Representative Institutions* (Budapest, 1971) pp. 126–30. Jarosz, *System wyborczy PRL*, pp. 298–320, is critical of Polish procedure. For voting, see Strashun, in *Sovetskoe gosudarstvo i pravo*, no. 7, 46–9. In Romania unmarked ballots are counted as votes for the candidate with strongest support; see *Scienteia*, 11 Mar 1975, in *ABSEES*, vi, no. 3 (July 1975) 254.

53. Ibid. See also *Yugoslav Survey*, Oct–Dec 1963, 2145–6; July–Sep 1965, 3177;

and Nov 1967, 14–15. Both Polish and Hungarian figures show a fall associated with transition to limited competition; see Wiatr, in *Essays on the Behavioral Study of Politics*, ed. Ranney, pp. 237–9. The 1958 turnout of 86 per cent was exceptionally low; since then the figure has varied between 96 and 98 per cent; see Radio Free Europe, *Polish background Report*, 24 Mar 1972. For Hungary, see Radio Free Europe, *Hungarian Background Report*, 24 May 1971; and *Nepszabadsag*, 17 June 1975, in *ABSEES*, vi, no. 4 (Oct 1975) 209.

54. Wiatr (in *Essays on the Behavioral Study of Politics*, ed. Ranney, pp. 241 and 246) shows that in the 1957 and 1958 Polish elections turn-out was higher in western and northern regions; for the 1965 elections, see S. Gebert, in *Problemy Rad Narodowych*, no. 7, 62–3. In the 1976 Polish elections, turn-out was markedly down in the troubled Baltic areas; see *Trybuna Ludu*, 23 Mar 1976. In Yugoslavia throughout the 1960s, turnout was highest in Slovenia and lowest in Macedonia or Montenegro; see *Yugoslav Survey*, Oct – Dec 1963, 2145–6, and July – Sep, 3177. This can largely be accounted for by differences in levels of education and general development.

55. For Polish regional variations, see Wiatr, in *Essays on the Behavioral Study of Politics*, ed. Ranney, pp. 246–7, and in *Studia socjologiczno-politiczne*, no. 4, 112 and 156. The fall in negative votes in Poland from 0·78 to 0·47 per cent in 1972 reflected the greater popularity of the Gierek leadership (see Radio Free Europe, *Polish Background Report*, 24 Mar 1972). In the Yugoslav elections of 1963, 1965 and 1967, Slovenia consistently returned the highest number of negative votes (5 to 8 per cent: see *Yugoslav Survey*, Oct – Dec 1963, 2145–6; July – Sep, 3177; and Nov 1967, 14–15). Romania's first competitive elections, in 1975, produced 1·2 per cent voting against, as compared with 0·25 per cent in 1969 (Radio Free Europe, *Romanian Background Report*, 14 Mar 1975). Cf. the increase between the 1967 and 1971 Hungarian elections (Radio Free Europe, *Hungarian Background Report*, 24 May 1971).

56. See Rusinow, in *American Universities Fieldstaff Reports*, SE Europe Series, xvi, no. 5, 14–19; and Singleton, *Twentieth Century Yugoslavia*, p. 147. Many of the successful independents have been traditionalist partisans. In the thirteen clear contests between official and unofficial candidates in Hungary in 1971, victory was divided equally; see Radio Free Europe, *Hungarian Background Report*, 24 May 1971. Markedly lower majorities result from contested seats; see J. Gronsky, 'Novy volebni system Madarske lidove Republiky', *Pravnik*, 1971, 1034.

57. See Gebert, *Problemy Rad Narodowych*, 1966, no. 7, 49, for 1961 and 1965 figures. It is significant that in the only defeat of a Polish parliamentary 'seat' candidate, in Nowy Sacz in 1957, none of the 'surplus' candidates was elected; see Pelczynski, in *Elections Abroad*, ed. Butler, pp. 170–1.

58. The total number of votes cast against 'seat' candidates in Poland has ranged from over 10 per cent in 1957 (in 1958 20 per cent was recorded in Warsaw's industrial constituencies) to 3–4 per cent throughout the 1960s. See Pelczynski, in *Elections Abroad*, ed. Butler, p. 169; Wiatr, in *Studia socjologiczno-politiczne*, no. 4, p. 163; Gebert, *Problemy Rad Narodowych*, 1966, no. 7, p. 69; Radio Free Europe, *Polish Background Report*, 19 May 1969.

59. See Wiatr, in *Studia sociologiczno-politiczne*, 1959, no. 4, 115 and 178–9; Pelczynski, in *Elections Abroad*, ed. Butler, pp. 172–3; Radio Free Europe

Polish Background Report, Appendix.

60. See Strashun, *Sovetskoe gosudarstvo i pravo*, 1973, no. 7, 45 (Yugoslavia and East Germany); Jarosz, *System wyborczy PRL*, pp. 191–8 (Poland); *Scienteia*, 21 Dec 1974, in *ABSEES*, VI, no. 2 (April 1975) 227 (Romania).

61. See M. Domagala, 'Ewolucja systemi wyborczej NDR', *Zeszyty ndukowy UL*, no. 99 (1973) 99 (East Germany); Jarosz, *System wyborczy PRL*, pp. 191–3 (Poland). Radio Free Europe, *Hungarian Background Report*, 25 Feb 1971, gives details of the 1970 law. The 1974 Yugoslav law endows social and political organisations with greater powers than they held in the 1960s. See Rusinow, in *American Universities Fieldstaff Report*, SE Europe Series, XVI, no. 4 10–13; Singleton, *Twentieth Century Yugoslavia*, pp. 274–5; *Yugoslav Survey*, Aug 1974, 45–6.

62. See Rusinow, XVI, no. 6, in *American Universities Fieldstaff Reports*, SE Europe Series, XVI, no. 6, 11–15 (Yugoslavia); Pelczynski, in *Elections Abroad*, ed. Butler, pp. 142–8, Jarosz, *System wyborczy PRL*, pp. 200–4, and Gebert, in *Problemy Rad Narodowych*, 1966, no. 7, 53 (Poland); Gronsky, in *Pravnik*, 1971, 1027–8, and Radio Free Europe, *Hungarian Background Report*, 13 June 1975 (Hungary). Where the local party presses unitedly for a candidate it is successful.

63. See Rusinow, in *American Universities Fieldstaff Reports*, XVI, no. 4, 12; *Yugoslav Survey*, Nov 1967, 17. For Hungary, see Radio Free Europe, *Hungarian Background Report*, 31 Mar 1971; in two-thirds of the contested seats in 1971 both candidates were officially sponsored.

64. Polish evidence is the most detailed: see Jaroz, *System wyborczy PRL*, pp. 239–41; Gebert, in *Problemy Rad Narodowych*, 1966, no. 7, p. 57; A. Patrzalek, 'Niektore instytucje prawa wyborczego PRL w swietle praktyki wyborow 1965', *Problemy Rad Narodowych*, 1966, no. 7, 97–8. For Hungary, see Radio Free Europe, *Hungarian Background Report*, 31 Mar 1971; for Yugoslav figures in 1965 and 1967, see *Yugoslav Survey*, July–Sep 1967, 3175, and Nov 1967, 17–18.

65. See Swearer, in *Midwest Journal of Political Science*, V, no. 2 142–5; Gilison, in *American Political Science Review*, LXII, no. 3, 814; Dinka and Skidmore, in *Political Science Quarterly*, Sep 1973, p. 397. For an analysis of the functions of 'classic' elections, see R. Rose and H. Mossawir, 'Voting and Elections', *Political Studies*, XV, no. 2 (June 1967).

66. The differences are often ones of campaign emphasis. Cf. *Partiinaya zhizn*, no. 8 (1974) 5–7, and Mote, *Soviet . . . Elections*, pp. 76–9 (USSR) with Wiatr, in *Studia socjologiczno-politiczne*, 1959, no. 4, 75–82, 125–30, and Gebert, in *Problemy Rad Narodowych*, 1966, no. 7, 71–2 (Poland). One of the objectives of the Hungarian election law of 1970 was to stimulate greater activity; see *Nepszabadsag*, 20 Sep 1970, in *ABSEES*, I, no. 3 (Jan 1971) 190–9. For 'stalactite' and 'stalagmite', see J. P. Nettl, *Political Mobilisation* (London, 1967) pp. 271–2.

67. Throughout the 1960s attendance at nomination meetings for the federal level was below 20; this accounted for some of the non-confirmations. See *Yugoslav Survey*, Oct–Dec 1963, 2144; July–Sep 1965, 3175; and November 1967, 17.

68. See Jarosz, *System wyborczy PRL*, pp. 230–7, Party Central Committee, *Nowe Drogi*, no. 4 (1972) 39, and J. Ptasinski, *Nowe Drogi*, no. 7 (1965) 47 (Poland);

Zivot strany, 20 Sep 1971 (Czechoslovakia); Hill, in *Soviet Studies*, XXVIII, no. 4, 592–3 (USSR). For extension of terms, see Grospic, in *Pravnik*, 1971, 779; and Radio Free Europe, *Hungarian Background Report*, 13 June 1975.

69. Soviet citizens thus experience elections for one-eighth of their lives; see Hill, in *Soviet Studies*, XXVIII, no. 4, 590. The separate or joint holding of national and local-level elections varies in these states independently of the type of election.

70. See Mote, *Soviet . . . Elections*, pp. 19, 64–72; Dinka and Skidmore, in *Political Science Quarterly*, Sep 1973, 403, 405 (Czechoslovakia).

71. See Medvedev, *On Socialist Democracy*, p. 143. Polish research in 1961 found that these media did little to increase public interest, and that all including survey interviewing tended to be identified as official agitation; see Gostowski, in *Polish Sociological Bulletin*, 1967, no. 1, 47, 50–1. In his 1958 Lodz survey (in *Public Opinion Quarterly*, Fall 1959, 374–5), Gostowski found that campaign propaganda had some effect on knowledge of candidates. For emphasis in Polish campaigns, see Wiatr, in *Studia socjologiczno-politiczne*, 1959, no. 4, 94–109, 137–46.

72. See the party call to voters in *Pravda*, 16 May 1970; trans. in *Current Digest of the Soviet Press*, 1970, no. 20, pp. 10–11. For Hungarian examples, see Kadar, Radio Budapest, 14 June 1975, in BBC *Summary of World Broadcasts, Eastern Europe*, 30 May 1975. The opportunity is usually taken to attack bourgeois elections; see Mote, *Soviet . . . Elections*, pp. 54–5, and Radio Free Europe, *Czechoslovak Situation Report*, 21 Jan 1971.

73. See Rusinow, in *American Universities Fieldstaff Reports*, SE Europe Series, XVI, no. 6, 14–19 (Yugoslavia); Pelczynski, in *Elections Abroad*, ed. Butler, pp. 161–2 (Poland); Radio Free Europe, *Hungarian Background Report*, 24 May 1971. For local focus, see Gebert, in *Problemy Rad Norodowych*, 1966, no. 7, 72 (Poland); and Nowak, in *Przeglad zachodny*, 1967, no. 6, 293 (East Germany).

74. One-third of Slovak voters attended these meetings in 1971; see Dinka and Skidmore, in *Political Science Quarterly*, Sep 1973, 403. 48 per cent of Hungarian voters did so in 1967; see Gronsky, in *Pravnik*, 1971, 1026. Attendance can drop a great deal, especially in local elections; Bereza, in *Studia socjologiczno-politiczne*, 1959, no. 2, 171, gives 10 per cent for one district of Warsaw in 1958. Officially attendance is seen as proof of political consciousness; see Chkhivadze, *The Soviet Form of Popular Government*, p. 104. For collective voting, see Radio Free Europe, *Czechoslovak Background Report* 27 Jan 1971.

75. See Gilison, in *American Political Science Review*, LXII, no. 3 816. For the somewhat lower rates elsewhere see Makhnenko, *State Law*, p. 296.

76. See Radio Free Europe, *Hungarian Background Report*, 24 May 1971 and 13 June 1975; Gebert, *Problemy Rad Narodowych*, 1966, no. 6, 70; Gilison, *British and Soviet Politics*, p. 85. It has been calculated that, at the Soviet rate, the number of people who in the course of a decade experience the office of deputy is about 6 million; see D. P. Hammer, *USSR: The Politics of Oligarchy* (Hinsdale, Ill., 1974) p. 152. For contrasting Soviet views, see *Partiinaya zhizn*, 1964, no. 11, 21–7; and Aimbetov et al., *Problemy*, pp. 99–100.

77. See D. E. Powell and P. Shoup, 'The Emergence of Political Science in Communist countries', *American Political Science Review*, LXIV, no. 2 (June

1970) 577, quoting a survey in Siberia published in 1967; also see Medvedev's very critical comments in *On Socialist Democracy*, p. 143. For the Czechoslovak poll (1008 respondents), see Piekalkiewicz, *Public Opinion Polling in Czechoslovakia*, p. 175. On political socialisation developments, see G. P. Hollander, *Soviet Political Indoctrination* (New York, 1972); and *Political Socialisation in Eastern Europe*, ed. I. Volyges (New York, 1975).

78. The 1958 poll in Lodz found that one-third of the 352 respondents could name at least one candidate; in 1961 two-thirds of 369 could do so and nearly 80 per cent of 434 expressed interest in the elections; see Gostowski, in *Public Opinion Quarterly*, Fall 1959, 375–80, and in *Polish Sociological Bulletin*, 1967, no. 1, 50–1. Gostowski's 1958 findings of the low level of correct attitudes were confirmed by Bereza, in *Studia socjologiczno-polityczne*, 1959, no. 2, 176. For comment on Yugoslav attitudes, see Rusinow, in *American Universities Fieldstaff Reports*, SE Europe Series, XVI, no. 4, 2.

79. Elections reach groups, such as housewives and pensioners, that are weakly integrated through socio-political organisations and economic mobilisation. Some see integration as the primary purpose of 'totalitarian' elections; see Milnor, *Elections and Political Stability*, p. 119.

80. See the party appeal to electors in *Pravda*, 16 May 1970, trans. in *Current Digest of the Soviet Press* 1970, no. 20, 10–11; Gierek, *Nowe Drogi*, 1972, no. 3, 21–2; and Kadar, quoted in Radio Free Europe, *Hungarian Background Report*, 13 June 1975.

81. See Chovanec, *Zastupitelska soustava CSSR*, pp. 116, 126–32 (Czechoslovakia). For the USSR, see Saifulin, *The Soviet Parliament*, pp. 35–42; and Hill, in *British Journal of Political Science*, II, no. 1, 49–64.

82. See Bezuglov, *Soviet Deputy*, pp. 27–32; Mote, *Soviet . . . Elections*, pp. 51–2; Swearer, in *Midwest Journal of Political Science*, V, no. 2, 134. For Czechoslovakia, see Chovanec, *Zastupitelska soustava CSSR*, p. 105 and Grospic, *Pravnik*, 1971, 777.

83. See Gilison, *British and Soviet Politics*, pp. 98–9. Research in the USSR has found that the worker and peasant deputies, i.e. those selected for their group representation, perform poorly; see V. P. Kazimirchuk et al., *Upravlenie, sotsiologiya, pravo* (Moscow, 1971) pp. 176–201, trans. in *Soviet Law and Government*, XI, no. 3 (Winter 1972–3) 208–23. One Estonian survey found that 77 per cent of voters were dissatisfied with their deputies; see Powell and Shoup, in *American Political Science Review*, LXIV, no. 2, 577.

84. See Bereza, in *Studia socjologiczno-polityczne*, 1959, no. 2, 168; Polish national survey of 1965, *Problemy Rad Narodowych*, 1969, no. 13, 49 and 74; and a Czechoslovak poll of July 1968 in Piekalkiewicz in *Public Opinion Polling in Czechoslovakia*, p. 179. For Yugoslavia, see Rusinow, in *American Universities Fieldstaff Reports*, SE Europe Series, XVI, no. 6, 8 and 11.

85. See B. Zawadska, 'Socjalistyczny mandat przedstawicielski', *Panstwo i Prawo*, 1973, no. 12, 60–4; Bihari, *Socialist Representative Institutions*, pp. 116–24. For local politicking, see Pelczynski, in *Elections Abroad*, ed. Butler, pp. 145–6 (Poland) and Rusinow, in *American Universities Fieldstaff Reports*, SE Europe Series, XVI, no. 6, 14–19 (Yugoslavia).

86. See Jarosz, *System wyborczy PRL*, p. 269 (Poland); Radio Free Europe, *Hungarian Background Report*, 13 June 1975; Chovanec, *Zastupitelska soustava CSSR*, p. 126 (Czechoslovakia). For the USSR, see E. M. Jacobs, 'The

Composition of Local Soviets', *Government and Opposition*, 1969, no. 4, 504 – 17; and *Sovety deputatov trudyashchikhsya*, 1975, no. 8, 19 – 23.
87. See Swearer, *Midwest Journal of Political Science*, v, no. 2, pp. 145 – 7; Party Central Committee call, *Pravda* 7 May 1966, trans. in *Current Digest of the Soviet Press*, 1966, no. 18, 31 – 2; Gierek, in *Nowe Drogi*, 1972, no. 3, 23; and Party Central Committee, *Nowe Drogi*, 1972, no. 4, 39. Leaders no longer stand for several seats, as was the case in the USSR in the 1930s; see Mote, *Soviet . . . Elections*, p. 31. Such votes can reflect popularity; see Radio Free Europe, *Polish Background Report*, 24 Mar 1972, on differentiation in the Polish elections of 1972.
88. See Vali, *Rift and Revolt*, pp. 417 – 18 (Hungary); Dinka and Skidmore, in *Political Science Quarterly*, Sep 1973, 413, and Radio Free Europe, *Czechoslovak Background Report*, 22 Jan 1971 (Czechoslovakia).
89. See V. F. Kotok, quoted in *Studies in Polish Political System* (Warsaw, 1967), ed. J. Wiatr, p. 134; also see Y. Shabanov's criticism of this view in *Problemy sovetskoi sotsialisticheskoi demokratii v period stroitelstva kommunizma* (Minsk, 1969) p. 143.
90. A standard 'explanation' of defeats is that they reveal nomination errors; see Chkhikvadze, *The Soviet State and Law*, p. 141.
91. See Wiatr, in *Studia socjologiczno-polityczne*, 1959, no. 4, 179 and 204; Pelczynski, in *Elections Abroad*, ed. Butler, pp. 164 – 5. For Hungary, see Kadar, in *Nepszabadsag*, 19 Feb 1971, quoted in *Hungarian Background Report*, 25 Feb 1971. Undeniably, many appeals still have plebiscitary overtones.
92. See Vali, *Rift and Revolt*, p. 417 (Hungary); Dinka and Skidmore, in *Political Science Quarterly*, Sep 1973, 400 (Czechoslovakia); Radio Free Europe, *Polish Situation Report*, 16 Mar 1972.
93. See Skilling, *Communist Governments*, pp. 125 – 35, and Ionescu, *Politics of the European Communist States*. For the USSR, see *Interest Groups in Soviet Politics*, ed. H. G. Skilling and W. Griffith. (Princeton, NJ, 1973).
94. See Mote, *Soviet . . . Elections*, pp. 61 – 3; H. W. Schwarze, *The GDR Today* (London, 1973) pp. 26 – 9; J. Kepa, *Nowe Drogi*, 1965, no. 7 (Poland); Rusinow, in *American Universities Fieldstaff Reports*, SE Europe Series, xvi, no. 6, 14 – 19 (Yugoslavia).
95. According to Y. Shabanov, quoted by Hill in *Soviet Studies*, xxviii, no. 4, 597.
96. See Wiatr's findings on the basis of 1957 and 1958 results, in *Essays on the Behavioral Study of Politics*, ed. Ranney, pp. 245 – 8.
97. For sources of information, see Churchward, *Contemporary Soviet Government*, pp. 112 – 15; and F. C. Barghoorn, *Politics in the USSR* (Boston, Mass., 1972) pp. 163 – 5. It is difficult to say more than that account is taken of election data; see Y. Shabanov citing party instructions, quoted by Hill in *Soviet Studies*, xxviii, no. 4, 597. Even referendums and organised public discussions make hardly any impact on policy; see V. F. Kotok, *Referendum v sisteme sotsialisticheskoi demokratii* (Moscow, 1964).
98. See Wiatr, in *Essays on the Behavioral Study of Politics*, ed. Ranney, p. 239. After the results of the 1957 elections in Poland, the two-thirds ceiling on 'surplus' candidates was reduced to one-half and made optional for parliamentary elections; see Jarosz, *System wyborczy PRL*, pp. 217 – 20. In the 1967 Hungarian elections, far fewer seats were contested than the leadership had hoped, and therefore nomination procedure was opened up and unmarked

ballots made invalid by the 1970 electoral law; see Gronsky, in *Pravnik*, 1971, 1014–15.

99. See V. F. Kotok, *Nakazy izbiratelei v sotsialisticheskom gosudarstve* (Moscow, 1967), pp. 84, 111, 113; A. T. Leizerov, 'A Study of the Effectiveness of Village and District Soviets in Belorussia', *Sovetskoe gosudarstvo i pravo*, 1974, no. 12, trans. in *Soviet Law and Government*, XIV, no. 1 (Summer 1975) esp. 66–8, 75, 88. A Polish survey of 1965 found fulfilment of electors' requests to be very mixed; see *Problemy Rad Narodowych*, 1969, no. 13, pp. 35–46.

100. See for instance, Makhnenko, *State Law*, pp. 341–64, 412–28.

101. Swearer (in *Midwest Journal of Political Science*, V, no. 2 134–45), Churchward (*Contemporary Soviet Government*, p. 108) and Milnor (*Elections and Political Stability*, p. 113) all emphasise the disbenefits.

102. These pressures have been increasingly evident since the economic reforms of the mid-1960s. Poland offers the clearest example of these developments; see A. Pravda, 'Gierek's Poland: Five Years On', *The World Today*, XXXII, no. 7 (July 1976) pp. 270–8.

103. See Klokocka, *Volby*, pp. 244–9.

104. The proposals formed part of a document prepared for the Fourteenth Party Congress, held clandestinely in Aug 1968; see *The Secret Vysocany Congress*, ed. Pelikan, pp. 234–37. For a similar but more far-reaching scheme, see Klokocka, *Volby*, pp. 269–85.

105. *The Secret Vysocany Congress*, ed. Pelikan, pp. 232, 236.

CHAPTER 10

1. For a full discussion of the points made here, see Richard Rose, 'Dynamic Tendencies in the Authority of Regimes', *World Politics*, XXI, no. 4 (1969) 602–28.

2. See Richard Rose and Derek W. Urwin, 'Social Cohesion, Political Parties and Strains in Regimes', *Comparative Political Studies*, II, no. 1 (1969) esp. 31–44.

3. For a further documentation of the argument of the first three parts of this chapter, see R. Rose 'On the Priorities of Citizenship in the Deep South and Northern Ireland', *Journal of Politics*, XXXVIII, no. 2 (1976) p. 257ff.

4. As social and economic rights cannot be guaranteed by the ballot or by the courts, it would not be appropriate to consider them further here. On the possible political consequences of overloaded claims upon economic resources, see R. Rose and B. Guy Peters, *Can Government Go Bankrupt?* (New York: Basic Books, forthcoming).

5. Western elections where one party has taken half the popular vote from 1945 to 1975 are: Australia, 1; Austria, 1; Germany, 1; Malta, 4; New Zealand, 3; Sweden, 1; and the United States, 4. See T. T. Mackie and R. Rose, *The International Almanac of Electoral History* (London: Macmillan, 1974).

6. See G. Lehmbruch, *Proporzdemokratie: politisches System und Politische Kultur in der Schweiz und in Österreich* (Tübingen: Mohr, 1967); and J. Steiner 'Non-violent Conflict Resolution in Democratic Systems: Switzerland', *Journal of Conflict Resolution*, XIII, no. 3 (1969).

7. See A. J. Peaslee, *Constitutions of Nations*, 2nd edition (The Hague: M. Nijhoff, 1956).

8. For detailed discussion and documentation of traditional Southern electoral practices, see V. O. Key Jr, *Southern Politics in State and Nation* (New York: Knopf, 1949).

9. The crucial civil-rights lawsuits were filed in the name of individuals, and not in the name of blacks as a social group or oppressed class. Legal procedures allowed courts to apply precedents establishing individual rights to subsequent plaintiffs, and to issue injunctions protecting groups of blacks threatened with infringement of individual rights.

10. See Mildred A. Schwartz, *Trends in White Attitudes toward Negroes* (Chicago: National Opinion Research Centre, 1967) p. 22ff.

11. Quoted in C. V. Hamilton, *The Bench and the Ballot* (New York: Oxford University Press, 1973) p. 43.

12. *The Shameful Blight: The Survival of Racial Discrimination in Voting in the South* (Washington, DC: The Washington Research Project, 1972) p. 13.

13. Cf. 'Black Impact on the 1976 Elections', *Focus*, IV, no. 12 (1976): and Robert Axelrod, 'Communication re Where the Votes Come From', *American Political Science Review*, LXVIII, no. 2, (1974) 718.

14. A phrase used by British soldiers to interpret the Act of Parliament authorising the arrest and internment without *habeas corpus* of United Kingdom subjects in Northern Ireland from 1971 to 1976. For a full discussion and documentation of the troubles of the province, see R. Rose, *Governing without Consensus: An Irish Perspective* (London: Faber, 1971), and *Northern Ireland: Time of Choice* (London: Macmillan, 1976).

15. *English Law – the New Dimension* (London: Stevens, 1974) p. 15. More generally, see Anthony Lester, *Democracy and Individual Rights*, Fabian Society Tract no. 390 (London, 1968); and Louis L. Jaffe, *English and American Judges as Lawmakers* (Oxford: Clarendon Press, 1969).

16. J. L. McCracken, quoted in Rose, *Governing without Consensus*, p. 218.

17. See Ian McAllister, *The 1975 Northern Ireland Convention Election*, University of Strathclyde Occasional Paper no. 14 (Glasgow, 1975) p. 25.

18. See Robert Fisk, *The Point of No Return: The Strike which Broke the British in Ulster* (London: Andre Deutsch, 1975).

19. Cf. James Callaghan, *A House Divided: The Dilemma of Northern Ireland* (London: Collins, 1973).

Notes on Contributors

JOEL D. BARKAN, Associate Professor of Political Science, University of Iowa. Doctorate in Political Science, University of California at Los Angeles. Formerly, visiting lecturer at the University of Dar es Salaam. Author of books on East and West African politics, and articles on the politics of the developing areas.

JEAN FRANÇOIS BAYART has written a doctoral thesis on the political system in the Cameroun, and has published numerous articles on different aspects of this subject in the *Revue française de science politique*, the *Revue française Africaine*, and in *African Affairs*. He is at present research attaché at the Centre d'Études et de Recherches Internationales in Paris.

GUY HERMET, Director, Centre d'Études et de Recherches Internationales, FNSP, Paris. Doctorate in Sociology, Sorbonne. Author of several books on Spain, and a variety of articles on modernising regimes and religious organisations in authoritarian regimes.

JUAN J. LINZ, Pelatiah Perit Professor of Political and Social Science, Yale University. Doctorate from Columbia University. A specialist in the comparative study of the breakdown and consolidation of non-democratic regimes. Author of many monographs concerned with historical and contemporary Spain, and, with S. M. Lipset, of pioneering studies in comparative voting behaviour. Chairman, Committee on Political Sociology, International Political Science Association/International Sociological Association.

DENIS MARTIN, Research officer of the Centre d'Études et de Recherches Internationales, FNSP, Paris. Doctorate in Sociology, Paris. Author of various articles on African politics and co-editor of the *Guide de recherches: L'Afrique noire* (Paris: A. Colin, 1973).

JOHN J. OKUMU, Professor of Political Science, University of Khartoum, Sunda. Doctorate in Political Science, University of California at Los Angeles, and post-doctoral fellow, Yale University; formerly at the University of Dar es Salaam. Co-author and editor of several studies of East African politics.

ELIZABETH PICARD, Research assistant at the Centre d'Études et de Recherches Internationales, FNSP, Paris. Licenciée in sociology and diploma of the Institut d'Études Politiques, Paris. Specialist in Middle East politics.

ALEX PRAVDA, Lecturer in Soviet and East European politics, University of Reading. Doctorate from Oxford. Author of studies of Czechoslovakian reform politics, and currently engaged in a comparative study of trade unions and politics in Communist states.

RICHARD ROSE, Professor of Politics, University of Strathclyde, Glasgow. Doctorate from Oxford. Author or editor of seven books about electoral politics and author of books about British, Irish and American politics. Secretary, Committee on Political Sociology, International Political Science Association International Sociological Association.

ALAIN ROUQUIÉ, Research Scholar of the Fondation Nationale des Sciences Politiques, Paris. Agrégé in Political Science, Sorbonne. Specialist in Latin American politics, and author of articles concerning the role of the military in politics.

PHILIPPE C. SCHMITTER, Professor of Political Science, University of Chicago. Doctorate from the University of California, Berkeley. Author of books and articles on Latin American politics, especially Brazil, studies of Iberian politics, and of European corporatism.

Index